LIFE OF ROBERT BURNS

AMS PRESS

NEW YORK

Alex. Nasmyth.   G. J. Stodart.

Robert Burns

THE LIFE

OF

ROBERT BURNS

BY

J. G. LOCKHART, D.C.L.

ENLARGED EDITION.

REVISED AND CORRECTED FROM THE LATEST TEXT OF THE
AUTHOR, WITH NEW ANNOTATIONS AND APPENDICES

BY

WILLIAM SCOTT DOUGLAS.

———

" OF HIM WHO WALKED IN GLORY AND IN JOY,
BEHIND HIS PLOUGH, UPON THE MOUNTAIN SIDE."

LONDON:
GEORGE BELL & SONS, YORK ST., COVENT GARDEN,
AND NEW YORK.
1892.

Library of Congress Cataloging in Publication Data

Lockhart, John Gibson, 1794-1854.
    The life of Robert Burns.

    Originally issued in series: Bohn's standard library.
    1. Burns, Robert, 1759-1796—Biography. I. Douglas,
William Scott, 1851-1883, ed. II. Title.
PR4331.L6 1974   821'.6[B]   70-144515
ISBN 0-404-08517-2

Reprinted from the edition of 1892, London
First AMS edition published in 1974
Manufactured in the United States of America

AMS PRESS INC.
NEW YORK, N.Y. 10003

PREFATORY NOTE.

IN the lapse of more than half a century since
Lockhart produced this work, some important
accessions have been made to the general stock of
knowledge concerning his illustrious theme. Nevertheless, abating sundry errors of chronology, and a
few misstatements of fact (here corrected, or pointed
out), his handy little volume has maintained its place
in public estimation, in the face of many a pretentious
new-comer. On all hands, the performance is admitted
to be a masterly one of its class; kind, yet impartial;
animated with a refined spirit of criticism; and, on
the whole, a graceful treatment of his subject.

The publishers having resolved to reproduce this
Biography as one of their "Standard Library" series,
engaged the present editor to revise and correct it
where necessary, and to supplement the original work
with fresh annotations and appendices, to render it
more complete, according to the requirements of the
day. In laying the results before the public, he trusts

that his long familiar acquaintance with the details treated of, and his desire to do justice to the departed biographer's able performance, will be made manifest to the reader, and justify the publishers' selection of

THE EDITOR.

EDINBURGH,
  May, 1882.

MEMOIR OF LOCKHART.

JOHN GIBSON LOCKHART was born in his father's manse at Cambusnethan, in the county of Lanark, in 1794. He was the son of the Rev. John Lockhart by his second wife Elizabeth Gibson, daughter of the Rev. Mr. Gibson, minister of St. Cuthbert's, Edinburgh.

In 1796 his father was transferred to the College Church, Glasgow, and in that city young Lockhart received his first education.

As a boy he had an insatiable appetite for reading, and, although far from being diligent in pursuing his proper school studies, yet the facility with which he acquired knowledge was such that he outstripped more industrious competitors, and won, by the unanimous award of the professors, the Snell Exhibition to Baliol College, Oxford, a prize worth £150 per annum, when he was only in his sixteenth year. He took honours as a first-class man in classics when nineteen, and graduated B.C.L. in the following year, exchanging that degree for the higher one of D.C.L. in 1834.

After spending some time in Germany, during which he acquired a knowledge of the language and a taste for its literature, he was called, in 1816, to the Scottish bar.

His peculiar temperament, however, unfitted him to become successful in this career. He lacked two essentials—readiness of language and self-possession, and we need not wonder at his want of success, nor that he abandoned the law to follow the bent of his genius, the pursuit of literature.

As a member of the little band of young Scotch Tories, who, under their chief, Wilson, began to dispute the literary supremacy of the Scotch Whigs, as represented by Jeffrey and the "Edinburgh Review," he early distinguished himself; and from the commencement of "Blackwood's Magazine," in 1817, Wilson and Lockhart were its chief supporters, and for seven or eight years following, very few numbers appeared without an article from the pen of the latter. He wrote on various subjects, amongst them being translations from the German and Spanish, and strong political articles against the Whigs. At this period party feeling ran high in Edinburgh, opponents did not always confine themselves to a war with paper, and at least one fatal catastrophe occurred, which left a lasting impression on Lockhart's mind.

It was through the political bias of young Lockhart, and his literary connection with Blackwood, that he became acquainted with Sir Walter Scott. Their first introduction to each other took place in 1818, from which time they became intimate friends, and when Scott, from pressure of other work, ceased to write the historical parts of the "Edinburgh Annual Register," he recommended the proprietors to employ Lockhart in his place. In 1819, "Peter's Letters to his Kinsfolk," which so graphically describes Scottish men and manners at that time, was published anonymously. In 1820, the author was married to Sophia, the eldest daughter of Scott, and for six years his home was Chiefswood, in the immediate neighbourhood of Abbotsford, where, doubtless, some of his happiest days were spent. There are few more pleasant passages in Scott's life than those describing his early walk to breakfast with the young couple, or his assisting at their modest dinner party by drawing up the wine from the well, in which it had been put to cool. It was during these six years that Lockhart's pen was unusually prolific.

In 1821, "Valerius," a Roman story of the highest merit, was published. It was a great success, and pronounced to be the best novel on classical manners ever written. In the same year appeared also "Adam Blair," a tale of Scottish domestic life, in which are to be found passages of exquisite pathos and powerful delineations of the passions. In 1823 was published "Reginald Dalton," a tale depicting English, and more especially University life; and his "Ancient Spanish Ballads," which, although not very close translations from the originals, yet surpass them in the peculiar characteristics of true ballad poetry. In 1824, "Matthew Wald" appeared.

Lockhart removed to London in 1826, having accepted the editorship of the "Quarterly Review," in which he succeeded Gifford. In his hands the "Review" not only maintained, but greatly increased its reputation, and during the twenty-seven years of his editorship his contributions were both numerous and valuable, noticeable among them being critical sketches of Theodore Hook, Campbell, and Southey.

In 1828 was published Lockhart's "Life of Burns" for "Constable's Miscellany," unquestionably the best that has yet appeared. In 1836 his "Life of Napoleon," for "Murray's Family Library" (pronounced to be a most fair and impartial history), and subsequently that of Sir Walter Scott, Lockhart's *magnum opus*—a work both of duty and love, remarkable for its truthful estimate of life and conduct, and the matchless skill in delineation and analysis which the author brought to his task. As a literary work it ranks in the first class, and, for the interest it creates as a biography, stands second only to Boswell's "Life of Johnson."

In 1843, as a reward for his services, Sir Robert Peel made him auditor of the Duchy of Cornwall, a sinecure appointment worth £600 a-year. At this time his literary income was considerable, and, as he had inherited some family property, he was in possession of a very comfortable subsistence.

The latter years of Lockhart's life were clouded by domestic calamity. The New Cemetery in the Harrow Road contains the dust of his hopeful boy, John Hugh Lockhart—the

" Hugh Littlejohn " of Sir Walter's " Tales of a Grandfather "
—who died December 15, 1831; also of Miss Anne Scott
(sister of Mrs. Lockhart), who died June 25, 1833 ; and finally
of Sophia—Mrs. Lockhart—who died May 17, 1837.   These
deaths were followed by the demise of both of Mrs. Lockhart's
brothers—Charles, at Teheran in Persia, in October, 1841,
and Sir Walter, on his passage home from India, in February,
1847.   The succession to the Baronetcy and estate of Abbotsford then devolved on Mr. Lockhart's son, Walter Scott, who
adopted the surname "Lockhart-Scott;" and whose only sister,
in August following, became the wife of James Robert Hope,
Esq., Q.C., London.   The youthful Baronet, however (third
of Abbotsford) died at Versailles on 10th January, 1853; the
Baronetcy then lapsed, and Mrs. Hope, with her husband,
under the adopted surname "Hope-Scott," succeeded to the
estate of Abbotsford.

These family bereavements, together with indifferent health,
and irregular habits of study, were telling hard on Mr. Lockhart's constitution, and he endeavoured, by spending a winter
in Italy, to recover his strength.   At first the result was
favourable, and he returned somewhat invigorated, though he
could not disguise from himself that old age was upon him.
He had intended, after Scott's death, never to re-visit Abbotsford, but a severe attack of diarrhœa in the October of 1853
completely shattered his constitution, and, feeling now in its
fullest force his desolate and lonely state, he turned to his
former home once more, and there, amidst those scenes which
had witnessed his youthful ambition and love, and which
genius has immortalized, his parting spirit was soothed by
filial love and attention.   He breathed his last in the arms
of his daughter on the 25th November, 1854, having shortly
before completed his 60th year.

It was an observation of the late lamented Mr. Thackeray
that shyness and reserve in a man are the result of coldness
and pride.   In whatever degree this may be correct when

applied generally, it certainly does not apply to Lockhart ; on the contrary, reserve with him sprang from excessive modesty. His failure at the bar is altogether attributable to this. Nature intended him for the study, not the rostrum, and it was only with the pen that he had been given a ready outlet for his thoughts.

Possessing an exterior of the finest type of manly beauty, gifted with a marvellous memory, a mind singularly acute, sagacious, and instructive, in the readiness with which it read men and their motives, he was eminently fitted to become a leader among them. His idiosyncracy, however, forbade it. It was only among his own immediate friends that he could display his immense wealth in knowledge, and his marvellous power in applying it, whether in playful raillery, subtle wit, glowing fancy, biting satire, or withering sarcasm. To those about him he was ever kind, affable, and sympathising, but those who sought his acquaintance only because he was a celebrity were often disappointed at their reception, for the deference and homage they wished to render to his talents and achievements caused him to shrink from accepting it, and to shut himself up, as it were, in the indomitable reserve which characterised him.

His mind was eminently practical ; quick to discern between the semblance and the reality ; unsparing to morbid sickly sentiment; tender to genuine feeling ; despising every species of vanity, pretension, and cant; unfailing in his homage to the humblest worth. His reserve never prevented his intellect from having fair play, but it greatly impeded the justice due to his nobler part.

Lockhart was laid beside his illustrious father-in-law, among the crumbling ruins of Dryburgh Abbey. His daughter, Mrs. Hope-Scott, had then but one child, Mary Monica, born in October, 1852. She afterwards gave birth to a son, Walter, in June, 1857, and to another daughter, Margaret Anne, in September, 1858 ; but on the 26th of the following month, she herself—the daughter of Lockhart, and grand-daughter of Scott—died at Edinburgh, and was buried in a vault of St. Margaret's Convent there. Her two infants, Walter, and Margaret Anne, were laid beside their mother in the same place of sepulture, in December of the same year.

Mary Monica Hope-Scott, through many years the sole heir of the estate of Abbotsford, is now (1882) the wife of the Hon. Joseph Constable Maxwell, a son of Lord Herries, and has children, one or more. Mr. Hope-Scott contracted a second marriage, but he and his wife are both dead; and so closes our little record of "The Abbotsford Family."

> "Be cheerful, sir,
> Our revels now are ended; these our actors,
> As I foretold you, were all spirits, and
> Are melted into air—into thin air."

THE AUTHOR'S PREFACE.

SOME apology must be deemed necessary for any new attempt to write the "Life of Burns." The present adventurer on that field has only this to offer—that Dr. Currie's Memoir cannot be, with propriety, detached from the collection of the Poet's works which it was expressly designed to accompany; and the regretted projector of "Constable's Miscellany"[1] sought in vain for any other narrative sufficiently detailed to meet the purposes of his publication.

The last reprint of Dr. Currie's Edition had the advantage of being superintended by Mr. Gilbert Burns; and that excellent man, availing himself of the labours of Cromek, Walker, and Peterkin, and supplying many blanks from the stores of his own recollection, produced at last a book, in which almost everything that should be—and some things that never should have been—told, of his brother's history, may be found.[2] There is, however, at least for indolent readers, no small inconvenience in the arrangement which Currie's Memoir, thus enlarged, presents. The frequent references to notes, appendices, and letters, not included in the same volume, are somewhat perplexing. And it may, moreover, be seriously questioned, whether Gilbert Burns's best method of answering many of his amiable author's unconscious mis-statements and exaggerations, would not have

---

[1] For which publication this Memoir was written. Mr. Archibald Constable died in July, 1827.

[2] [Gilbert's revisal appeared in 1820, after five years' promise, and the result was very disappointing. Mr. Lockhart's flattering reference to it here can be explained only by a conjecture that his knowledge of its contents was derived from the "prospectus"—not from a personal perusal of the performance.]

been to expunge them altogether from a work with which posterity were to connect, in any shape or measure, the authority of his own name.

As to criticism on Burns's poetry, no one can suppose that anything of consequence, remains to be added on a subject which has engaged successively the pens of Mackenzie, Heron, Currie, Scott, Jeffrey, Walker, Wordsworth, Campbell, and Wilson.

The humble purpose of the following Essay was, therefore, no more than to compress, within the limits of a single small volume, the substance of materials already open to all the world, and sufficient, in every point of view, for those who have leisure to collect, and candour to weigh them.

For any little touches of novelty that may be discovered in a Narrative, thus unambitiously undertaken, the writer is indebted to respectable authorities, which shall be cited as he proceeds. As to the earlier part of Burns's history, Currie and Walker appear to have left little unexplored ; it is chiefly concerning the incidents of his closing years that their accounts have been supposed to admit of a supplement.

J. G. L.

London, *April*, 1828.

October, 1829.

A new edition of this Narrative being called for, the author has corrected some errors, obligingly pointed out to him by Mr. H. Paul, Mr. Sillar, and others. He has also been enabled to fill up some *lacunæ* from Burns's MS. correspondence with the late Lady Harriet Don, sister of the Earl of Glencairn ; and, above all, he has to acknowledge, with a lively sense of gratitude, the kindness of Mr. James Burnes of Montrose, in intrusting him with an interesting and valuable series of the Poet's Letters to his relatives in the North of Scotland, from which various extracts are interwoven in the following pages.

CONTENTS.

LIFE OF ROBERT BURNS.

CHAPTER I.

"My father was a farmer upon the Carrick Border,
And carefully he brought me up in decency and order."

ROBERT BURNS was born on the 25th of January, 1759, in a clay-built cottage, about two miles to the south of the town of Ayr, and in the immediate vicinity of the Kirk of Alloway, and the "Auld Brig o' Doon." About a week afterwards, part of the frail dwelling, which his father had constructed with his own hands, gave way at midnight; and the infant poet and his mother were carried through the storm, to the shelter of a neighbouring hovel.

The father, William *Burnes* (for so he spelt his name), was the son of a farmer in Kincardineshire, whence he removed at nineteen years of age,[1] in consequence of domestic embarrassments. The farm on which the family lived formed part of the estate forfeited, after the Rebellion of 1715, by the noble house of Keith-Maris-

---

[1] [Dr. Currie, on the authority of Gilbert Burns, says "in his nineteenth year," but subsequent investigations prove that he left his native district for the southern parts of Scotland in 1748, when he must have been twenty-seven years old. Robert, the father of William Burnes, was evidently then alive, although not one of the "Burns-genealogists" has discovered the date of his death. A headstone in Glenbervie churchyard is said to record the death of the grandfather (James) in 1743, and of the grandmother (Margaret Falconer) in 1749.]

chal; and the poet took pleasure in believing that his humble ancestors shared the principles and the fall of their chiefs. " Though my fathers " (said he after his fame was established) " had not illustrious honours and vast properties to hazard in the contest—though they left their humble cottages only to add so many units more to the unnoted crowd that followed their leaders, yet what they could they did, and what they had they lost. With unshaken firmness, and unconcealed political attachments, they shook hands with ruin, for what they esteemed the cause of their king and their country." [1] Indeed, after William Burnes settled in the west of Scotland, there prevailed a vague notion that he himself had *been out* in the insurrection of 1745-6; but though Robert would fain have interpreted his father's silence in favour of a tale which flattered his imagination, his brother Gilbert always treated it as a mere fiction; and such it was. [2] It is easy to suppose,

---

[1] Letter to Lady Winifred Constable, December 16, 1789, here first published in part.

[2] [There exists no recorded remark of Burns importing that he gave credence to, or even was aware of this " mere fiction " which the timid Gilbert took some pains to argue down, probably to avert attention from what he knew to be no fiction; to wit, the fact that his " forefathers " had been actively engaged in the older rebellion of 1715, and had suffered hardships in consequence. Gilbert affected to wonder how his brother had been misled in the account he gives of the Jacobitism of his ancestors, "knowing that his father was yet unborn in 1715!" This glaring *non sequitur* Gilbert supplemented with a curious reminiscence, thus:— " Among a collection of parish certificates in my father's possession, I have read one stating that ' the bearer had no hand in the late wicked rebellion.'" The collection of certificates referred to still exists in the hands of Gilbert's representatives, but the one just quoted is not in the bundle. The earliest of these, in favour of William Burnes, is signed by three landowners of Kincardineshire, and dated May 9, 1748, when "the bearer" was about to migrate southwards in search of employment; and he is therein designated " the son of an honest farmer of this neighbourhood, and a very well inclined lad himself."]

See APPENDIX A, Paternal Ancestry of Burns.

that when any obscure northern stranger fixed himself in those days in the Low Country, such rumours were likely enough to be circulated concerning him.

William Burnes laboured for some years in the neighbourhood of Edinburgh as a gardener, and then found his way into Ayrshire. At the time when Robert was born, he was gardener and overseer to a gentleman of small estate, Mr. Ferguson of Doonholm; but resided on a few acres of land, which he had on lease from another proprietor, and where he had originally intended to establish himself as a nurseryman. He married Agnes Brown in December, 1757, and the poet was their first-born.

William Burnes seems to have been, in his humble station, a man eminently entitled to respect. He had received the ordinary learning of a Scottish parish school, and profited largely, both by that, and by his own experience in the world. " I have met with few " (said the poet, in 1787, after he himself had seen a good deal of mankind) " who understood men, their manners, and their ways, equal to my father." He was a strictly religious man. There exists in his handwriting [1] a little manual of theology, in the form of a dialogue, which he drew up for the use of his children, and from which it appears that he had adopted more of the Arminian than of the Calvinistic *doctrine;* a circumstance not to be wondered at, when we consider that he had been educated in a district which was never numbered among the strongholds of the Presbyterian church. The affectionate reverence with which his children ever regarded him, is attested by all who have described him as he ap-

---

[1] [Not in the penmanship of William Burnes, but in that of the teacher, John Murdoch, who appears to have extended the document from rough scrolls, or from the dictation of the father, while the children were being reared at Mount Oliphant. The " little manual," printed from the original possessed by Gilbert's son, was published by M'Kie of Kilmarnock in 1875.]

peared in his domestic circle; but there needs no evidence, beside that of the poet himself, who has painted, in colours that will never fade, "the saint, the father, and the husband," of the "Cotter's Saturday Night."

Agnes Brown, the wife of this good man, is described as "a very sagacious woman, without any appearance of forwardness, or awkwardness of manner;"[1] and it seems that, in features, and, as he grew up, in general address, the poet resembled her more than his father. She had an inexhaustible store of ballads and traditionary tales, and appears to have nourished his infant imagination by this means, while her husband paid more attention to "the weightier matters of the law."

These worthy people laboured hard for the support of an increasing family. William was occupied with Mr. Ferguson's service, and Agnes, like the "Wyfe of Auchtermuchtie," who ruled

"Baith calvis and kye,
And a' the house baith in and out,"—

contrived to manage a small dairy as well as her children. But though their honesty and diligence merited better things, their condition continued to be very uncomfortable; and our poet (in his Autobiography) accounts distinctly for his being born and bred "a very poor man's son," by the remark, that "stubborn ungainly integrity, and headlong, ungovernable irascibility, are disqualifying circumstances."

These defects of temper did not, however, obscure the sterling worth of William Burnes in the eyes of Mr. Ferguson; who, when the gardener expressed a wish to try his fortune on a farm of his, then vacant, and confessed at the same time his inability to meet the charges of stocking it,

---

[1] Letter of Mr. Mackenzie, surgeon at Irvine. Morison, vol. ii., p. 261.

at once advanced £100 towards the removal of the difficulty. Burnes accordingly removed to this farm (that of
Mount Oliphant, in the parish of Ayr) at Whitsuntide,
1766, when his eldest son was between six and seven years
of age. But the soil proved to be of a most ungrateful
description; and Mr. Ferguson dying, and his affairs falling
into the hands of a harsh *factor* (who afterwards sat for his
picture in the "Twa Dogs"), Burnes was glad to give up
his bargain at the end of six years.[1] He then removed
about ten miles to a larger and better farm, that of Lochlea,
in the parish of Tarbolton. But here, after a short interval
of prosperity, some unfortunate misunderstanding took
place as to the conditions of the lease; the dispute was referred to arbitration; and, after three years of suspense, the
result involved Burnes in ruin. The worthy man lived to
know this decision; but death saved him from witnessing
its necessary consequences. He died of consumption on the
13th February, 1784. Severe labour, and hopes only renewed to be baffled, had at last exhausted a robust but
irritable structure and temperament of body and of mind.

In the midst of the harassing struggles which found this
termination, William Burnes appears to have used his utmost exertions for promoting the mental improvement of
his children—a duty rarely neglected by Scottish parents,
however humble their station, and scanty their means.
Robert was sent, in his sixth year, to a small school at
Alloway Miln, about a mile from the house in which he was

---

[1] [This is a mistake. The Burnes family lived at Mount Oliphant exactly eleven years, *i.e.* from Whitsunday, 1766, to Whitsunday, 1777.
Entry to the soil was obtained at Martinmas, 1765, and by the terms of
the lease, its currency might come to a close in six years; but if the
tenant failed to exercise his option of then removing, he was held bound
to remain for at least six years more. Gilbert's narrative states that his
father "attempted to fix himself in a better farm at the end of the first
six years, but failing in that attempt, he continued for six years more."]

born; but Campbell, the teacher, being in the course of a few months removed to another situation, Burnes and four or five neighbours engaged Mr. John Murdoch to supply his place, lodging him by turns in their own houses, and ensuring to him a small payment of money quarterly. Robert Burns, and Gilbert his next brother, were the aptest and favourite pupils of this worthy man, who survived till very lately,[1] and whose letter, published at length by Currie, detailed with honest pride the part which he had in the early education of our poet. He became the frequent inmate and confidential friend of the family, and speaks with enthusiasm of the virtues of William Burnes, and of the peaceful and happy life of his humble abode.

" He was," says Murdoch, " a tender and affectionate father; he took pleasure in leading his children in the path of virtue; not in driving them, as some parents do, to the performance of duties to which they themselves are averse. He took care to find fault but very seldom; and therefore, when he did rebuke, he was listened to with a kind of reverential awe. A look of disapprobation was felt; a reproof was severely so; and a stripe with the *taws*, even on the skirt of the coat, gave heartfelt pain, produced a loud lamentation, and brought forth a flood of tears. . . .

" He had the art of gaining the esteem and good-will of those that were labourers under him. I think I never saw him angry but twice; the one time it was with the foreman of the band, for not reaping the field as he was desired; and the other time, it was with an old man, for using smutty inuendoes and *double entendres*. . . .

" In this mean cottage, of which I myself was at times an inhabitant, I really believe there dwelt a larger portion

---

[1] [The excellent teacher died in London at the age of seventy-seven, in the year 1824. He was in poor circumstances, eking out his professional earnings by keeping a little stationery shop.]

of content than in any palace in Europe. The 'Cotter's Saturday Night' will give some idea of the temper and manners that prevailed there."

The boys, under the joint tuition of Murdoch and their father, made rapid progress in reading, spelling, and writing; they committed psalms and hymns to memory with extraordinary ease—the teacher taking care (as he tells us) that they should understand the exact meaning of each word in the sentence ere they tried to get it by heart. "As soon," says he, " as they were capable of it, I taught them to turn verse into its natural prose order ; sometimes to substitute synonymous expressions for poetical words; and to supply all the ellipses. Robert and Gilbert were generally at the upper end of the class, even when ranged with boys by far their seniors. The books most commonly used in the school were the 'Spelling Book,' the New Testament, the Bible, 'Mason's Collection of Prose and Verse,' 'Fisher's English Grammar.'—Gilbert always appeared to me to possess a more lively imagination, and to be more of the wit, than Robert. I attempted to teach them a little church-music. Here they were left far behind by all the rest of the school. Robert's ear, in particular, was remarkably dull, and his voice untunable. It was long before I could get them to distinguish one tune from another. Robert's countenance was generally grave, and expressive of a serious, contemplative, and thoughtful mind. Gilbert's face said, ' Mirth, with thee I mean to live;' and certainly, if any person who knew the two boys had been asked which of them was the most likely to court the Muses, he would never have guessed that Robert had a propensity of that kind."—(*Currie*, vol. i., p. 89.)

" At those years," says the poet himself, in 1787, " I was by no means a favourite with anybody. I was a good deal noted for a retentive memory, a stubborn sturdy something in my disposition, and an enthusiastic idiot-piety. I say *idiot* piety, because I was then but a child. Though it cost the schoolmaster some thrashings, I made an excellent English scholar; and by the time I was ten or eleven years of age, I was a critic in substantives, verbs, and particles. In my infant and boyish days, too, I owed much to an old woman who resided in the family, remarkable for her ignorance, credulity, and superstition. She had, I suppose, the largest collection in the country of tales and songs concerning devils, ghosts, fairies, brownies, witches, warlocks, spunkies, kelpies, elf-candles, dead-lights, wraiths, apparitions, cantraips, giants, enchanted towers, dragons, and other trumpery.[1] This cultivated the latent seeds of poetry; but had so strong an effect on my imagination, that to this hour, in my nocturnal rambles, I sometimes keep a sharp look-out in suspicious places; and though nobody can be more sceptical than I am in such matters, yet it often takes an effort of philosophy to shake off these idle terrors. The earliest composition that I recollect taking pleasure in, was 'The Vision of Mirza,' and a hymn of Addison's, beginning, 'How are thy servants blest, O Lord!' I particularly remember one half-stanza, which was music to my boyish ear:

> 'For though on dreadful whirls we hung
> High on the broken wave——'

I met with these pieces in 'Mason's English Collection,' one of my school-books. The two first books I ever read

---

[1] Mr. Robert Chambers tells me that this woman's name was Jenny Wilson, and that she outlived Burns, with whom she was a great favourite. [Chambers afterwards corrected this information on the authority of Mrs. Begg, youngest sister of the poet. The name of this aged inmate was Betty Davidson; she was connected by ties of relationship with the Browns of Carrick—direct relatives of the bard's mother. By invitation, she passed a few months from time to time under the roof of William Burnes, both at Alloway and Mount Oliphant.]

in private, and which gave me more pleasure than any two
books I ever read since, were, 'The Life of Hannibal,' and
'The History of Sir William Wallace.' Hannibal gave
my young ideas such a turn, that I used to strut in raptures up and down after the recruiting drum and bagpipe,
and wish myself tall enough to be a soldier; while the story
of Wallace poured a tide of Scottish prejudice into my
veins, which will boil along there till the floodgates of life
shut in eternal rest." [1]

And speaking of the same period and books to Mrs.
Dunlop, he says, "For several of my earlier years I had
few other authors; and many a solitary hour have I stole
out, after the laborious vocations of the day, to shed a tear
over their glorious but unfortunate stories. In those boyish
days, I remember, in particular, being struck with that part
of Wallace's story where these lines occur—

> 'Syne to the Leglen wood, when it was late,
> To make a silent and a safe retreat.'

"I chose a fine summer Sunday, the only day my line of
life allowed, and walked half a dozen miles to pay my
respects to the Leglen wood, with as much devout enthusiasm as ever pilgrim did to Loretto; and explored every
den and dell where I could suppose my heroic countyman
to have lodged." [2]

Murdoch continued his instructions until the family had

---

[1] Autobiography. Currie, vol. i., p. 38. [Hannibal was lent by
Murdoch; and Wallace was borrowed, some considerable time afterwards, from a blacksmith in the vicinity of Mount Oliphant—Kirkpatrick by name. According to Mrs. Begg, his daughter Nelly was the
"sweet, sonsie lass" referred to by the poet, as his partner on the harvest
field when he was yet under fifteen, and who first charmed him into love
and song.]

[2] [Leglen wood is on the estate of Auchencruive, some three miles above
the town of Ayr, in the heart of a peninsula formed by a peculiar bend
of the river.]

been about two years at Mount Oliphant, when he left for a time that part of the country. "There being no school near us," says Gilbert Burns, "and our little services being already useful on the farm, my father undertook to teach us arithmetic in the winter evenings by candle-light—and iu this way my two elder sisters received all the education they ever received."

Gilbert tells an anecdote which must not be omitted here, since it furnishes an early instance of the liveliness of his brother's imagination. Murdoch, being on a visit to the family, read aloud one evening part of the tragedy of Titus Andronicus; the circle listened with the deepest interest until he came to Act ii., sc. 5, where Lavinia is introduced "with her hands cut off, and her tongue cut out." At this the children entreated, with one voice, in an agony of distress, that their friend would read no more. "If you will not hear the play out," said William Burnes, "it need not be left with you."—"If it be left," cries Robert, "I will burn it." His father was about to chide him for this return to Murdoch's kindness, but the good young man interfered, saying he liked to see so much sensibility, and left "The School for Love," in place of his truculent tragedy. At this time Robert was nine years of age.

"Nothing," continues Gilbert Burns, "could be more retired than our general manner of living at Mount Oliphant; we rarely saw anybody but the members of our own family. There were no boys of our own age, or near it, in the neighbourhood. Indeed, the greatest part of the land in the vicinity was at that time possessed by shop-keepers, and people of that stamp, who had retired from business, or who kept their farm in the country at the same time that they followed business in town. My father was for some time almost the only companion we had. He conversed familiarly on all subjects with us, as if we had been men; and was at great pains, while we accompanied him in the labours of the farm, to lead the conversation to such subjects as might tend to increase our knowledge, or confirm us in virtuous habits. He borrowed 'Salmon's Geographical Grammar' for us, and endeavoured to make us acquainted with the situation and history of the different countries in the world; while, from a book-society in Ayr, he procured for us the reading of 'Derham's Physico- and Astro-Theology,' and 'Ray's Wisdom of God in the Creation,' to give us some idea of astronomy and natural history. Robert read all these books with an avidity and industry scarcely to be equalled. My father had been a subscriber to 'Stackhouse's History of the Bible.' From this Robert collected a competent knowledge of ancient history; for *no book was so voluminous as to slacken his industry, or so antiquated as to damp his researches.*" A collection of letters, by eminent English authors, is mentioned as having fallen into Burns's hands much about the same time, and greatly delighted him.

When he was about thirteen or fourteen years old, his father sent him and Gilbert "week about, during the summer quarter," to the parish school of Dalrymple, two or three miles distant from Mount Oliphant, for the improvement of their penmanship. The good man could not pay two fees; or his two boys could not be spared at the same time from the labour of the farm ! [1]

---

[1] [These little sojournings, during the summer season of 1772, in the village of Dalrymple, were of some importance in the formation of our poet's after-habits. A lad about his own age, the son of a well-to-do farmer named Candlish, at Porclewan, situated betwixt Mount Oliphant and that village, happened to contract an intimacy with Robert Burns about this period. This was James Candlish, who afterwards distinguished himself, first as a debater in juvenile clubs, and thereafter as a medical lecturer in Glasgow and in Edinburgh. Their friendship was farther cemented by the circumstance that in the summer following they met at the Ayr Grammar School, where the poet spent some weeks by

"We lived very poorly," says the poet. "I was a dexterous ploughman for my age; and the next eldest to me (Gilbert) could drive the plough very well, and help me to thrash the corn. A novel-writer might perhaps have viewed these scenes with some satisfaction, but so did not I. My indignation yet boils at the recollection of the scoundrel factor's insolent letters, which used to set us all in tears."

Gilbert Burns gives his brother's situation at this period in greater detail—"To the buffetings of misfortune," says he, "we could only oppose hard labour and the most rigid economy. We lived very sparingly. For several years butcher's meat was a stranger in the house, while all the members of the family exerted themselves to the utmost of their strength, and rather beyond it, in the labours of the farm. My brother, at the age of thirteen, assisted in thrashing the crop of corn, and at fifteen was the principal labourer on the farm, for we had no hired servant, male or female. The anguish of mind we felt at our tender years, under these straits and difficulties, was very great. To think of our father growing old (for he was now above fifty),[1] broken down with the long-continued fatigues of his life, with a wife and five other children, and in a declining state of circumstances, these reflections produced in my brother's mind and mine sensations of the deepest distress. I doubt not but the hard labour and sorrow of this period of his life, was in a great measure the cause of that depression of spirits with which Robert was so often afflicted through

invitation from Murdoch (then recently appointed to a mastership there). Two letters, addressed by Burns to Candlish in after-life, are contained in his published correspondence; and during the Ellisland period we find the poet characterizing him as "the earliest friend, except my only brother, that I have on earth, and one of the worthiest fellows that ever any man called by the name of friend."]

[1] [He was born in 1721, consequently at the time of which Gilbert is now speaking (1772), William Burnes was just fifty-one.]

his whole life afterwards. At this time he was almost
constantly afflicted in the evenings with a dull headache,
which, at a future period of his life, was exchanged for a
palpitation of the heart, and a threatening of fainting and
suffocation in his bed, in the night-time."

The year after this, Burns was able to gain three weeks
of respite, one before, and two after the harvest, from the
labours which were thus straining his youthful strength.
His tutor Murdoch was now established in the town of Ayr,
and the boy spent one of those weeks in revising the English
grammar with him ; the other two were given to French.
He laboured enthusiastically in the new pursuit, and came
home at the end of a fortnight with a dictionary and a
" Télémaque," of which he made such use in his leisure
hours, by himself, that in a short time (if we may believe
Gilbert) he was able to understand any ordinary book of
French prose. His progress, whatever it really amounted
to, was looked on as something of a prodigy ; and a writing-
master in Ayr, a friend of Murdoch, insisted that Robert
Burns must next attempt the rudiments of the Latin tongue.
He did so, but with little perseverance we may be sure,
since the results were of no sort of value. Burns's Latin
consisted of a few scraps of hackneyed quotations, such as
many that never looked into Ruddiman's Rudiments can
apply on occasion, quite as skilfully as he ever appears to
have done. The matter is one of no importance ; we might
perhaps safely dismiss it with parodying what Ben Jonson
said of Shakespeare ; he had little French and no Latin ;
and yet it is proper to mention, that he is found, years after
he left Ayrshire, writing to Edinburgh in some anxiety
about a copy of Molière.

He had read, however, and read well, ere his sixteenth
year elapsed, no contemptible amount of the literature
of his own country. In addition to the books which have
already been mentioned, he tells us that, before the family

quitted Mount Oliphant, he had read "the 'Spectator,' some plays of Shakespeare, Pope (the 'Homer' included), 'Tull and Dickson on Agriculture,' 'Locke on the Human Understanding,' 'Justice's British Gardener's Directory,' 'Boyle's Lectures,' 'Taylor's Scripture Doctrine of Original Sin,' 'A Select Collection of English Songs,' 'Harvey's Meditations' (a book which has ever been very popular among the Scottish peasantry), and the Works of Allan Ramsay;" and Gilbert adds to this list, "Pamela" (the first novel either of the brothers read), two stray volumes of "Peregrine Pickle," two of "Count Fathom," and a single volume of "some English historian," containing the reign of James I. and his son. The "Collection of Songs," says Burns, "was my *vade mecum*. I pored over them, driving my cart, or walking to labour, song by song, verse by verse; carefully noticing the true tender or sublime, from affectation or fustian; and I am convinced I owe to this practice much of my critic-craft, such as it is."—(*Autobiography*.)

He derived, during this period, considerable advantages from the vicinity of Mount Oliphant to the town of Ayr—a place then, and still, distinguished by the residence of many respectable gentlemen's families, and a consequent elegance of society and manners, not common in remote provincial situations. To his friend Mr. Murdoch he no doubt owed, in the first instance, whatever attentions he received there from people older as well as higher than himself: some such persons appear to have taken a pleasure in lending him books, and surely no kindness could have been more useful to him than this. As for his coevals, he himself says, very justly, "It is not commonly at that green age that our young gentry have a due sense of the distance between them and their ragged playfellows. *My* young superiors," he proceeds, "never insulted the *clouterly* appearance of my plough-boy carcass, the two extremes of which were often exposed to all the inclemencies of all the seasons. They would give me stray volumes of books : among them, even then, I could pick up some observation ; and one whose heart I am sure not even the Munny[1] Begum scenes have tainted, helped me to a little French. Parting with these, my young friends and benefactors, as they occasionally went off for the East or West Indies, was often to me a sore affliction,—but I was soon called to more serious evils." The condition of the family during the last two years of their residence at Mount Oliphant, when the struggle which ended in their removal was rapidly approaching its crisis, has been already described ; nor need we dwell again on the untimely burden of sorrow, as well as toil, which fell to the share of the youthful poet, and which would have broken altogether any mind wherein feelings like his had existed, without strength like his to control them.

The removal of the family to Lochlea, in the parish of Tarbolton, took place when Burns was in his sixteenth year.[2] He had some time before this made his first attempt in verse, and the occasion is thus described by himself in his Autobiography :—" This kind of life—the cheerless gloom of a hermit, with the unceasing moil of a galley-slave, brought me to my sixteenth year ; a little before which period I first committed the sin of Rhyme. You know our country custom of coupling a man and woman together as partners in the labours of harvest. In my fifteenth autumn my partner

---

[1] The allusion here is to one of the sons of Dr. John Malcolm, afterwards highly distinguished in the service of the East India Company.

[2] [One error in chronology begets many more. In the year 1777, when the Burnes family removed to Lochlea, the poet was, of course, in his *nineteenth* year, that is to say, he had completed his eighteenth year on 25th January preceding. "A little before my sixteenth year," means the autumn of 1773—the same year in which his visit to Murdoch at Ayr took place.]

was a bewitching creature, a year younger than myself.
My scarcity of English denies me the power of doing her
justice in that language; but you know the Scottish idiom
—she was a *bonnie, sweet, sonsie lass*. In short, she, altogether unwittingly to herself, initiated me in that delicious
passion, which, in spite of acid disappointment, gin-horse
prudence, and book-worm philosophy, I hold to be the first
of human joys, our dearest blessing here below ! How she
caught the contagion, I cannot tell : you medical people
talk much of infection from breathing the same air, the
touch, &c.; but I never expressly said I loved her. Indeed,
I did not know myself why I liked so much to loiter
behind with her, when returning in the evening from our
labours; why the tones of her voice made my heart-
strings thrill like an Æolian harp; and particularly why
my pulse beat such a furious ratann, when I looked
and fingered over her little hand, to pick out the cruel
nettle-stings and thistles. Among her other love-inspiring
qualities, she sang sweetly; and it was her favourite reel,
to which I attempted giving an embodied vehicle in rhyme.
I was not so presumptuous as to imagine that I could make
verses like printed ones, composed by men who had Greek
and Latin; but my girl sang a song, which was said to be
composed by a small country laird's son, on one of his
father's maids, with whom he was in love; and I saw
no reason why I might not rhyme as well as he; for,
excepting that he could smear sheep, and cast peats, his
father living in the moorlands, he had no more scholar-craft
than myself.

" Thus with me began love and poetry; which at times
have been my only, and till within the last twelve months,
have been my highest enjoyment." [1]

---

[1] [The autobiography from which these quotations are made was addressed to Dr. Moore at the end of July, 1787. Exactly one year before

The earliest of the poet's productions is the little ballad

> " O, once I loved a bonie lass,
>   Aye! and I love her still;
> And whilst that honour warms my breast,
>   I'll love my handsome Nell," &c.

Burns himself characterizes it as "a very puerile and silly performance;" yet it contains here and there lines of which he need hardly have been ashamed at any period of his life :—

> " She dresses ay sae clean and neat,
>   Baith decent and genteel,
> *And then there's something in her gait*
>   *Gars ony dress look weel."*

" Silly and puerile as it is," said the poet, long afterwards, " I am always pleased with this song, as it recalls to my mind those happy days when my heart was yet honest, and my tongue sincere . . . I composed it in a wild enthusiasm of passion, and to this hour I never recollect it but my heart melts, my blood sallies, at the remembrance." (*MS. Common-place Book, August,* 1783.)

In his first epistle to Lapraik (1785) he says,

> " Amaist as soon as I could spell,
> I to the crambo-jingle fell,
>   Tho' rude and rough ;
> *Yet crooning to a body's sel'*
>   *Does weel eneugh.*'

And in some nobler verses, entitled, " On my Early Days," we have the following passage :

> " I mind it weel in early date,
> When I was beardless, young and blate,

---

that date, he published his poems in Kilmarnock to raise funds to enable him to go abroad. It is observable here that the poet does not confess to having experienced any love-enjoyment in the interval.]

> And first could thrash the barn,
> Or haud a yokin' o' the pleugh,
> *An' tho' forfoughten sair eneugh,*
> *Yet unco proud to learn—*
> *When first among the yellow corn*
> *A man I reckon'd was,*
> *An' wi' the lave ilk marry morn*
> *Could rank my rig and lass—*
> Still shearing and clearing
> The tither stookit raw,
> Wi' claivers and haivers
> Wearing the day awa,—
>
> E'en then a wish, I mind its power,
> A wish that to my latest hour
> Shall strongly heave my breast,
> That I, for poor auld Scotland's sake,
> Some useful plan or book could make,
> Or sing a sang, at least :
> *The rough bur-thistle spreading wide*
> *Amang the bearded bear,*
> *I turn'd the weeder-clips aside,*
> *And spared the symbol dear.*" [1]

He is hardly to be envied who can contemplate without emotion this exquisite picture of young nature and young genius. It was amidst such scenes that this extraordinary being felt those first indefinite stirrings of immortal ambition, which he has himself shadowed out under the magnificent image of the " blind gropings of Homer's Cyclops, around the walls of his cave." (*Autob.*, 1787.)

---

[1] These verses form a portion of the poetic epistle, addressed to Mrs Scott, " Gudewife o' Wauchope House," from Edinburgh, in March, 1787.]

CHAPTER II.

"O enviable early days,
   When dancing thoughtless pleasure's maze,
      To care and guilt unknown!
   How ill exchang'd for riper times,
   To feel the follies or the crimes
      Of others—or my own!"

AS has been already mentioned, William Burnes now
quitted Mount Oliphant for Lochlea, in the parish of
Tarbolton, where, for some little space, fortune appeared to
smile on his industry and frugality. Robert and Gilbert
were employed by their father as regular labourers—he
allowing them £7 of wages each *per annum;* from which
sum, however, the value of any home-made clothes received
by the youths was exactly deducted. Robert Burns's
person, inured to daily toil, and continually exposed to all
varieties of weather, presented, before the usual time, every
characteristic of robust and vigorous manhood. He says
himself, that he never feared a competitor in any species of
rural exertion; and Gilbert Burns, a man of uncommon
bodily strength, adds, that neither he, nor any labourer he
ever saw at work, was equal to the youthful poet, either in
the corn-field, or the severer tasks of the thrashing-floor.
Gilbert says, that Robert's literary zeal slackened considerably after their removal to Tarbolton. He was separated
from his acquaintances of the town of Ayr, and probably
missed not only the stimulus of their conversation, but the
kindness that had furnished him with his supply, such as
it was, of books. But the main source of his change of

habits about this period was, it is confessed on all hands, the precocious fervour of one of his own turbulent passions.

" In my seventeenth year," [1] says Burns, " to give my manners a brush, I went to a country dancing-school. My father had an unaccountable antipathy against these meetings ; and my going was, what to this moment I repent, in opposition to his wishes. My father was subject to strong passions ; from that instance of disobedience in me, he took a sort of dislike to me, which I believe was one cause of the dissipation which marked my succeeding years. I say dissipation, comparatively with the strictness, and sobriety, and regularity of Presbyterian country life ; for though the Will-o'-wisp meteors of thoughtless whim were almost the sole lights of my path, yet early ingrained piety and virtue kept me for several years afterwards within the line of innocence.[2] The great misfortune of my life was to

---

[1] [The bard's own dates in his autobiography are worthy of the reader's attention, because, while they are in all respects correct, they have been disregarded by his biographers and annotators, down to nearly the present day. Dr. Currie, under the direction of Gilbert Burns, set their authority aside, and even in one important instance had the temerity to alter, because it interfered with his own theories. The "seventeenth" year of Burns was the one he was least likely ever to forget. It was then he made his memorable excursion to Kirkoswald, where he first was taught " to look unconcernedly on a large tavern bill, and to mix without fear in a drunken squabble." It was also in that year (1775) that the incident narrated by himself, given in the text, took place, and the truth of which Gilbert's long comment in the next footnote was meant to impugn. It was of this year also that Robert used these words in his narrative of that period :—" My father, worn out by early hardship, was unfit for labour. There was a freedom in his lease in two years more, and to weather these we retrenched expenses. We lived very poorly."]

[2] " I wonder," says Gilbert, " how Robert could attribute to our father that lasting resentment of his going to a dancing-school against his will, of which he was incapable. I believe the truth was, that about this time he began to see the dangerous impetuosity of my brother's passions, as

want an aim. I saw my father's situation entailed on me perpetual labour. The only two openings by which I could enter the temple of Fortune, were the gate of niggardly economy, or the path of little chicaning bargain-making. The first is so contracted an aperture, I could never squeeze myself into it;—the last I always hated—there was contamination in the very entrance ! Thus abandoned of aim or view in life, with a strong appetite for sociability, as well from native hilarity, as from a pride of observation and remark; a constitutional melancholy or hypochondria-cism that made me fly solitude; add to these incentives to social life, my reputation for bookish knowledge, a certain wild logical talent, and a strength of thought, something like the rudiments of good sense; and it will not seem

---

well as his not being amenable to counsel, which often irritated my father, and which he would naturally think a dancing school was not likely to correct. But he was proud of Robert's genius, which he bestowed more expense on cultivating than on the rest of the family—and he was equally delighted with his warmth of heart, and conversational powers. He had indeed that dislike of dancing-schools which Robert mentions ; but so far overcame it during Robert's first month of attendance, that he permitted the rest of the family that were fit for it, to accompany him during the second month.   Robert excelled in dancing, and was for some time distractedly fond of it."

[The dancing-school experience referred to by Gilbert at the close of his note belonged to the Tarbolton period of his history, when the father was prostrated by his last illness, and all the children had very much their own way. The poet tells us that even during his Irvine days, his father was "visibly far gone in a consumption." The "country dancing-school" spoken of in the text is understood to have been at Dalrymple in the year 1775 ; and it is more than probable that neither Gilbert nor any younger member of the family were made aware of Robert's secret adventure. Dr. Currie has sadly weakened the force of the poet's own words in this part of the narrative. In the MS. it stands thus :—"My going was, what to this hour I repent, *in absolute defiance of his commands:* from that instance of *rebellion*, he took a kind of dislike to me," &c.]

surprising that I was generally a welcome guest where I
visited, or any great wonder that, always where two or three
met together, there was I among them. But far beyond
all other impulses of my heart, was *un penchant pour l'ador-
able moitié du genre humain.* My heart was completely
tinder, and was eternally lighted up by some goddess or
other; and, as in every other warfare in this world, my
fortune was various, sometimes I was received with favour,
and sometimes I was mortified with a repulse. At the
plough, scythe, or reaphook, I feared no competitor, and
thus I set absolute want at defiance; and as I never cared
farther for my labours than while I was in actual exercise,
I spent the evenings in the way after my own heart. A
country lad seldom carries on a love adventure without an
assisting confidant. I possessed a curiosity, zeal, and
intrepid dexterity, that recommended me as a proper second
on these occasions, and I dare say, I felt as much pleasure
in being in the secret of half the loves of the parish of
Tarbolton, as ever did statesman in knowing the intrigues
of half the courts of Europe." [1]

In regard to the same critical period of Burns's life, his
excellent brother writes as follows :—" The seven years we

---

[1] [There is some parenthetical matter contained in the long passage
above quoted from the autobiography, and that peculiarity has caused
considerable confusion to chronologists. It opens, as we have seen, with
incidents and allusions which can refer only to the Mount Oliphant period
of the writer's history, and farther on the reference to his constitutional
hypochondria operating as an incentive to social excitement is equally
applicable to that time. The same may be said regarding his extensive
practice in epistolary correspondence coupled with his dexterity in directing the love-adventures of his companions, for he says, in the paragraph
immediately following, that such was the direct result of his visit to
Kirkoswald. It is only in his concluding sentence that he slides into
Tarbolton matters by anticipation; and in the next paragraph he resumes
his narrative of the earlier period, by detailing another incident of his
" seventeenth year."]

lived in Tarbolton parish (extending from the seventeenth to the twenty-fourth of my brother's age)[1] were not marked by much literary improvement; but, during this time, the foundation was laid of certain habits in my brother's character, which afterwards became but too prominent, and which malice and envy have taken delight to enlarge on. Though, when young, he was bashful and awkward in his intercourse with women, yet when he approached manhood, his attachment to their society became very strong, and he was constantly the victim of some fair enslaver. The symptoms of his passion were often such as nearly to equal those of the celebrated Sappho. I never indeed knew that he *fainted, sunk, and died away;* but the agitations of his mind and body exceeded anything of the kind I ever knew in real life. He had always a particular jealousy of people who were richer than himself, or who had more consequence in life. His love, therefore, rarely settled on persons of this description. When he selected any one out of the sovereignty of his good pleasure to whom he should pay his particular attention, she was instantly invested with a sufficient stock of charms, out of the plentiful stores of his own imagination; and there was often a great dissimilitude between his fair captivator, as she appeared to others, and as she seemed when invested with the attributes he gave her.[2] One generally reigned paramount in his affections; but as Yorick's affections flowed out towards Madame de L—— at the remise door, while the eternal vows of Eliza were upon him, so Robert was frequently

---

[1] [Really, from the 19th to the 26th, *i e.*, from 1777 to 1784.]

[2] [Gilbert's own words (as still to be seen in the MS.) are much better than Dr. Currie's paraphrase quoted in the text. In the original it stands thus:—" and there was often a great disparity between his fair captivator and her attributes." For these fourteen words, Currie substitutes precisely double the number, with only half the effect.]

encountering other attractions, which formed so many
underplots in the drama of his love."

Thus occupied with labour, love, and dancing, the youth
" without an aim " found leisure occasionally to clothe the
sufficiently various moods in his mind in rhymes.   It was
as early as seventeen, he tells us, that he wrote some stanzas
which begin beautifully :

> " I dream'd I lay where flowers were springing
>   Gaily in the sunny beam ;
> Listening to the wild birds singing,
>   By a falling crystal stream.
> Straight the sky grew black and daring,
>   Thro' the woods the whirlwinds rave,
> Trees with aged arms were warring,
>   O'er the swelling *drumlie* wave.
> Such was life's deceitful morning, &c." [1]

On comparing these verses with those on " Handsome
Nell," the advance achieved by the young bard in the
course of two short years must be regarded with admiration,
nor should a minor circumstance be entirely overlooked,
that in the piece which we have just been quoting, there
occurs but one Scotch word.   It was about this time also,
that he wrote a ballad of much less ambitious vein, which,
years after, he says, he used to con over with delight, because of the faithfulness with which it recalled to him the
circumstances and feelings of his opening manhood.

> " My father was a farmer
>   Upon the Carrick border,
> And carefully he bred me
>   In decency and order.
> He bade me act a manly part,
>   Though I had ne'er a farthing ;
> For without an honest manly heart
>   No man was worth regarding.

---

[1] [These verses refer to, and were composed during, the darkest period
at Mount Oliphant—a year before the removal to Lochlea.]

" Then out into the busy world
  My course I did determine ;
Though to be rich was not my wish,
  Yet to be great was charming ;
My talents they were not the worst,
  Nor yet my education ;
Resolv'd was I at least to try
  To mend my situation.

*   *   *   *

" No help, nor hope, nor view had I,
  Nor person to befriend me ;
So I must toil, and sweat, and moil,
  And labour to sustain me :
To plough and sow, and reap and mow,
  My father bred me early ;
For one (he said) to labour bred
  Was a match for fortune fairly.

" Thus all obscure, unknown and poor,
  Through life I'm doom'd to wander,
Till down my weary bones I lay
  In everlasting slumber :
No view, nor care, but shun whate'er
  Might breed me pain or sorrow,
I live to-day as well's I may,
  Regardless of to-morrow." &c.

These are the only two of his very early productions in
which we have nothing expressly about love. The rest
were composed to celebrate the charms of those rural
beauties who followed each other in the dominion of his
fancy—or shared the capacious throne between them ; and
we may easily believe, that one who possessed, with other
qualifications, such powers of flattering, feared competitors
as little in the diversions of his evenings as in the toils of
his day.

The rural lover, in those districts, pursues his tender
vocation in a style, the especial fascination of which town-
bred swains may find it somewhat difficult to comprehend.

After the labours of the day are over, nay, very often after he is supposed by the inmates of his own fireside to be in his bed, the happy youth thinks little of walking many long Scotch miles to the residence of his mistress, who, upon the signal of a tap at her window, comes forth to spend a soft hour or two beneath the harvest moon, or if the weather be severe (a circumstance which never prevents the journey from being accomplished), amidst the sheaves of her father's barn. This "chappin' out," as they call it, is a custom which parents commonly wink at, if they do not openly approve of the observance; and the consequences are far, very far, more frequently quite harmless, than persons not familiar with the peculiar manners and feelings of our peasantry may find it easy to believe. Excursions of this class form the theme of almost all the songs which Burns is known to have produced about this period,—and such of these juvenile performances as have been preserved, are, without exception, beautiful. They show how powerfully his boyish fancy had been affected by the old rural minstrelsy of his own country, and how easily his native taste caught the secret of its charm. The truth and simplicity of nature breathe in every line—the images are always just, often originally happy—and the growing refinement of his ear and judgment, may be traced in the terser language and more mellow flow of each successive ballad.

The best of his songs written at this time is that beginning,—

> "It was upon a Lammas night,
>   When corn rigs are bonie,
> Beneath the moon's unclouded light,
>   I held awa to Annie.
>
> The time flew by wi' tentless heed,
>   Till, 'tween the late and early,
> Wi' sma' persuasion she agreed
>   To see me through the barley," &c.

The heroine of this ditty is supposed to have been a daughter of the poet's friend—"rude, rough, ready-witted Rankine."

We may let him carry on his own story. "A circumstance," says he, "which made some alteration on my mind and manners was, that I spent my nineteenth[1] summer on a smuggling coast, a good distance from home, at a noted school [Kirkoswald], to learn mensuration, surveying, dialling, &c., in which I made a good progress. But I made a greater progress in the knowledge of mankind. The contraband trade was at that time very successful, and it sometimes happened to me to fall in with those who carried it on. Scenes of swaggering riot and roaring dissipation were till this time new to me; but I was no enemy to social life. Here, though I learnt to fill my glass, and to mix without fear in a drunken squabble, yet I went on with a high hand with my geometry, till the sun entered Virgo, a month which is always a carnival in my bosom, when a charming *filette*, who lived next door to the school, overset my trigonometry, and set me off at a tangent from the sphere of my studies. I, however, struggled on with my *sines* and *cosines* for a few days more; but stepping into the garden one charming noon to take the sun's altitude, there I met my angel, like

> ' Proserpine, gathering flowers,
> Herself a fairer flower.'——

"It was in vain to think of doing any more good at school. The remaining week I staid I did nothing but craze the faculties of my soul about her, or steal out to meet her; and the two last nights of my stay in this

---

[1] [This word "nineteenth" distinctly reads "seventeenth" in the author's manuscript. It is the alteration of date before noted, which Currie admits he made "by the suggestion of Gilbert Burns," but for which no grounds whatever have been stated.]

country, had sleep been a mortal sin, the image of this modest and innocent girl had kept me guiltless.

"I returned home very considerably improved. My reading was enlarged with the very important addition of Thomson's and Shenstone's works; I had seen human nature in a new phasis; and I engaged several of my school-fellows to keep up a literary correspondence with me. This improved me in composition. I had met with a collection of letters by the wits of Queen Anne's reign, and I pored over them most devoutly; I kept copies of any of my own letters that pleased me; and a comparison between them and the composition of most of my correspondents flattered my vanity. I carried this whim so far, that though I had not three farthings' worth of business in the world, yet almost every post brought me as many letters as if I had been a broad plodding son of day-book and ledger.

"My life flowed on much in the same course till the twenty-third year.[1] *Vive l'amour, et vive la bagatelle*, were my sole principles of action. The addition of two more authors to my library gave me great pleasure : Sterne and M'Kenzie—'Tristram Shandy' and 'The Man of Feeling'—were my bosom favourites. Poesy was still a darling walk for my mind; but it was only indulged in according to the humour of the hour. I had usually half a dozen or more pieces on hand; I took up one or other, as it suited the momentary tone of the mind, and dismissed the work as it bordered on fatigue. My passions, once lighted up, raged like so many devils, till they found vent in rhyme; and then the conning over my verses, like a spell, soothed all into quiet."

---

[1] [This proves the exactness of the poet's own dates in his auto-biography. Here he refers to the six months he spent in Irvine; his "twenty-third year" was, of course, 1781, and so we find "December 27, 1781" is the date of the published letter he wrote from Irvine to his father.]

Of the rhymes of those days, a few, when he penned his Autobiography, had appeared in print. "Winter, a Dirge," an admirably versified piece, is of their number; the "Death of Poor Mailie," "Mailie's Elegy," and "John Barleycorn;" and one charming song, inspired by the nymph of Kirkoswald, whose attractions put an end to his trigonometry.

> "Now westlin' winds, and slaughtering guns,
>   Bring Autumn's pleasant weather;
> The moorcock springs, on whirring wings,
>   Amang the blooming heather. . . .
> O Peggy dear, the evening's clear,
>   Thick flies the skimming swallow;
> The sky is blue, the fields in view,
>   All fading green and yellow;
> Come let us stray our gladsome way," &c.

"John Barleycorn"[1] is a good old ballad, very cleverly new-modelled and extended; but the "Death" and "Elegy of Poor Mailie" deserve more attention. The expiring animal's admonitions touching the education of the "poor toop lamb, my son and heir," and the "yowie, sillie thing," her daughter, are from the same peculiar vein of sly homely wit, embedded upon fancy, which he afterwards dug with a bolder hand in the "Twa Dogs," and perhaps to its utmost depth, in his "Death and Doctor Hornbook." It need scarcely be added, that poor Mailie was a real personage, though she did not actually die until some time after her last words were written. She had been purchased by Burns in a frolic, and became exceedingly attached to his person.

> "Thro' all the town she trotted by him,
> A lang half-mile she could descry him;

---

[1] [Of several of Burns's effusions that have been translated into the German language, we are informed that no one delighted the illustrious Goethe more than "John Barleycorn." It became his favourite post-prandial ditty.]

> Wi' kindly bleat, when she did spy him,
>   She ran wi' speed;
> A friend mair faithfu' ne'er came nigh him,
>   Than Mailie dead."

These little pieces are in a much broader dialect than any of their predecessors. His merriment and satire were, from the beginning, Scotch.

Notwithstanding the luxurious tone of some of Burns's pieces produced in those times, we are assured by himself (and his brother unhesitatingly confirms the statement), that no positive vice mingled in any of his loves, until after he reached his twenty-third year. He has already told us, that his short residence "away from home" at Kirkoswald, where he mixed in the society of sea-faring men and smugglers, produced an unfavourable alteration on some of his habits; but in 1781-2 he spent six months at Irvine; and it is from this period that his brother dates a serious change.

"As his numerous connections," says Gilbert, "were governed by the strictest rules of virtue and modesty (from which he never deviated till his twenty-third year), he became anxious to be in a situation to marry.[1] This was not likely to be the case while he remained a farmer, as the

---

[1] [The writings of the poet in reference to this period of his early life furnish no clue to the name or social position of the young woman he was thus anxious to marry; and not till half a century after his death did any of his family, or Tarbolton associates, venture to throw some light on the matter. Four drafts of love-letters in the poet's hand-writing, addressed to "My dear E.," found among his papers at his death, were published in Currie's first edition (1800) as having been written "about the year 1780." These were withdrawn from the second, and all subsequent editions, and were not even restored by Gilbert in 1820. The details of that early love-attachment of Burns, as revealed by his youngest sister, Mrs. Begg, would occupy more space than a footnote can supply, and therefore we refer the reader to Appendix B. for particulars on this theme.]

stocking of a farm required a sum of money he saw no probability of being master of for a great while. He and I had for several years taken land of our father, for the purpose of raising flax on our own account; and in the course of selling it, Robert began to think of turning flax-dresser, both as being suitable to his grand view of settling in life, and as subservient to the flax-raising." [1] Burns accordingly went to a half-brother of his mother's, by name Peacock, a flax-dresser in Irvine, with the view of learning this new trade, and for some time he applied himself diligently; but misfortune after misfortune attended him. The shop accidentally caught fire during the carousal of a new-year's-day morning, and Robert " was left, like a true poet, not worth a sixpence."—" I was obliged," says he, " to give up this scheme; the clouds of misfortune were gathering thick round my father's head; and what was worst of all, he was visibly far gone in a consumption; and to crown my distresses, a *belle fille* whom I adored, and who had pledged her soul to meet me in the field of matrimony, jilted me, with peculiar circumstances of mortification.[2] The finishing evil that brought up the rear of

---

[1] Mr. Sillar assured Mr. Robert Chambers that this notion originated with William Burnes, who thought of becoming entirely a lint-farmer; and, by way of keeping as much of the profits as he could within his family, of making his eldest son a flax-dresser.

[2] Some letters referring to this affair are omitted in the " General Correspondence " of Gilbert's edition, for what reason I know not, They are surely as well worth preserving as many in the Collection, particularly when their early date is considered. The first of them begins thus :—" I verily believe, my dear E., that the pure genuine feelings of love are as rare in the world as the pure genuine principles of virtue and piety. This, I hope, will account for the uncommon style of all my letters to you. By uncommon, I mean their being written in such a serious manner, which, to tell you the truth, has made me often afraid lest you should take me for some zealous bigot, who conversed with his mistress as he would converse with his minister. I don't know

this infernal file, was, my constitutional melancholy being
increased to such a degree, that for three months I was in
a state of mind scarcely to be envied by the hopeless
wretches who have got their mittimus—'Depart from me,
ye cursed ! ' " The following letter, addressed by Burns to
his father, three days before the unfortunate fire took
place, will show abundantly that the gloom of his spirits
had little need of that aggravation. When we consider by
whom, to whom, and under what circumstances, it was
written, the letter is every way a remarkable one :—

how it is, my dear; for though, except your company, there is nothing
on earth gives me so much pleasure as writing to you, yet it never gives
me those giddy raptures so much talked of among lovers. I have often
thought, that if a well-grounded affection be not really a part of virtue,
'tis something extremely akin to it. Whenever the thought of my E.
warms my heart, every feeling of humanity, every principle of generosity,
kindles in my breast. It extinguishes every dirty spark of malice and
envy, which are but too apt to invest me. I grasp every creature in the
arms of universal benevolence, and equally participate in the pleasures
of the happy, and sympathise with the miseries of the unfortunate. I
assure you, my dear, I often look up to the divine Disposer of events,
with an eye of gratitude for the blessing which I hope He intends to
bestow on me, in bestowing you."

What follows is from Burns's Letter in answer to that in which the
young woman intimated her final rejection of his vows.—" I ought in
good manners to have acknowledged the receipt of your letter before
this time, but my heart was so shocked with the contents of it, that I
can scarcely yet collect my thoughts so as to write to you on the subject.
I will not attempt to describe what I felt on receiving your letter. I
read it over and over, again and again; and though it was in the
politest language of refusal, still it was peremptory; ' you were sorry
you could not make me a return, but you wish me ' (what, without you,
I never can obtain) all kind of happiness.' It would be weak and un-
manly to say that without you I never can be happy; but sure I am,
that sharing life with you, would have given it a relish, that, wanting
you, I never can taste." In such excellent English did Burns woo his
country maidens, in at most his twentieth year, [or, more probably,
his twenty-third year].

"Irvine, 27 Dec., 1781.

"Honoured Sir,—I have purposely delayed writing, in the hope that I should have the pleasure of seeing you on New-year's-day; but work comes so hard upon us, that I do not choose to be absent on that account, as well as for some other little reasons, which I shall tell you at meeting. My health is nearly the same as when you were here, only my sleep is a little sounder; and, on the whole, I am rather better than otherwise, though I mend by very slow degrees. The weakness of my nerves has so debilitated my mind that I dare neither review past wants, nor look forward into futurity; for the least anxiety or perturbation in my breast produces most unhappy effects on my whole frame. Sometimes, indeed, when for an hour or two my spirits are lightened, I *glimmer* a little into futurity; but my principal, and indeed my only pleasurable employment, is looking backwards and forwards in a moral and religious way. I am quite transported at the thought, that ere long, perhaps very soon, I shall bid an eternal adieu to all the pains and uneasiness, and disquietudes of this weary life; for I assure you I am heartily tired of it; and, if I do not very much deceive myself, I could contentedly and gladly resign it.

> ' The soul, uneasy, and confined at home,
> Rests and expatiates in a life to come.'

"It is for this reason I am more pleased with the 15th, 16th, and 17th verses of the 7th chapter of Revelations, than with any ten times as many verses in the whole Bible, and would not exchange the noble enthusiasm with which they inspire me for all that this world has to offer.[1]

---

[1] The verses of Scripture here alluded to, are as follows :—

"15. Therefore are they before the throne of God, and serve him day and night in his temple; and he that sitteth on the throne shall dwell among them.

As for this world, I despair of ever making a figure in it. I am not formed for the bustle of the busy, nor the flutter of the gay. I shall never again be capable of entering into such scenes. Indeed, I am altogether unconcerned at the thoughts of this life. I foresee that poverty and obscurity probably await me, and I am in some measure prepared and daily preparing, to meet them. I have just time and paper to return you my grateful thanks for the lessons of virtue and piety you have given me, which were so much neglected at the time of giving them, but which I hope have been remembered ere it is yet too late. Present my dutiful respects to my mother, and my compliments to Mr. and Mrs. Muir;[1] and, with wishing you a merry New-year's-day I shall conclude.

> "I am, honoured Sir, your dutiful son,
>
> "ROBERT BURNS."

"P.S.—My meal is nearly out; but I am going to borrow, till I get more."

"This letter," says Dr. Currie, "written several years before the publication of his Poems, when his name was as obscure as his condition was humble, displays the philosophic melancholy which so generally forms the poetical temperament, and that buoyant and ambitious spirit which indicates a mind conscious of its strength. At Irvine, Burns at this time possessed a single room for his lodgings, rented, perhaps, at the rate of a shilling a week. He passed

---

"16. They shall hunger no more, neither thirst any more; neither shall the sun light on them, nor any heat.

"17. For the Lamb that is in the midst of the throne shall feed them, and shall lead them unto living fountains of waters, and God shall wipe away all tears from their eyes."

[1] [This was the worthy couple who inhabited Tarbolton Mill, on the Faile water, referred to as "Willie's Mill," in "Death and Dr. Hornbook."]

his days in constant labour as a flax-dresser, and his food consisted chiefly of oatmeal, sent to him from his father's family. The store of this humble, though wholesome nutriment, it appears, was nearly exhausted, and he was about to borrow till he should obtain a supply. Yet even in this situation, his active imagination had formed to itself pictures of eminence and distinction. His despair of making a figure in the world, shows how ardently he wished for honourable fame; and his contempt of life, founded on this despair, is the genuine expression of a youthful and generous mind. In such a state of reflection, and of suffering, the imagination of Burns naturally passed the dark boundaries of our earthly horizon, and rested on those beautiful representations of a better world, where there is neither thirst, nor hunger, nor sorrow, and where happiness shall be in proportion to the capacity of happiness."

Unhappily for himself and for the world, it was not always in the recollections of his virtuous home and the study of his Bible, that Burns sought for consolation amidst the heavy distresses which " his youth was heir to." Irvine is a small seaport; and here, as at Kirkoswald, the adventurous spirits of a smuggling coast, with all their jovial habits, were to be met with in abundance. " He contracted some acquaintance," says Gilbert, " of a freer manner of thinking and living than he had been used to, whose society prepared him for overleaping the bounds of rigid virtue, which had hitherto restrained him."

I owe to Mr. Robert Chambers, author of " Traditions of Edinburgh," the following note of a conversation which he had in June, 1826, with a respectable old citizen of this town:—"Burns was, at the time of his residence among us, an older-looking man than might have been expected from his age—very darkly complexioned, with a strong eye—of a thoughtful appearance, amounting to what might be called a gloomy attentiveness; so much so, that when in company which did not call forth his brilliant powers of conversation, he might often be seen, for a considerable space together, leaning down on his palm, with his elbow resting on his knee. He was in common silent and reserved; but when he found a man to his mind, he constantly made a point of attaching himself to his company, and endeavouring to bring out his powers. It was among women alone that he uniformly exerted himself and uniformly shone. People remarked even then, that when Robert Burns did speak, he always spoke to the point, and in general with a sententious brevity. His moody thoughtfulness, and laconic style of expression, were both inherited from his father, who, for his station in life, was a very singular person."

Burns himself thus sums up the results of his residence at Irvine:—"From this adventure I learned something of a town life; but the principal thing which gave my mind a turn, was a friendship I formed with a young fellow, a very noble character, but a hapless son of misfortune. He was the son of a simple mechanic; but a great man in the neighbourhood, taking him under his patronage, gave him a genteel education, with a view of bettering his situation in life. The patron dying just as he was ready to launch out into the world, the poor fellow in despair went to sea; where, after a variety of good and ill fortune, a little before I was acquainted with him, he had been set ashore by an American privateer, on the wild coast of Connaught, stripped of everything. . . . . . . His mind was fraught with independence, magnanimity, and every manly virtue. I loved and admired him to a degree of enthusiasm, and of course strove to imitate him. In some measure I succeeded; I had pride before, but he taught it to flow in proper channels. His knowledge of the world was vastly superior to mine; and I was all attention to learn. He was the only man I ever saw who was a greater fool than myself, where woman was the presiding star; but he spoke of illicit love with the levity of a sailor—which hitherto I had regarded with horror. *Here his friendship did me a mischief.*" Professor Walker, when preparing to write his Sketch of the Poet's Life, was informed by an aged inhabitant of Irvine, that Burns's chief delight while there was in discussing religious topics, particularly in those circles which usually gather in a Scotch churchyard after service. The senior added, that Burns commonly took the high Calvinistic side in such debates; and concluded with a boast "that the lad" was indebted to himself in a great measure for the gradual adoption of "more liberal opinions." [1] It was during the same period, that the poet was first initiated in the mysteries of freemasonry, "which was," says his brother, "his first introduction to the life of a boon companion." He was introduced to St. David's Lodge of Tarbolton by John Rankine, a very dissipated man, of considerable talents, to whom he afterwards indited a poetical epistle, which will be noticed in its place. [2]

"Rhyme," Burns says, "I had given up;" (on going to

---

[1] [This anecdote from Walker is to be received with caution. There never was a time when Burns sympathized with Calvinistic views. The other information gleaned by Chambers in Irvine, is more characteristic of Robert Burns. See note, page 42, infra.]

[2] [The epithet, "very dissipated man," here employed against "the wale o' cocks for fun an' drinking," is much too strong; for although he was somewhat "rough, rude, an' ready-witted," his memory was long respected in the district. He outlived our bard nearly fourteen years, his head-stone in Galston churchyard showing that he died on February 2, 1810. In a very curious triplet, the poet thus anticipated Rankine's survival of himself:—

> "He who of Rankine sang lies stiff and dead,
> And a green grassy hillock hides his head,—
> Alas! alas! a devilish change indeed!"]

Irvine;) "but meeting with Fergusson's 'Scottish Poems,' I strung anew my wildly-sounding lyre with emulating vigour." Neither flax-dressing nor the tavern could keep him long from his proper vocation. But it was probably this accidental meeting with Fergusson, that in a great measure finally determined the "Scottish" character of Burns's poetry ; and, indeed, but for the lasting sense of this obligation, and some natural sympathy with the personal misfortunes of Fergusson's life, it would be difficult to account for the very high terms in which Burns always mentions his productions.

Shortly before Burns went to Irvine, he, his brother Gilbert, and some seven or eight young men besides, all of the parish of Tarbolton, had formed themselves into a society which they called the Bachelor's Club ; and which met one evening in every month for the purposes of mutual entertainment and improvement. That their cups were but modestly filled is evident; for the rules of the club did not permit any member to spend more than threepence at a sitting. A question was announced for discussion at the close of each meeting ; and at the next they came prepared to deliver their sentiments upon the subject-matter thus proposed. Burns and David Sillar (to whom the "Epistle to Davie, a brother-poet" was afterwards addressed, and who subsequently published a volume of verses not without merit) were employed by the rest to draw up the regulations of the Society : and some stanzas prefixed to *Sillar's* scroll of Rules "first introduced Burns and him to each other as brother rhymers."[1] Of the sort of questions discussed, we

---

[1] I quote from a letter of Mr. Sillar, 29th November, 1828, the lines·—

> "Of birth and blood we do not boast,
> No gentry does our Club afford,
> But ploughmen and mechanics, we
> In nature's simple dress record :

may form some notion from the minute of one evening, still extant in Burns's hand-writing.—QUESTION FOR HALLOWE'EN (Nov. 11, 1780).—" Suppose a young man, bred a farmer, but without any fortune, has it in his power to marry either of two women, the one a girl of large fortune, but neither handsome in person, nor agreeable in conversation, but who can manage the household affairs of a farm well enough ; the other of them a girl every way agreeable in person, conversation, and behaviour, but without any fortune : which of them shall he choose ? " Burns, as may be guessed, took the imprudent side in this discussion.

" On one solitary occasion," says he, " we resolved to meet at Tarbolton in July, on the race-night and have a dance in honour of our society. Accordingly, we did meet, each one with a partner, and spent the night in such innocence and merriment, such cheerfulness and good-humour, that every brother will long remember it with delight." There can be no doubt that Burns would not have patronised this sober association so long, unless he had experienced at its assemblies the pleasure of a stimulated mind ; and as little, that to the habit of arranging his thoughts and expressing them in somewhat of a formal shape, thus early cultivated, we ought to attribute much of that conversational skill which, when he first mingled with the upper world, was generally considered as the most remarkable of all his personal accomplishments.—Burns's associates of the Bachelor's Club, must have been young men possessed of talents and acquirements, otherwise such minds as his and

---

Let nane e'er join us who refuse
To aid the lads that haud the ploughs,
To choose their friends and wale their wives,
To ease the labours of their lives."

These lines, therefore (hitherto ascribed to Burns), are in fact the lawful property of Mr. Sillar.

Gilbert's could not have persisted in measuring themselves
against theirs; and we may believe, that the periodical display of the poet's own vigour and resources, at these club
meetings, and (more frequently than his father approved)
at the Free Mason Lodge of Tarbolton, extended his rural
reputation; and, by degrees, prepared persons not immediately included in his own circle, for the extraordinary
impression which his poetical efforts were ere long to create
all over "the Carrick border."

Mr. David Sillar[1] gives an account of the beginning of
his own acquaintance with Burns, and introduction into this
Bachelor's Club, which will always be read with much
interest.—"Mr. Robert Burns was some time in the parish
of Tarbolton prior to my acquaintance with him. His
social disposition easily procured him acquaintance; but a
certain satirical seasoning with which he and all poetical
geniuses are in some degree influenced, while it set the
rustic circle in a roar, was not unaccompanied with its kindred attendant, suspicious fear. I recollect hearing his
neighbours observe, 'he had a great deal to say for himself,'
and that they 'suspected his principles.' He wore the only
tied hair in the parish; and in the church, his plaid, which
was of a particular colour, I think *fillemot*, he wrapped in

---

[1] David Sillar, a native of Tarbolton, became in 1784 a schoolmaster
at Irvine; and having, in the course of a long life, realized considerable
property, was appointed chief magistrate of that town. I regret that, in
the former edition of this narrative (pp. 43, 44, 46 of the Miscellany
edition, and pp. 50, 51, 54 of the 8vo), some misstatements concerning this
member of the Tarbolton Club were inserted. These, in as far as he
pointed them out, are now omitted or corrected. Bailie Sillar was certainly not at Irvine during Burns's residence there. [A native of that
town informed us, that in his later years Sillar grew very penurious, and
even refused to subscribe for the erection of the poet's mausoleum at
Dumfries, as well as of the Ayr monument. He inherited a large sum
consequent on the death of two brothers whom he survived. He himself
paid the debt of nature in 1830.]

a particular manner round his shoulders. These surmises, and his exterior, had such a magnetical influence on my curiosity, as made me particularly solicitous of his acquaintance. Whether my acquaintance with Gilbert was casual or premeditated, I am not now certain. By him I was introduced, not only to his brother, but to the whole of that family, where in a short time, I became a frequent, and, I believe, not unwelcome visitant. After the commencement of my acquaintance with the bard, we frequently met upon Sundays at church, when, between sermons, instead of going with our friends or lasses to the inn, we often took a walk in the fields. In these walks, I have frequently been struck with his facility in addressing the fair sex: and many times, when I have been bashfully anxious how to express myself, he would have entered into conversation with them with the greatest ease and freedom ; and it was generally a death-blow to our conversation, however agreeable, to meet a female acquaintance. Some of the few opportunities of a noon-tide walk that a country life allows her laborious sons, we spent on the banks of the river, or in the woods in the neighbourhood of Stair, a situation peculiarly adapted to the genius of a rural bard. Some book (generally one of those mentioned in his letter to Mr. Murdoch) he always carried and read, when not otherwise employed. It was likewise his custom to read at table. In one of my visits to Lochlea, in time of a sowen supper, he was so intent on reading, I think Tristram Shandy, that his spoon falling out of his hand, made him exclaim, in a tone scarcely imitable, ' Alas, poor Yorick ! ' Such was Burns, and such were his associates, when I was admitted a member of the Bachelors' Club.'' [1]

---

[1] Letter to Mr. Aiken of Ayr, in Morison's Burns, vol. ii., pp. 257-260. [Mr. Lockhart omitted Sillar's closing paragraph, which the editor considers to be of some importance, as proving that Burns, long

The misfortunes of William Burnes thickened apace, as has already been seen, and were approaching their crisis at the time when Robert came home from his flax-dressing experiment at Irvine. I have been favoured with copies of some letters addressed by the poet soon afterwards to his cousin, "Mr. James Burness, writer in Montrose," which cannot but gratify every reader.[1] They are worthy of the strong understanding and warm heart of Burns; and, besides opening a pleasing view of the manner in which domestic affection was preserved between his father and the relations from whom the accidents of life had separated that excellent person in boyhood, they appear to me—written by a young and unknown peasant in a wretched hovel, the abode of poverty, care, and disease— to be models of native good taste and politeness.

"Lochlea, 21st June, 1783.

"DEAR SIR,—My father received your favour of the 10th curt.; and as he has been for some months very poorly in

---

before his residence in Irvine, had adopted the most liberal views in matters ecclesiastical. The omitted portion is as follows:—"Burns had in his youth paid considerable attention to the arguments for and against the doctrine of 'original sin,' then making considerable noise in the neigh-bourhood of Ayr; and having perused Dr. Taylor's work on that subject, and also a favourite book called 'Letters concerning the Religion essential to Man,' his opinions, when he came to Tarbolton, were consequently favourable to what you Ayr people call 'the moderate side.' The reli-gious views of the people of Tarbolton at that time were purely those of their fathers, derived from the 'Westminster Confession,' and taught by each generation to the succeeding one, uncontaminated by reading, reflection, and discussion. The slightest insinuation of Taylor's opinions made his neighbours suspect Burns, and even avoid him, as 'an heretical and dangerous companion.' Such was Burns," &c.]

[1] [Mr. Lockhart seems not to have been aware that these letters, ad-dressed by the poet to his cousin in Montrose, had already been given to the public by Gilbert Burns in his re-issue of Dr. Currie's edition of the "Life and Works of Burns," 1820.]

health, and is, in his own opinion, and indeed in almost everybody else's, in a dying condition; he has only, with great difficulty, written a few farewell lines to each of his brothers-in-law. For this melancholy reason, I now hold the pen for him, to thank you for your kind letter, and to assure you, Sir, that it shall not be my fault if my father's correspondence in the North die with him. My brother writes to John Caird; and to him I must refer you for the news of our family. I shall only trouble you with a few particulars relative to the present wretched state of this country. Our markets are exceedingly high; oatmeal 17d. and 18d. per peck, and not to be got even at that price. We have indeed been pretty well supplied with quantities of white peas from England and elsewhere; but that resource is likely to fail us; and what will become of us then, particularly the very poorest sort, Heaven only knows. This country, till of late, was flourishing incredibly in the manufacture of silk, lawn, and carpet weaving; and we are still carrying on a good deal in that way, but much reduced from what it was. We had also a fine trade in the shoe way, but now entirely ruined, and hundreds driven to a starving condition on account of it. Farming is also at a very low ebb with us. Our lands, generally speaking, are mountainous and barren; and our land-holders, full of ideas of farming gathered from the English and the Lothians, and other rich soils in Scotland, make no allowance for the odds of the quality of land, and consequently stretch us much beyond what, in the event, we will be found able to pay. We are also much at a loss for want of proper methods in our improvements of farming. Necessity compels us to leave our old schemes, and few of us have opportunities of being well informed in new ones. In short, my dear sir, since the unfortunate beginning of this American war, and its as unfortunate conclusion, this country has been, and still is, decaying very fast. Even in higher life, a couple of our Ayrshire noblemen, and the major parts of our knights and squires, are all insolvent. A miserable job of a Douglas, Heron & Co. Bank, which no doubt you have heard of, has undone numbers of them; and imitating English and French, and other foreign luxuries and fopperies, has ruined as many more. There is a great trade of smuggling carried on along our coasts, which, however destructive to the interests of the kingdom at large, certainly enriches this corner of it; but too often at the expense of our morals. However, it enables individuals to make, at least for a time, a splendid appearance; but Fortune, as is usual with her when she is uncommonly lavish of her favours, is generally even with them at the last; and happy were it for numbers of them if she would leave them no worse than when she found them.

" My mother sends you a small present of a cheese; 'tis but a very little one, as our last year's stock is sold off; but if you could fix on any correspondent in Edinburgh or Glasgow, we would send you a proper one in the season. Mrs. Black promises to take the cheese under her care so far, and then to send it to you by the Stirling carrier.

" I shall conclude this long letter with assuring you, that I shall be very happy to hear from you, or any of our friends in your country, when opportunity serves. My father sends you, probably for the last time in this world, his warmest wishes for your welfare and happiness; and my mother and the rest of the family desire to enclose their compliments to you, Mrs. Burness, and the rest of your family, along with,

" Dear Sir, your affectionate cousin,

" ROBERT BURNESS." [1]

---

[1] [It is to be observed here that this cousin of our poet, had, through some freak of fancy, adopted the double *ss* in the spelling of his surname, contrary to use and wont in the various branches of the family. The

In the second of these letters, the Poet announces the death of his father. It is dated Lochlea, 17th February, 1784:—" DEAR COUSIN,—I would have returned you my thanks for your kind favour of the 13th December sooner, had it not been that I waited to give you an account of that melancholy event, which, for some time past, we have from day to day expected. On the 13th curt. I lost the best of fathers. Though, to be sure, we have had long warning of the impending stroke, still the feelings of nature claim their part ; and I cannot recollect the tender endearments and parental lessons of the best of friends and the ablest of instructors, without feeling what perhaps the calmer dictates of reason would partly condemn. I hope my father's friends in your country will not let their connection in this place die with him. For my part I shall ever with pleasure—with pride, acknowledge my connection with those who were allied by the ties of blood and friendship to a man whose memory I will ever honour and revere. I expect, therefore, my dear Sir, you will not neglect any opportunity of letting me hear from you, which will ever very much oblige,

" My dear cousin, yours sincerely,

" ROBERT BURNESS."

Among other evils from which the excellent William Burnes, thus escaped, was an affliction that would, in his eyes, have been severe. Our youthful poet had not, as he confesses, come unscathed out of the society of those persons of " liberal opinions " with whom he consorted in Irvine; and he expressly attributes to their lessons, the

---

poet's father, like his ancestors, spelled his name " Burnes," as if the surname had two syllables; but he pronounced it as one syllable. The poet however, through the habit of corresponding with this cousin, adopted the double *ss*, probably in compliment to his relative.]

scrape into which he fell soon after "he put his hand to the plough again." He was compelled, according to the then all but universal custom of rural parishes in Scotland, to do penance in church, before the congregation, in consequence of the birth of an illegitimate child; and whatever may be thought of the propriety of such exhibitions, there can be no difference of opinion as to the culpable levity with which he describes the nature of his offence, and the still more reprehensible bitterness with which, in his Epistle to Rankine,[1] he inveighs against the clergyman, who, in rebuking him, only performed what was then a regular part of the clerical duty, and a part of it that could never have been at all agreeable to the worthy man whom he satirizes under the appellation of "Daddie Auld." "The Poet's Welcome to an Illegitimate Child" was composed on the same occasion—a piece in which some very manly feelings are expressed, along with others which it can give no one pleasure to contemplate. There is a song in honour of the same occasion, or a similar one, about the same period, "The Rantin' Dog the Daddie o't," which exhibits the poet as glorying, and only glorying, in his shame.[2]

---

[1] There is much humour in some of the verses; as,

> " 'Twas ae night lately, in my fun,
> I gaed a roving wi' the gun,
> An' brought a paitrick to the grun,'
> 　　　A bonnie hen,
> And, as the twilight was begun,
> 　　　Thought nane wad ken," &c.

[2] [The biographer here has made some inconsiderate misstatements, for which he was severely reflected on by Sir Harris Nicolas in a memoir of the poet prefixed to his "Aldine edition" of the Poems. He properly pointed out that the song called "The Rantin' Dog the Daddie o't," equally with the "Poet's Welcome," is remarkable for the tenderness it displays towards both mother and child. Some other composition of the bard on this topic must have been hanging in Mr. Lockhart's

When I consider his tender affection for the surviving members of his own family, and the reverence with which he ever regarded the memory of the father whom he had so recently buried, I cannot believe that Burns has thought fit to record in verse all the feelings which this exposure excited in his bosom. " To waive (in his own language) the quantum of the sin," he who, two years afterwards, wrote the " Cotter's Saturday Night," had not, we may be sure, hardened his heart to the thought of bringing additional sorrow and unexpected shame to the fireside of a widowed mother. But his false pride recoiled from letting his jovial associates guess how little he was able to drown the whispers *of the still small voice*, and the fermenting bitterness of a mind ill at ease within itself, escaped (as may be too often traced in the history of satirists) in the shape of angry sarcasms against others, who, whatever their private errors might be, had at least done him no wrong. It is impossible not to smile at one item of consolation which Burns proposes to himself on this occasion :—

> " —— The mair they talk, *I'm kenn'd the better ;*
>   E'en let them clash ! "

This is indeed a singular manifestation of " the last infirmity of noble minds."

---

memory ; if not the " Epistle to Rankine," it may have been the " Reply to a Tailor." Certainly the words quoted from the " Welcome,"

> " The mair they talk, I'm kenn'd the better ! "

display a singular manifestation of the poet's early aspiration,

> " To be rich was not my wish, yet to be great was charming ! "

but at the same time they do not justify the harsh allegation challenged by Sir Harris.]

CHAPTER III.

"The star that rules my luckless lot
Has fated me the russet coat,
And damn'd my fortune to the groat ;
        But in requit,
Has bless'd me wi' a random shot
        O' country wit."

THREE months before the death of William Burnes,
Robert and Gilbert took the farm of Mossgiel, in the
neighbouring parish of Mauchline, with the view of pro-
viding a shelter for their parents in the storm, which they
had seen gradually thickening, and knew must soon burst ;
and to this place the whole family removed on William's
death.[1] "It was stocked by the property and individual
savings of the whole family (says Gilbert), and was a joint
concern among us. Every member of the family was
allowed ordinary wages for the labour he performed on the
farm. My brother's allowance and mine was £7 per annum
each. And during the whole time this family concern
lasted, as well as during the preceding period at Lochlea,
Robert's expenses never, in any one year, exceeded his
slender income."

"I entered on this farm," says the poet, "with a full re-

---

[1] The farm consisted of 119 acres, and the rent was £90. [But it is
by no means certain that the family shifted their *residence* to Mossgiel
till Whitsunday following. Indeed, the presumption is all against such
a supposition, because their predecessor at Mossgiel was entitled to retain
possession of the house there until 25 May.]

solution, *Come, go to ! I will be wise.* I read farming books,
I calculated crops, I attended markets, and, in short, in
spite of the *devil, and the world, and the flesh,* I believe I
should have been a wise man ; but the first year, from
unfortunately buying bad seed, the second, from a late
harvest, we lost half our crops. This overset all my wisdom,
and I returned *like the dog to his vomit, and the sow that was
washed, to her wallowing in the mire."*—(*Autob.*, 1787).

"At the time that our poet took the resolution of becoming *wise,* he procured," says Currie, "a little book of
blank paper, with the purpose expressed on the first page,
of making farming memorandums. These *farming memoranda* are curious enough," that biographer slyly adds,
"and a specimen may gratify the reader." [1]

Specimens accordingly he gives ; as,

> " O why the deuce should I repine
>   And be an ill-foreboder ?
> I'm twenty-three, and five foot nine—
>   I'll go and be a sodger," &c.

> " O leave novells, ye Mauchline belles,
>   Ye're safer at your spinning wheel ;
> Such witching books are baited hooks
>   For rakish rooks—like Rob Mossgiel.

> Your fine Tom Jones and Grandisons,
>   They make your youthful fancies reel,
> They heat your veins, and fire your brains,
>   And then ye're prey for Rob Mossgiel," &c.

The four years [2] during which Burns resided on this cold

---

[1] [This quotation from Dr. Currie's first vol., page 355, has hitherto
appeared in every edition of the present work (through some misappre-
hension of the author) as if the words were those of Gilbert Burns, and
formed part of his narrative. But the words are distinctly Currie's own,
and in the present text, the proper correction is made accordingly.]

[2] [Why *four* years ? The poet's residence there, from Whitsunday,
1784, to Whitsunday, 1786, when his poems were at the press to raise

and ungrateful farm of Mossgiel, were the most important
of his life. It was then that his genius developed its
highest energies; on the works produced in those years his
fame was first established, and must ever continue mainly
to rest: it was then also that his personal character came
out in all its brightest lights, and in all but its darkest
shadows; and indeed, from the commencement of this
period, the history of the man may be traced, step by step, in
his own immortal writings.

Burns now began to know that Nature had meant him
for a poet; and diligently, though as yet in secret, he
laboured in what he felt to be his destined vocation.
Gilbert continued for some time to be his chief, often
indeed his only confidant;[1] and anything more interesting
and delightful than this excellent man's account of the
manner in which the poems included in the first of his
brother's publications were composed, is certainly not to be
found in the annals of literary history.

The reader has already seen, that long before the earliest
of these poems was known beyond the domestic circle, the
strength of Burns's understanding, and the keenness of his
wit, as displayed in his ordinary conversation, and more particularly at masonic meetings and debating clubs (of which

---

funds to help him off to Jamaica, embraced a period of two years only.
He continued there till the following November, when he removed to
Edinburgh; and from that time till Whitsunday, 1788, when he entered
on possession of Ellisland, he cannot well be said to have been a resident
at Mossgiel.]

[1] [This statement requires to be considerably qualified. We have seen
that Gilbert knew nothing of Robert's first dancing-school escapade; we
shall see that although residing under the same roof with his brother,
when the latter cantered off to Edinburgh on horseback, on his first
journey to that city, he allowed Dr. Currie to tell the world that the
journey was performed on foot; moreover, the poet wrote his Autobiography in the parlour of Mossgiel, and Gilbert was only made aware of
its existence some years after his brother's death.]

he formed one in Mauchline, on the Tarbolton model, immediately on his removal to Mossgiel) had made his name known to some considerable extent in the country about Tarbolton, Mauchline, and Irvine ; and thus prepared the way for his poetry. Professor Walker gives an anecdote on this head, which must not be omitted : Burns already numbered several clergymen among his acquaintances; indeed, we know from himself, that at this period he was not a little flattered, and justly so no question, with being permitted to mingle occasionally in their society. One of these gentlemen told the Professor, that after entering on the clerical profession, he had repeatedly met Burns in company, " where," said he, " the acuteness and originality displayed by him, the depth of his discernment, the force of his expressions, and the authoritative energy of his understanding, had created a sense of his power, of the extent of which I was unconscious, till it was revealed to me by accident. On the occasion of my second appearance in the pulpit, I came with an assured and tranquil mind, and though a few persons of education were present, advanced some length in the service with my confidence and self-possession unimpaired ; but when I saw Burns, who was of a different parish, unexpectedly enter the church, I was affected with a tremor and embarrassment, which suddenly apprised me of the impression which my mind, unknown to itself, had previously received." The Professor adds, that the person who had thus unconsciously been measuring the stature of the intellectual giant, was not only a man of good talents and education, but " remarkable for a more than ordinary portion of constitutional firmness." [1]

Every Scotch peasant, who makes any pretension to

---

[1] Life prefixed to Morison's Burns, p. 45. [The minister here referred to was Dr. Alex. Niven, of Dunkeld. Born in 1759, he died in November, 1833.]

understanding, is a theological critic—at least such *was* the
case—and Burns, no doubt, had long ere this time distinguished himself considerably among those hard-headed
groups that may usually be seen gathered together in the
churchyard after the service is over.   It may be guessed,
that from the time of his residence at Irvine, his strictures
were too often delivered in no reverent vein.   " Polemical
divinity," says he, in his Autobiography, 1787, " about this
time, was putting the country half mad,[1] and I, ambitious
of shining in conversation-parties on Sundays, at funerals,

---

[1] The following account of the *Buchanites*, a set of fanatics, now forgotten, who made much noise in the South and West of Scotland, about
the period in question, is taken from one of the Poet's letters to his
cousin (Mr. Burnes of Montrose), with which I have been favoured since
this narrative was first published.   [This letter first made its public
appearance in the present work.]   It is dated Mossgiel, August, 1784.
" We have been surprised with one of the most extraordinary pheno-
mena in the moral world, which, I dare say, has happened in the course
of this half century.   We have had a party of the Presbytery Relief,
as they call themselves, for some time in this country.   A pretty thriving
society of them has been in the burgh of Irvine for some years past, till
about two years ago, a Mrs. Buchan from Glasgow came among them,
and began to spread some fanatical notions of religion among them,
and, in a short time, made many converts among them, and, among
others, their preacher, one Mr. Whyte, who, upon that account, has been
suspended and formally deposed by his brethren.   He continued, however, to preach in private to his party, and was supported, both he, and
their spiritual mother, as they affect to call old Buchan, by the contributions of the rest, several of whom were in good circumstances; till,
in spring last, the populace rose and mobbed the old leader Buchan, and
put her out of the town; on which, all her followers voluntarily quitted
the place likewise, and with such precipitation, that many of them never
shut their doors behind them; one left a washing on the green, another
a cow bellowing at the crib without meat, or any body to mind her; and,
after several stages, they are fixed at present in the neighbourhood of
Dumfries.   Their tenets are a strange jumble of enthusiastic jargon;
among others, she pretends to give them the Holy Ghost by breathing
on them, which she does with postures and practices that are scandalously

&c., used a few years afterwards to puzzle Calvinism with so much heat and indiscretion, that I raised the hue and cry of heresy against me, which has not ceased to this hour." There are some plain allusions to this matter in Mr. David Sillar's letter, already quoted ; and a friend has told Allan Cunningham " that he first saw Burns on the afternoon of the Monday of a Mauchline Sacrament, lounging on horseback at the door of a public-house, holding forth on religious topics to a whole crowd of country people, who presently became so much shocked with his levities, that they fairly hissed him from the ground." [1]

To understand Burns's situation at this time, at once

---

indecent ; they have likewise disposed of all their effects, and hold a community of goods, and live nearly an idle life, carrying on a great farce of pretended devotion in barns and woods, where they lodge and lie all together, and hold likewise a community of women, as it is another of their tenets that they can commit no moral sin. I am personally acquainted with most of them, and I can assure you the above mentioned are facts.

" This, my dear Sir, is one of the many instances of the folly of leaving the guidance of sound reason and common sense in matters of religion. " Whenever we neglect or despise these sacred monitors, the whimsical notions of a perturbated brain are taken for the immediate influences of the Deity, and the wildest fanaticism, and the most inconsistent absurdities, will meet with abettors and converts. Nay, I have often thought that the more out of the way and ridiculous the fancies are, if once they are sanctified under the sacred name of Religion, the unhappy mistaken votaries are the more firmly glued to them. "

[1] [This suspicious-looking anecdote, furnished on the questionable authority of Allan Cunningham, the present editor would be disposed to delete from the book, as bearing no marks of truth in its face. There is nothing approaching to this in Sillar's account. He only tells us that Burns's " principles were suspected by the neighbours, who regarded him with a kind of suspicious fear, as he had *a good deal to say for himself*." The poet's own reference to his ambition of shining on Sundays between sermons, and at funerals, &c., is connected with the Mount Oliphant period of his early life. Some expressions in one of his letters to Candlish clearly allude to those opportunities of puzzling Calvinism

patronized by a number of clergymen, and attended with
" a hue-and-cry of heresy," we must remember his own
words, that " polemical divinity was putting the country
half-mad." Of both the parties which, ever since the
Revolution of 1688, have pretty equally divided the Church
of Scotland, it so happened that some of the most zealous
and conspicuous leaders and partisans were then opposed to
each other, in constant warfare, in this particular district ;
and their feuds being of course taken up among their con-
gregations, and spleen and prejudice at work, even more
furiously in the cottage than in *the manse*, he who, to the
annoyance of the one set of belligerents, could talk like
Burns, might count pretty surely, with whatever alloy
his wit happened to be mingled, in whatever shape the
precious " circulating medium " might be cast, on the applause and countenance of the enemy. And it is needless
to add, they were the less scrupulous sect of the two that
enjoyed the co-operation, such as it was then, and far
more important, as in the sequel it came to be, of our
poet.

William Burnes, as we have already seen, though a most
exemplary and devout man, entertained opinions very
different from those which commonly obtained among the
rigid Calvinists of his district. The worthy and pious old
man himself, therefore, had not improbably infused into
his son's mind its first prejudice against these persons ;
though, had he lived to witness the manner in which
Robert assailed them, there can be no doubt his sorrow
would have equalled their anger. The jovial spirits with
whom Burns associated at Irvine, and afterwards, were

---

at Dalrymple, and perhaps at Ayr, when both the youths were in
attendance there for a time. " I am still," writes Burns to him in 1787,
" the old man with his deeds, as when we were sporting about the lady-
thorn."]

of course habitual deriders of the manners, as well as the
tenets of the

> "Orthodox, orthodox, wha believe in John Knox."

We have already observed the effect of the young poet's
own first collision with the ruling powers of Presbyterian
discipline; but it was in the very act of settling at Mossgiel
that Burns formed the connection, which, more than any
circumstance besides, influenced him as to the matter now
in question. The farm belonged to the estate of the Earl
of Loudoun, but the brothers held it on a sub-lease from
Mr. Gavin Hamilton, writer (*i.e.* attorney), in Mauchline,
a man, by every account, of engaging manners, open, kind,
generous, and high-spirited, between whom and Robert
Burns, in spite of considerable inequality of condition, a
close and intimate friendship was ere long formed. Just
about this time it happened that Hamilton was at open
feud with Mr. Auld, the minister of Mauchline (the same
who had already *rebuked* the poet),[1] and the ruling elders

---

[1] [Mr. L. is certainly a little hasty here. There is no evidence that
Burns was rebuked within the church of Mauchline, prior to the summer of 1786. It may be that the Kirk-session records of a former
similar transaction have been lost; but the likelihood is that the poet,
who assuredly did undergo penance of this kind on account of his
child by Elizabeth Paton of Largieside, was gallant enough to stand by
the side of the mother, and she did not belong to Mauchline parish. In
fact, the little "misbegot" was neither conceived nor born within
"Daddie Auld's" jurisdiction. In a song which our poet composed on
the occasion, the point we contend for is pretty clearly admitted, thus:—

> "Before the congregation wide
>   I pass'd the muster fairly,
> My handsome Betsey by my side,
>   We gat our ditty rarely!
> But for her sake, this vow I make,
>   And solemnly I swear it!
> That while I own a single crown,
>   She's welcome to a share o't."]

of the parish, in consequence of certain irregularities in his personal conduct and deportment, which, according to the usual strict notions of kirk-discipline, were considered as fairly demanding the vigorous interference of these authorities. The notice of this person, his own landlord, and, as it would seem, one of the principal inhabitants of the village of Mauchline at the time, must, of course, have been very flattering to our polemical young farmer. He espoused Gavin Hamilton's quarrel warmly. Hamilton was naturally enough disposed to mix up his personal affair with the standing controversies whereon Auld was at variance with a large and powerful body of his brother clergymen; and by degrees the Mauchline *writer's* ardent *protégé* came to be as vehemently interested in the church-politics of Ayrshire, as he could have been in politics of another order, had he happened to be a freeman of some open borough, and his patron a candidate for the honour of representing it in St. Stephen's.

Cromek has been severely criticized for some details of Gavin Hamilton's dissensions with his parish minister;[1] but perhaps it might have been well to limit the censure to the tone and spirit of the narrative, since there is no doubt that these petty squabbles had a large share in directing the early energies of Burns's poetical talents. Even in the west of Scotland, such matters would hardly excite much notice now-a-days, but they were quite enough to produce a world of vexation and controversy forty years ago; and the English reader, to whom all such details are denied, will certainly never be able to comprehend either the merits or the demerits of many of Burns's most remarkable productions. Since I have touched on this matter at all, I may as well add, that Hamilton's family, though professedly adhering (as, indeed, if they were to be Christians

---

[1] " Reliques," p. 164—" Edinburgh Review," Vol. XIII. p. 273.

at all in that district, they must needs have done) to the Presbyterian Establishment, had always lain under a strong suspicion of Episcopalianism. Gavin's great grandfather had been curate of Kirkoswald in the troubled times that preceded the Revolution, and incurred great and lasting popular hatred, in consequence of being supposed to have had a principal hand in bringing a thousand of the "Highland host" into that region in 1677-8. The district was commonly said not to have entirely recovered the effects of that savage visitation in less than a hundred years; and the descendants and representatives of the Covenanters, whom the curate of Kirkoswald had the reputation at least of persecuting, were commonly supposed to regard with anything rather than ready goodwill, his descendant, the witty writer of Mauchline. A well-nursed prejudice of this kind was likely enough to be met by counter-spleen, and such seems to have been the truth of the case. The lapse of another generation has sufficed to wipe out every trace of feuds, that were still abundantly discernible, in the days when Ayrshire first began to ring with the equally zealous applause and vituperation of—

> " Poet Burns,
> And his priest-skelping turns."

It is impossible to look back now to the civil war, which then raged among the churchmen of the west of Scotland, without confessing, that on either side there was much to regret, and not a little to blame. Proud and haughty spirits were unfortunately opposed to each other; and in the superabundant display of zeal as to doctrinal points, neither party seems to have mingled much of the charity of the Christian temper. The whole exhibition was most unlovely—the spectacle of such indecent violence among the leading Ecclesiastics of the district, acted unfavourably on many men's minds—and no one can doubt, that in the

at best unsettled state of Robert Burns's principles, the unhappy effect must have been powerful indeed as to him.

Macgill and Dalrymple, the two ministers of the town of
Ayr, had long been suspected of entertaining heterodox
opinions on several points, particularly the doctrine of
original sin, and the Trinity; and the former at length
published an essay, which was considered as demanding the
notice of the church courts. More than a year was spent
in the discussions which arose out of this; and at last Dr.
Macgill was fain to acknowledge his errors, and promise
that he would take an early opportunity of apologizing for
them to his own congregation from the pulpit—which promise, however, he never performed. The gentry of the
country took, for the most part, the side of Macgill, who
was a man of cold unpopular manners, but of unreproached
moral character, and possessed of some accomplishments,
though certainly not of distinguished talents. The bulk of
the lower orders espoused, with far more fervid zeal, the
cause of those who conducted the prosecution against this
erring doctor. Gavin Hamilton, and all persons of his
stamp, were of course on the side of Macgill; Auld, and
the Mauchline elders, were his enemies. Mr. Robert
Aiken, a writer in Ayr, a man of remarkable talents, particularly in public speaking, had the principal mangement
of Macgill's cause before the Presbytery, and, I believe,
also before the Synod. He was an intimate friend of
Hamilton, and through him had about this time formed an
acquaintance, which soon ripened into a warm friendship,
with Burns. Burns, therefore, was from the beginning a
zealous, as in the end he was perhaps the most effective,
partisan of the side on which Aiken had staked so much of
his reputation. Macgill, Dalrymple, and their brethren,
suspected, with more or less justice, of leaning to heterodox
opinions, are the "New Light" pastors of his earliest satires.

The prominent antagonists of these men, and chosen

champions of the "Auld Light" in Ayrshire, it must now be admitted on all hands, presented, in many particulars of personal conduct and demeanour, as broad a mark as ever tempted the shafts of a satirist. These men prided themselves on being the legitimate and undegenerate descendants and representatives of the haughty Puritans, who chiefly conducted the overthrow of Popery in Scotland, and who ruled for a time, and would fain have continued to rule, over both king and people, with a more tyrannical dominion than ever the Catholic priesthood itself had been able to exercise amidst that high-spirited nation. With the horrors of the Papal system for ever in their mouths, these men were in fact as bigoted monks, and almost as relentless inquisitors, in their hearts, as ever wore cowl and cord— austere and ungracious of aspect, coarse and repulsive of address and manners—very Pharisees as to the lesser matters of the law, and many of them, to all outward appearance at least, overflowing with pharisaical self-conceit, as well as monastic bile. That admirable qualities lay concealed under this ungainly exterior, and mingled with and checked the worst of these gloomy passions, no candid man will permit himself to doubt; and that Burns has grossly overcharged his portraits of them, deepening shadows that were of themselves sufficiently dark, and excluding altogether those brighter, and perhaps softer, traits of character, which redeemed the originals within the sympathies of many of the worthiest and best of men, seems equally clear. Their bitterest enemies dared not at least to bring against them, even when the feud was at its height of fervour, charges of that heinous sort, which they fearlessly, and I fear justly, preferred against their antagonists. No one ever accused them of signing the Articles, administering the sacraments, and eating the bread of a Church, whose fundamental doctrines they disbelieved, and, by insinuation at least, disavowed.

The law of Church-patronage was another subject on which controversy ran high and furious in the district at the same period; the actual condition of things on this head being upheld by all the men of the New Light, and condemned as equally at variance with the precepts of the gospel, and the rights of freemen, by not a few of the other party, and, in particular, by certain conspicuous zealots in the immediate neighbourhood of Burns. While this warfare raged, there broke out an intestine discord within the camp of the faction which he loved not. Two of the foremost leaders of the Auld Light party quarrelled about a question of parish-boundaries; the matter was taken up in the Presbytery of Irvine, and there, in the open court, to which the announcement of the discussion had drawn a multitude of the country people, and Burns among the rest, the reverend divines, hitherto sworn friends and associates, lost all command of temper, and abused each other *coram populo*, with a fiery virulence of personal invective, such as has long been banished from all popular assemblies, wherein the laws of courtesy are enforced by those of a certain unwritten code.

" The first of my poetic offspring that saw the light," says Burns, " was a burlesque lamentation on a quarrel between two reverend Calvinists, both of them *dramatis personæ* in my ' Holy Fair.' I had a notion myself that the piece had some merit; but to prevent the worst, I gave a copy of it to a friend who was very fond of such things, and told him I could not guess who was the author of it, but that I thought it pretty clever. With a certain description of the clergy, as well as laity, it met with a roar of applause."

This was the " Holy Tuilyie, or Twa Herds," a piece not given either by Currie or Gilbert Burns, though printed by Mr. Paul, and omitted, certainly for no very intelligible reason, in editions where "The Holy Fair," "The Ordination," &c. found admittance. The two herds, or pastors, were Mr. Moodie, minister of Riccarton, and that favourite victim of Burns's, John Russell, then minister in Kilmarnock, and afterwards of Stirling.

"From this time," Burns says, "I began to be known in the country as a maker of rhymes . . . . . 'Holy Willie's Prayer' next made its appearance, and alarmed the kirk-session so much, that they held several meetings to look over their spiritual artillery, and see if any of it might be pointed against profane rhymers"———: and to a place among profane rhymers, the author of this terrible infliction had unquestionably established his right.   Sir Walter Scott speaks of it as "a piece of satire more exquisitely severe than any which Burns ever afterwards wrote—but unfortunately cast in a form too daringly profane to be received into Dr. Currie's collection."[1]   Burns's reverend editor, Mr. Paul, nevertheless, presents "Holy Willie's Prayer" at full length; and even calls on the friends of religion to bless the memory of the poet who took such a judicious method of "leading the liberal mind to a rational view of the nature of prayer."[2]

"This," says that bold commentator, "was not only the prayer of Holy Willie, but it is merely the metrical version of every prayer that is offered up by those who call themselves the pure reformed church of Scotland.   In the course of his reading and polemical warfare, Burns embraced and defended the opinions of Taylor of Norwich, Macgill, and that school of divines.   He could not reconcile his mind to

---

[1] "Quarterly Review," No. 1, p. 22.

[2] I leave this passage as it stood originally; but am happy in having it in my power to add, on Mr. Paul's own authority, that he had no hand either in selecting the poems for the edition in question, or superintending the printing of it. He merely contributed the brief memoir prefixed, and critical notes appended to it; and "considered his contributions as a *jeu-d'esprit.*" After this explanation, my test may safely be left to the interpretation of every candid reader.

that picture of the Being, whose very essence is love, which is drawn by the high Calvinists, or the representatives of the Covenanters—namely, that he is disposed to grant salvation to none but a few of their sect; that the whole Pagan world, the disciples of Mahomet, the Roman Catholics, the Lutherans, and even the Calvinists who differ from them in certain tenets, must, like Korah, Dathan, and Abiram, descend to the pit of perdition, man, woman, and child, without the possibility of escape; but such are the identical doctrines of the Cameronians of the present day, and such was Holy Willie's style of prayer. The hypocrisy and dishonesty of the man, who was at the time a reputed saint, were perceived by the discerning penetration of Burns, and *to expose them he considered it his duty*. The terrible view of the Deity exhibited in that able production is precisely the same view which is given of him, in different words, by many devout preachers at present. They inculcate, that the greatest sinner is the greatest favourite of heaven—that a reformed bawd is more acceptable to the Almighty than a pure virgin, who has hardly ever transgressed even in thought—that the lost sheep alone will be saved, and that the ninety-and-nine out of the hundred will be left in the wilderness, to perish without mercy—that the Saviour of the world loves the elect, not from any lovely qualities which they possess, for they are hateful in his sight, but 'he loves them because he loves them.' Such are the sentiments which are breathed by those who are denominated High Calvinists, and from which the soul of a poet who loves mankind, and who has not studied the system in all its bearings, recoils with horror. . . . The gloomy, forbidding representation which they give of the Supreme Being, has a tendency to produce insanity, and lead to suicide." [1]—*Life of Burns*, pp. 40-41.

---

[1] According to every account, Holy Willie was no very consistent

Mr. Paul may be considered as expressing in the above, and in other passages of a similar tendency, the sentiments with which even the most audacious of Burns's anti-Calvinistic satires were received among the Ayrshire divines of the New Light. That performances so blasphemous should have been, not only pardoned, but applauded by ministers of religion, is a singular circumstance, which may go far to make the reader comprehend the exaggerated state of party feeling in Burns's native county, at the period when he first appealed to the public ear; nor is it fair to pronounce sentence upon the young and reckless satirist, without taking into consideration the undeniable fact—that in his worst offences of this kind, he was encouraged and abetted by those who, to say nothing more about their professional character and authority, were almost the only persons of liberal education whose society he had any opportunity of approaching at the period in question. Had Burns received, at this time, from his clerical friends and patrons, such advice as was tendered, when rather too late, by a layman who was as far from bigotry on religious subjects as any man in the world, this great genius might have made his first approaches to the public notice in a very different character.

"Let your bright talents"—(thus wrote the excellent John Ramsay of Ochtertyre, in October, 1787)—"let those bright talents which the Almighty has bestowed on you, be henceforth employed to the noble purpose of supporting the

___

character. I find it stated in Cromek's MSS. that he met with his death by falling, when drunk, into a wet ditch; and indeed this story seems to be alluded to in more than one of Burns's own letters. [On this latter point the author seems to be mistaken; nay, we are almost certain that the tippling saint survived the poet. But assuredly before "The Kirk's Alarm," was composed, in 1789, Holy Willie had been convicted of "robbing the plate," that is, of stealing money from the church-door collections for the poor.]

cause of truth and virtue. An imagination so varied and
forcible as yours may do this in many different modes;
nor is it necessary to be always serious, which you have
been to good purpose; good morals may be recommended
in a comedy, or even in a song. Great allowances are due
to the heat and inexperience of youth;—and few poets can
boast, like Thomson, of never having written a line, which,
dying, they would wish to blot. In particular, I wish you to
keep clear of the thorny walks of satire, which makes a man
an hundred enemies for one friend, and is doubly dangerous
when one is supposed to extend the slips and weaknesses of
individuals to their sect or party. About modes of faith,
serious and excellent men have always differed: and there
are certain curious questions, which may afford scope to
men of metaphysical heads, but seldom mend the heart
or temper. Whilst these points are beyond human ken,
it is sufficient that all our sects concur in their views
of morals. You will forgive me for these hints." Few
such hints, it is likely, ever reached his ears in the days
when they might have been most useful—days of which the
principal honours and distinctions are thus alluded to by
himself :—

> " I've been at drunken writers' feasts;
> Nay, been bitch-fou 'mang goodly priests."

It is amusing to observe how soon even really Bucolic
bards learn the tricks of their trade: Burns knew already
what lustre a compliment gains from being set in sarcasm,
when he made Willie call for special notice to

> ——" Gauin Hamilton's deserts, ...
> He drinks, and swears, and plays at cartes;
> Yet has sae mony takin' arts
>   Wi' great and sma',
> Frae God's ain priests the people's hearts
>   He steals awa," &c.

Nor is his other patron, Aiken, introduced with inferior

skill, as having merited Willie's most fervent execrations
by his "glib-tongued" defence of the heterodox doctor of
Ayr:

> "Lord! visit them wha did employ him,
> And for thy people's sake destroy 'em."

Burns owed a compliment to this gentleman's elocu-
tionary talents. "I never knew there was any merit in
my poems," said he, "until Mr. Aiken *read them* into
repute."

Encouraged by the "roar of applause" which greeted
these pieces, thus orally promulgated and recommended,
he produced in succession various satires, wherein the same
set of persons were lashed; as, "The Ordination;" "The
Kirk's Alarm," &c. &c.; and last, and best undoubtedly,
"The Holy Fair," [1] in which, unlike the others that have
been mentioned, satire keeps its own place, and is subservient to the poetry of Burns.   This was, indeed, an extraordinary performance: no partisan of any sect could
whisper that malice had formed its principal inspiration, or
that its chief attraction lay in the boldness with which
individuals, entitled and accustomed to respect, were held
up to ridicule; it was acknowledged, amidst the sternest
mutterings of wrath, that national manners were once
more in the hands of a national poet; and hardly denied
by those who shook their heads the most gravely over the
indiscretions of particular passages, or even by those who
justly regretted a too prevailing tone of levity in the treatment of a subject essentially solemn, that the Muse of

---

[1] [The "Holy Fair," according to the poet's own holograph copy
included in a folio version book of his poems, transcribed in 1785-86,
was composed in "August, 1785;" consequently, it was the *first and
best* of the satires here named. "The Ordination" was produced in
February, 1786, and "The Kirk's Alarm" was a composition of the
Ellisland period, so late as August, 1789.]

"Christ's Kirk on the Green" had awakened, after the slumber of ages, with all the vigour of her regal youth about her, in "the auld clay biggin'" of Mossgiel. "The Holy Fair," however, created admiration, not surprise, among the circle of domestic friends who had been admitted to watch the steps of his progress in an art, of which, beyond that circle, little or nothing was heard until the youthful poet produced at length a satirical masterpiece. It is not possible to reconcile the statements of Gilbert and others, as to some of the minutiæ of the chronological history of Burns's previous performances; but there can be no doubt, that although from choice or accident his first provincial fame was that of a satirist, he had, some time before any of his philippics on the Auld Light divines made their appearance, exhibited to those who enjoyed his personal confidence, a range of imaginative power hardly inferior to what "The Holy Fair" itself displays; and, at least, such a rapidly improving skill in poetical language and versification, as must have prepared them for witnessing, without wonder, even the most perfect specimens of his art.

Gilbert says, "that among the earliest of his poems" was the "Epistle to Davie," and Mr. Walker believes that this was written very soon after the death of William Burnes. This piece is in the very intricate and difficult measure of "The Cherry and the Slae;" and, on the whole, the poet moves with ease and grace in his very unnecessary trammels; but young poets are careless beforehand of difficulties which would startle the experienced; and great poets may overcome any difficulties if they once grapple with them; so that I should rather ground my distrust of Gilbert's statement, if it must be literally taken, on the celebration of "Jean" with which the epistle terminates: and after all, she is celebrated in the concluding stanzas, which may have been added some time after the first draught.[1] The gloomy circumstances of the poet's personal condition, as described in this piece, were common, it cannot be doubted, to all the years of his youthful history; so that no particular date is to be founded upon these; and if this was the first, certainly it was not the last occasion, on which Burns exercised his fancy in the colouring of the very worst issue that could attend a life of unsuccessful toil.

> " The last o't, the warst o't
> Is only just to beg—"

But Gilbert's recollections, however on trivial points inaccurate, will always be more interesting than any thing that could be put in their place.

" Robert," says he, " often composed without any regular plan. When any thing made a strong impression on his mind, so as to rouse it to poetic exertion, he would give way to the impulse, and embody the thought in rhyme. If he hit on two or three stanzas to please him, he would then think of proper introductory, connecting, and conclud-

---

[1] [Judging from internal evidence, it seems impossible that this celebrated " Epistle " could have been completed, as ultimately presented to the public, till pretty far on in the year 1785. Nevertheless, it is unnecessary to call in question Gilbert's recorded impression that it was during the summer of 1784 that Robert repeated to him some of its best paragraphs. It is of this very poem Gilbert speaks when he mentions that the middle portion of a long composition was often the first part his brother executed, just as the thoughts arose in his mind; and that introductory and closing passages might happen to be composed after long intervals of time from his first conceptions of the piece in question. It must have been so with the " Epistle to Davie." The poem opens with winter scenery, and " January " is the month attached to the printed composition. The first winter passed by the poet in Mossgiel was that of 1785; and as Mr. Lockhart well remarks the references to the writer's consuming passion for Jean Armour occupy the closing stanzas only. It is very questionable if the poet had either seen, or spoken to, Jean at the opening of the year 1785, although before its close his devotion to her had reached its climax.]

ing stanzas; hence the middle of a poem was often first produced. It was, I think, in summer, 1784, when, in the interval of harder labour, he and I were weeding in the garden (kail-yard), that he repeated to me the principal part of this epistle (to Davie). I believe the first idea of Robert's becoming an author was started on this occasion. I was much pleased with the epistle, and said to him I was of opinion it would bear being printed, and that it would be well received by people of taste; that I thought it at least equal, if not superior, to many of Allan Ramsay's epistles; and that the merit of these, and much other Scotch poetry, seemed to consist principally in the knack of the expression—but here, there was a strain of interesting sentiment, and the Scotticism of the language scarcely seemed affected, but appeared to be the natural language of the poet; that, besides, there was certainly some novelty in a poet pointing out the consolations that were in store for him when he should go a-begging. Robert seemed very well pleased with my criticism, and we talked of sending it to some magazine, but as this plan afforded no opportunity of knowing how it would take, the idea was dropped.

"It was, I think, in the winter following, as we were going together with carts for coal to the family (and I could yet point out the particular spot), that the author first repeated to me the 'Address to the Deil.' The curious idea of such an address was suggested to him, by running over in his mind the many ludicrous accounts and representations we have, from various quarters, of this august personage. 'Death and Doctor Hornbook,' though not published in the Kilmarnock edition, was produced early in the year 1785. The schoolmaster of Tarbolton parish, to eke up the scanty subsistence allowed to that useful class of men, had set up a shop of grocery goods. Having accidentally fallen in with some medical books, and become most hobby-horsically attached to the study of medicine, he had added the sale of a few medicines to his little trade. He had got a shop bill printed, at the bottom of which, overlooking his own incapacity, he had advertised, 'that 'advice would be given in common disorders at the shop gratis.' Robert was at a mason-meeting in Tarbolton, when the Dominie unfortunately made too ostentatious a display of his medical skill. As he parted in the evening from this mixture of pedantry and physic, at the place where he describes his meeting with Death, one of those floating ideas of apparitions, he mentions in his Auto-biography, crossed his mind : this set him to work for the rest of the way home. These circumstances he related when he repeated the verses to me next afternoon, as I was holding the plough, and he was letting the water off the field beside me. The ' Epistle to John Lapraik ' was pro-duced exactly on the occasion described by the author. He says in that poem, ' On Fasten-e'en we had a rockin'' I believe he has omitted the word "rocking" in the glossary. It is a term derived from those primitive times, when the country-women employed their spare hours in spinning on the rock, or distaff. This simple implement is a very portable one, and well fitted to the social inclina-tion of meeting in a neighbour's house : hence the phrase of *going a-rocking* or *with the rock*. As the connection the phrase had with the implement was forgotten when the rock gave place to the spinning-wheel, the phrase came to be used by both sexes on social occasions, and men talk of going with their rocks as well as women. It was at one of these *rockings* at our house, when we had twelve or fifteen young people with their *rocks*, that Lapraik's song beginning, ' When I upon thy bosom lean,' was sung, and we were in-formed who was the author.[1] The verses to the ' Mouse '

---

[1] Burns was never a fastidious critic ; but it is not very easy to under-

and 'Mountain Daisy' were composed on the occasions mentioned, and while the author was holding the plough ; I could point out the particular spot where each was composed. Holding the plough was a favourite situation with Robert for poetic compositions, and some of his best verses were produced while he was at that exercise. Several of the poems were produced for the purpose of bringing forward some favourite sentiment of the author. He used to remark to me, that he could not well conceive a more mortifying picture of human life, than a man seeking work. In casting about in his mind how this sentiment might be brought forward, the elegy, 'Man was made to mourn,' was composed. Robert had frequently remarked to me, that he thought there was something peculiarly venerable in the phrase, ' Let us worship God ' used by a decent sober head of a family introducing family worship. To this sentiment of the author the world is indebted for the ' Cotter's Saturday Night.' The hint of the plan, and title of the poem, were taken from Fergusson's ' Farmer's Ingle.'

" When Robert had not some pleasure in view, in which I was not thought fit to participate, we used frequently to walk together, when the weather was favourable, on the Sunday afternoon (those precious breathing-times to the labouring part of the community), and enjoyed such Sundays as would make one regret to see their number abridged. It was in one of these walks that I first had the pleasure of hearing the author repeat the ' Cotter's Saturday Night.' I do not recollect to have read or heard anything by which I was more highly *electrified*. The fifth and sixth stanzas,

---

stand his admiration of Lapraik's poetry. Emboldened by Burns's success, he too published : but the only one of his productions that is ever remembered now is this ; and even this survives chiefly because Burns has praised it. The opening verse, however, is pretty. [Since 1828, it has been discovered that even the song thus praised by Burns, had been stolen by Lapraik from an old magazine.]

and the eighteenth, thrilled with peculiar ecstasy through my soul."—*Currie*, vol. iii., p. 445

The poems mentioned by Gilbert Burns in the above extract, are among the most popular of his brother's performances ; and there may be a time for recurring to some of their peculiar merits as works of art. It may be mentioned here, that John Wilson, alias Dr. Hornbook, was not merely compelled to shut up shop as an apothecary, or druggist rather, by the satire which bears his name; but so irresistible was the tide of ridicule, that his pupils, one by one, deserted him, and he abandoned his school craft also. Removing to Glasgow, and turning himself successfully to commercial pursuits, Dr. Hornbook survived the local storm which he could not effectually withstand, and was often heard in his latter days, when waxing cheerful and communicative over a bowl of punch " in the Saltmarket," to bless the lucky hour in which the dominie of Tarbolton provoked the castigation of Robert Burns. In those days the Scotch universities did not turn out doctors of physic by the hundred, according to the modern fashion introduced by the necessities of the French revolutionary war; Mr. Wilson's was probably the only medicine-chest from which salts and senna were distributed for the benefit of a considerable circuit of parishes; and his advice, to say the least of the matter, was perhaps as good as could be had, for love or money, among the wise women who were the only rivals for his practice. The poem which drove him from Ayrshire was not, we may believe, either expected or designed to produce any such serious effect. Poor Hornbook and the poet were old acquaintances and in some sort rival wits at the time in the mason-lodge.[1]

---

[1] [If John Wilson engaged in "commercial pursuits" at Glasgow, it was for no long period, as he was soon appointed to the office of "Session Clerk" of Gorbals parish in that city, which situation he held till his death on 13th January, 1839.]

In "Man was made to Mourn," whatever might be the casual idea that set the poet to work, it is but too evident, that he wrote from the habitual feelings of his own bosom. The indignation with which he through life contemplated the inequality of human condition, and particularly,—and who shall say, with absolute injustice?—the contrast between his own worldly circumstances and intellectual rank, was never more bitterly, nor more loftily expressed, than in some of these stanzas :—

> " See yonder poor o'erlabour'd wight,
>   So abject, mean, and vile,
> Who begs a brother of the earth
>   To give him leave to toil !
> If I'm design'd yon lordling's slave—
>   By Nature's laws design'd ;
> Why was an independent wish
>   E'er planted in my mind ? "

The same feeling, strong, but triumphed over in the moment of inspiration, as it ought ever to have been in the plain exercise of such an understanding as his, may be read in every stanza of the " Epistle to Davie " :—

> " It's no in titles nor in rank,
> It's no in wealth like Lon'on bank,
>   To purchase peace and rest ;
> It's no in books, it's no in lear,
>   To mak us truly blest. . . . . . .
> Think ye, that such as you and I,
> Wha drudge and drive through wet and dry,
>   Wi' never-ceasing toil ;
> Think ye, are we less blest than they,
> Wha scarcely tent us in their way,
>   As hardly worth their while ?" . . . .

In " Man was made to Mourn," Burns appears to have taken many hints from an ancient ballad, entitled " The Life and Age of Man," which begins thus :—

" Upon the sixteenth hunder year of God, and fifty-three,
Frae Christ was born, that bought us dear, as writings testifie :
On January, the sixteenth day, as I did lie alone,
With many a sigh and sob did say—Ah ! man is made to moan !"

" I had an old grand-uncle," says the poet, in one of his
letters to Mrs. Dunlop, " with whom my mother lived in
her girlish years ; the good old man, for such he was, was
blind long ere he died ; during which time his highest enjoyment was to sit down and cry, while my mother would
sing the simple old song of ' The Life and Age of Man.' "[1]

The " Cotter's Saturday Night " is, perhaps, of all Burns's
pieces, the one whose exclusion from the collection, were such
things possible now-a-days, would be the most injurious, if
not to the genius, at least to the character, of the man.   In
spite of many feeble lines, and some heavy stanzas, it
appears to me, that even his genius would suffer more in
estimation, by being contemplated in the absence of this
poem, than of any other single performance he has left us.
Loftier flights he certainly has made, but in these he remained but a short while on the wing, and effort is too
often perceptible ; here the motion is easy, gentle, placidly

---

[1] [This old ballad may be seen at length in Cromek's " Select Scottish
Songs" (1810), Preface to vol. i. The verses of Burns, are said in his earliest
manuscript thereof to be "A song, to the tune of *Peggy Bawn*,"—a plaintive Irish air ; whereas Cromek, at page 280 of the " Reliques," tells us
it was composed to the tune of " John o' Badenyond."   Probably the
bard's mother sang the ancient words to that curious Strathspey tune.
Referring to the latter in connection with this anecdote, Southey
thus remarks in his work called " The Doctor " :—" It is certain
that this old song was in Burns's mind when he composed to the same
cadence those well-known stanzas, of which the burthen is, ' Man was
made to mourn.'   But the old man's tears were tears of piety, not of regret, while he thus listened and wept ; and his heart was not so much in
the past as his hopes were in the future.   Burns must have been conscious
in his better hours—and he had many such—that he inherited the feeling,
if not the sober piety, so touchingly displayed in this family anecdote."]

undulating. There is more of the conscious security of
power, than in any other of his serious pieces of considerable length ; the whole has the appearance of coming in a
full stream from the fountain of the heart—a stream that
soothes the ear, and has no glare on the surface. It is delightful to turn from any of the pieces which present so
great a genius as writhing under an inevitable burden, to
this, where his buoyant energy seems not even to feel the
pressure. The miseries of toil and penury, who shall affect
to treat as unreal ? Yet they shrink to small dimensions in
the presence of a spirit thus exalted at once, and softened,
by the pieties of virgin love, filial reverence, and domestic
devotion.

That he who thus enthusiastically apprehended, and thus
exquisitely painted, the artless beauty and solemnity of the
feelings and thoughts that ennoble the life of the Scottish
peasant, could witness observances in which the very highest
of these redeeming influences are most powerfully and gracefully displayed, and yet describe them in a vein of unmixed
merriment—that the same man should have produced
the "Cotter's Saturday Night" and the "Holy Fair"
about the same time—will ever continue to move wonder
and regret.

"The annual celebration of the Sacrament of the Lord's
Supper in the rural parishes of Scotland, has much in it,"
says the unfortunate Heron, "of those old Popish festivals,
in which superstition, traffic, and amusement used to be
strangely intermingled. Burns saw and seized in it one of
the happiest of all subjects to afford scope for the display of
that strong and piercing sagacity, by which he could almost
intuitively distinguish the reasonable from the absurd, and
the becoming from the ridiculous ; of that picturesque
power of fancy which enables him to represent scenes, and
persons, and groups, and looks, and attitudes, and gestures,
in a manner almost as lively and impressive, even in words,

as if all the artifices and energies of the pencil had been employed; of that knowledge which he had necessarily acquired of the manners, passions, and prejudices of the rustics around him; of whatever was ridiculous, no less than whatever was affectingly beautiful in rural life."[1] This is very good so far as it goes; but who ever disputed the exquisite graphic truth of the poem to which the critic refers? The question remains as it stood; is there then nothing besides a strange mixture of superstition, traffic, and amusement, in the scene which such an annual celebration in a rural parish of Scotland presents? Does nothing of what is "affectingly beautiful in rural life" make a part in the original which was before the poet's eyes? Were "Superstition," "Hypocrisy," and "Fun," the only influences which he might justly have impersonated? It would be hard, I think, to speak so even of the old Popish festivals to which Mr. Heron alludes; it would be hard, surely, to say it of any festival in which, mingled as they may be with sanctimonious pretenders, and surrounded with giddy groups of onlookers, a mighty multitude of devout men are assembled for the worship of God, beneath the open heaven, and above the graves of their fathers.

Let us beware, however, of pushing our censure of a young poet, mad with the inspiration of the moment, from whatever source derived, too far. It can hardly be doubted that the author of the " Cotter's Saturday Night " had felt, in his time, all that any man can feel in the contemplation of the most sublime of the religious observances of his country; and as little, that had he taken up the subject of this rural sacrament in a solemn mood, he might have produced a piece as gravely beautiful, as his " Holy Fair " is quaint, graphic, and picturesque. A scene of family wor-

---

[1] Heron's " Memoirs of Burns " (Edinburgh, 1797), p. 14.

ship, on the other hand, I can easily imagine to have come from his hand as pregnant with the ludicrous as that "Holy Fair" itself. The family prayers of the Saturday's night, and the rural celebration of the Eucharist, are parts of the same system—the system which has made the people of Scotland what they are—and what, it is to be hoped, they will continue to be. And when men ask of themselves what this great national poet really thought of a system in which minds immeasurably inferior to his can see so much to venerate, it is surely just that they should pay more attention to what he has delivered under the gravest sanction. In noble natures, we may be sure, the source of tears lies nearer the heart than that of smiles.

Mr. Hamilton Paul does not desert his post on occasion of the "Holy Fair;" he defends that piece as manfully as "Holy Willie;" and, indeed, expressly applauds Burns for having endeavoured to explode "abuses discountenanced by the General Assembly." The General Assembly would no doubt say, both of the poet and the commentator, *non tali auxilio.*

"Hallowe'en," a descriptive poem, perhaps even more exquisitely wrought than the "Holy Fair," and containing nothing that could offend the feelings of anybody, was produced about the same period. Burns's art had now reached its climax; but it is time that we should revert more particularly to the personal history of the poet.

He seems to have very soon perceived, that the farm of Mossgiel could at the best furnish no more than the bare means of existence to so large a family; and wearied with the "prospects drear," from which he only escaped in occasional intervals of social merriment, or when gay flashes of solitary fancy, for they were no more, threw sunshine on everything, he very naturally took up the notion of quitting Scotland for a time, and trying his fortune in the West Indies, where, as is well known, the managers of the plantations are, in the great majority of cases, Scotchmen of Burns's own rank and condition. His letters show that on two or three different occasions, long before his poetry had excited any attention, he had applied for, and nearly obtained appointments of this sort, through the intervention of his acquaintances in the sea-port of Irvine.[1] Petty acci-

---

[1] It can scarcely fail to strike an informed reader that the author is here laying a convenient, although probably a very hollow, groundwork to afford him a means of escape from a dilemma that he must now approach, but which he has hardly the nerve to encounter fairly. There is not a shadow of authority for the allegation he starts with, namely, that several of the bard's letters, written long before his poetry had excited any attention, show that he had applied for, and nearly obtained, appointments in the West Indies. Mr. Lockhart is here about to make the first public announcement of the recent discovery of a relic of Burns of more than usual importance. It was found in the hands of then existing near relatives of the poet's "Highland Mary," universally understood to have been a "very early" sweetheart of the poet, whose untimely death while they were betrothed lovers, he never ceased to bewail, and whose memory he had embalmed in at least two published lyrics of surpassing beauty. This relic was a pocket-bible in two small volumes, a parting gift to the deceased, bearing an inscription in the bard's own easily identified penmanship, giving the donor's name and address—"Mossgiel"— with masonic emblems of secrecy attached, but undated. Each volume is also inscribed with a verse from Scripture, indicating that the parties were solemnly sworn to the performance of certain vows.

How did the biographer acquit himself in the blaze of light thus suddenly let in upon the veiled mystery of this part of the poet's history? Not certainly with the candour one would have expected from such an author. In the order of chronology he had now to discuss the love-story of Jean Armour, which here he is pleased to designate "the last of the poet's Ayrshire love-stories." When that story reached its hapless close, Burns had been only two years a tenant of Mossgiel,—where then was room to be found for the love-story of Mary Campbell? That central episode in the poet's career could not be omitted from a biography intended to rank as a standard one of its class. He could not shut his eyes, or the eyes of his readers, to the bard's own account of his brief intercourse with Highland Mary, which in all its phases is inextricably mixed up with the arrangements to emigrate to the West Indies. And neither could he hide from himself the circumstance that the unfortunate outcome of the

dents, not worth describing, interfered to disappoint him from time to time : but at last a new burst of misfortune rendered him doubly anxious to escape from his native land; and, but for an accident, which no one will call petty, his arrangements would certainly have been completed.

But we must not come quite so rapidly to the last of his Ayrshire love-stories.

How many lesser romances of this order were evolved and completed during his residence at Mossgiel, it is needless to inquire ; that they were many, his songs prove, for in those days he wrote no love-songs on imaginary heroines. "Mary Morison," "Behind yon hills where Stinsiar flows," "On Cessnock bank there lives a lass," belong to this period;"[1] and there are three or four inspired by Mary Campbell—the object of by far the deepest passion that Burns ever knew, and which he has accordingly immortalized in the noblest of elegiacs.

In introducing to Mr. Thomson's notice the song—

" Will you go to the Indies, my Mary,
    And leave auld Scotia's shore ?—
Will you go to the Indies, my Mary,
    Across the Atlantic roar ? "

---

poet's first attachment to Jean Armour, created this very resolution to go to Jamaica! Perhaps it was delicacy towards the feelings of the poet's widow—then still alive—that prevented Lockhart from "speaking out" on this subject, and on this occasion ; or perhaps it had been an understood proviso with all the biographers, from Currie downwards, that inquiries into this very inviting theme, must, in the interests of propriety, be suppressed and treated as impertinent. Neither Cunningham, Hogg, Chambers, nor John Wilson, who succeeded Lockhart as biographers of Burns during the next twenty years, ventured to face the difficulty opened up by the recovery of Mary's bible ; indeed, not one of them seems to have discerned the difficulty at all ! Honest " Christopher North " was the only consistent man among them, for he ignored altogether the circumstance of the recovered relic, and treated the Mary-episode as an event that happened before the poet's " twenty-third year."]

[[1] Not so; all the songs here named belong to the Tarbolton period.]

Burns says, " In my very early years, when I was thinking of going to the West Indies, I took this farewell of a dear girl; " and in a note on a similar composition of which the living Mary was the subject—

> " For her I'll dare the billows' roar,
> For her I'll trace a distant shore,
> That Indian wealth may lustre throw
> Around my Highland lassie, O."

he says,—" This was a composition of mine in very early life, before I was known at all in the world. My Highland lassie was a warm-hearted, charming young creature as ever blessed a man with generous love. After a pretty long tract of the most ardent reciprocal affection, we met by appointment on the second Sunday of May, in a sequestered spot by the banks of Ayr, where we spent a day in taking a farewell before she should embark for the West Highlands, to arrange matters among her friends for our projected change of life. At the close of the autumn following, she crossed the sea to meet me at Greenock, where she had scarce landed when she was seized with a malignant fever, which hurried my dear girl to her grave in a few days, before I could even hear of her illness; " and Mr. Cromek, speaking of the same " day of parting love," gives, though without mentioning his authority, some further particulars which no one would willingly believe to be apocryphal. " This adieu," says that zealous inquirer into the details of Burns's story, " was performed with all those simple and striking ceremonials, which rustic sentiment has devised to prolong tender emotions, and to inspire awe. The lovers stood on each side of a small purling brook—they laved their hands in the limpid stream—and, holding a Bible between them, pronounced their vows to be faithful to each other. They parted— never to meet again." (" Reliques," p. 238). It is proper to add, that Mr. Cromek's story, which even Allan Cunningham was disposed to receive with suspicion, has been confirmed very strongly by the accidental discovery of a Bible, presented by Burns to " Mary Campbell," which was found in the possession of her sister at Ardrossan. Upon the boards of the first volume is inscribed, in Burns's handwriting,—" And ye shall not swear by my name falsely, I am the Lord.—Levit. chap. xix. v. 12." On the second volume,—" Thou shalt not forswear thyself, but shalt perform unto the Lord thine oaths.—St. Matth. chap. v. 33." And, on a blank leaf of either—" Robert Burns, Mossgiel," with his *mason-mark.*[1]

How lasting was the poet's remembrance of this pure love, and its tragic termination, will be seen hereafter.

Highland Mary, however, seems to have died ere her lover had made any of his more serious attempts in poetry. In the Epistle to Mr. Sillar, the very earliest, according to Gilbert, of these Essays, the poet celebrates " his Davie and his Jean." [2]

This was Jean Armour, the daughter of a respectable man, a mason in the village of Mauchline, where she was at the time the reigning toast,[3] and who afterwards became

---

[1] [On 25th January, 1841, this interesting pair of volumes, together with a lock of Mary's fair shining hair, were deposited in the Poet's Monument at Alloway. A handsome monument also was erected over the grave of Mary, in the West Churchyard at Greenock, in 1842. Neither date nor year of her death is inscribed thereon.]

[2] See Appendix C—Burns's " Highland Mary."

[3]   " In Mauchline there dwells six proper young belles,
          The pride of the place and its neighbourhood a' ;
        Their carriage and dress, a stranger would guess,
          In Lon'on or Paris they'd gotten it a' :

      " *Miss Miller* is fine, *Miss Markland's* divine,
          Miss Smith she has wit, and *Miss Betty* is braw ;
        There's beauty and fortune to get wi' *Miss Morton*,
          But *Armour's* the jewel for me o' them a'."

the wife of our poet. There are numberless allusions to her maiden charms in the best pieces which he produced at Mossgiel.

The time is not yet come, in which all the details of this story can be expected.[1] Jean Armour found herself "as ladies wish to be that love their *lords*." And how slightly such a circumstance might affect the character and reputation of a young woman in her sphere of rural life at that period, every Scotchman will understand—to any but a Scotchman, it might, perhaps, be difficult to explain. The manly readiness with which the young rustics commonly come forward to avert, by marriage, the worst consequences

---

[1] The poet's widow died within four years after the above passage was penned; and since that event, details more or less acceptable to the public have been poured forth abundantly concerning the "bonie Jean" who was fated to be the wife of Burns, "for better or for worse." There are many different versions of the story which narrates the circumstance that first brought the celebrated pair together; but the following, which is Jean's own, as communicated to Mr. John McDiarmid, may be depended on as correct:—"The first time I ever saw Burns was in Mauchline. His family then lived in Mossgiel, about a mile from the village. I was then spreading clothes in a bleach-green along with some other girls, when the poet passed in his way to call on Mr. Hamilton. He had a little dog which ran on the clothes, and I scolded, and threw something at the animal. Burns said, 'Lassie, if ye thought ought o' me, ye wadna hurt my dog!'—I thought to mysel—'I wadna think much o' you at ony rate!' I saw him afterwards at a dancing-room, and we fell acquainted."

In the "dancing-room" story, the "little dog" turns up again. Mauchline Race takes place annually in the month of April; and in a promiscuous dance on that occasion, in 1785, Burns and Miss Armour chanced to meet in the same diversion, although not as partners. Some merriment was created by the poet's dog getting into the room, and tracking his footsteps as he swung about; and the poet remarked to his partner, in a very audible voice, with a leer at Miss Armour—"I wish I could fa' in wi' some lassie who would love me as well as my dog does!" At the next casual meeting with Jean, the latter sympathizingly asked him if he had not yet fallen in with a lass to like him as well as his dog? Thereafter the pair became inseparable associates.

of such indiscretions, cannot be denied; nor, perhaps, is there any class of society, in any country, in which *matri-monial* infidelity is less known than among the female peasantry of Scotland.

Burns's worldly circumstances were in a most miserable state when he was informed of Miss Armour's condition; and the first announcement of it staggered him like a blow. He saw nothing for it but to fly the country at once; and, in a note to James Smith of Mauchline, the confidant of his amour, he thus wrote :—"Against two things I am fixed as fate—staying at home, and owning her conjugally. The first, by Heaven, I will not do!—the last, by hell, I will never do!—A good God bless you, and make you happy, up to the warmest weeping wish of parting friendship! . . . . . If you see Jean, tell her I will meet her; so help me God in my hour of need."

The lovers met accordingly; and the result of the meeting was what was to be anticipated from the tenderness and the manliness of Burns's feelings. All dread of personal inconvenience yielded at once to the tears of the woman he loved, and, ere they parted, he gave into her keeping a written acknowledgment of marriage, which, when produced by a person in Miss Armour's condition, is, according to the Scots law, to be accepted as legal evidence of an *irregular* marriage having really taken place; it being of course understood that the marriage was to be formally avowed as soon as the consequences of their imprudence could no longer be concealed from her family.

The disclosure was deferred to the last moment, and it was received by the father of Miss Armour with equal surprise and anger. Burns, confessing himself to be unequal to the maintenance of a family, proposed to go immediately to Jamaica, where he hoped to find better fortunes. He offered, if it were rejected, to abandon his farm, which was ere now a hopeless concern, and earn bread at least for his wife and children as a daily labourer at home ; but nothing could appease the indignation of Armour, who, Professor Walker hints, had entertained previously a very bad opinion of Burns's whole character. By what arguments he prevailed on his daughter to take so strange and so painful a step, we know not; but the fact is certain, that, at his entreaty, she destroyed the document, which must have been to her the most precious of her possessions—the only evidence of her marriage.

It was under such extraordinary circumstances that Miss Armour became the mother of twins.[1]

---

[1] The comments of the Rev. Hamilton Paul, on this delicate part of the poet's story, are too meritorious to be omitted.

"The scenery of the Ayr," says he, " from Sorn to the ancient burgh at its mouth, though it may be equalled in grandeur, is scarcely anywhere surpassed in beauty. To trace its meanders, to wander amid its green woods, to lean over its precipitous and rocky banks, to explore its coves, to survey its Gothic towers, and to admire its modern edifices, is not only highly delightful, but truly inspiring. If the poet, in his excursions along the banks of the river, or in penetrating into the deepest recesses of the grove, be accompanied by his favourite fair one, whose admiration of rural and sylvan beauty is akin to his own, however hazardous the experiment, the bliss is ecstatic. To warn the young and unsuspecting of their danger, is only to stimulate their curiosity. The well-meant dissuasive of Thomson is more seductive in its tendency than the admirers of that poet's morality are aware :—

> ' Ah ! then, ye Fair,
> Be greatly cautious of your sliding hearts ;
> Dare not the infectious sigh—nor in the bower,
> Where woodbines flaunt and roses shed a couch,
> While evening draws her crimson curtain round,
> Trust your soft minutes with betraying man.'

We are decidedly of opinion, that the inexperienced fair will be equally disposed to disregard this sentimental prohibition, and to accept the invitation of another bard, whose libertinism is less disguised,—

> ' Will you go to the bower I have shaded for you,
> Your bed shall be roses bespangled with dew ? '

——' To dear deluding woman, the joy of joys,'" continues Mr. Paul,

Burns's love and pride, the two most powerful feelings of his mind, had been equally wounded. His anger and grief together drove him, according to every account, to the verge of absolute insanity; and some of his letters on this occasion, both published and unpublished, have certainly all the appearance of having been written in as deep a concentration of despair as ever preceded the most awful of human calamities. His first thought had been, as we have seen, to fly at once from the scene of his disgrace and misery; and this course seemed now to be absolutely necessary. He was summoned to find security for the maintenance of the children whom he was prevented from legitimating, and such was his poverty that he could not satisfy the parish officers. I suppose security for some four or five pounds a year was the utmost that could have been demanded from a person of his rank; but the man who had in his desk the immortal poems to which we have been referring above, either disdained to ask, or tried in vain to find, pecuniary assistance in this hour of need; and the only alternative that presented itself to his view was America or a jail.

Who can ever learn without grief and indignation, that it was the victim of *such* miseries who at this moment, could pour out such a strain as the *Lament ?*

> " O thou pale orb, that silent shines,
>   While care-untroubled mortals sleep!
> Thou seest a wretch that inly pines,
>   And wanders here to wail and weep!

" Burns was partial in the extreme. This was owing, as well to his constitutional temperament, as to the admiration which he drew from the female world, and the facility with which they met his advances. But his aberrations must have been notorious, when a man in the rank of Miss Armour's father refused his consent to his permanent union with his unfortunate daughter. Among the lower classes of the community, subsequent marriage is reckoned an ample atonement for former indiscretion, and ante-nuptial incontinency is looked upon as scarcely a transgression."

With woe I nightly vigils keep,
　Beneath thy wan unwarming beam;
And mourn, in lamentation deep,
　How *life* and *love* are all a dream.

" No idly feigned poetic plaints,
　My sad love-lorn lamentings claim;
No shepherd's pipe—Arcadian strains;
　No fabled tortures, quaint and tame.
The plighted faith; the mutual flame;
　The oft attested Pow'rs above;
The *promised Father's tender name;*
　These were the pledges of my love!"

CHAPTER IV.

"He saw misfortune's cauld *nor'-wast*
Lang mustering up a bitter blast;
A jillet brak his heart at last,
        Ill may she be !
So, took a berth afore the mast,
        And owre the sea."

JAMAICA was now his mark; and after some little time and trouble, the situation of assistant-overseer on the estate of a Dr. Douglas in that colony, was procured for him by one of his friends in the town of Irvine. Money to pay for his passage, however, he had not; and it at last occurred to him, that the few pounds requisite for this purpose might be raised by the publication of some of the finest poems that ever delighted mankind.

His landlord, Gavin Hamilton, Mr. Aiken, and other friends, encouraged him warmly; and after some hesitation, he at length resolved to hazard an experiment which might perhaps better his circumstances; and, if any tolerable number of subscribers were procured, could not make them worse than they were already. His rural patrons exerted themselves with success in the matter; and so many copies were soon subscribed for, that Burns entered into terms with a printer[1] in Kilmarnock, and began to copy out his performances for

---

[1] John Wilson, printer. Among other jokes, Burns made the man print the "Epitaph on Wee Johnie;" without giving him any hint that "*Wee Johnie*" was *John Wilson*.

the press. He carried his MSS. piecemeal to the printer; and, encouraged by the ray of light which unexpected patronage had begun to throw on his affairs, composed, while the printing was in progress, some of the best poems of the collection. The tale of the "Twa Dogs," for instance, with which the volume commenced, is known to have been written in the short interval between the publication being determined on and the printing begun. His account of the business, in his Autobiography, is as follows:—

"I gave up my part of the farm to my brother: in truth, it was only nominally mine; and made what little preparation was in my power for Jamaica. But before leaving my native land, I resolved to publish my poems. I weighed my productions as impartially as was in my power: I thought they had merit; and it was a delicious idea that I should be called a clever fellow, even though it should never reach my ears—a poor negro-driver—or, perhaps, a victim to that inhospitable clime, and gone to the world of spirits. I can truly say, that, *pauvre inconnu* as I then was, I had pretty nearly as high an idea of myself and of my works as I have at this moment, when the public has decided in their favour. It ever was my opinion, that the mistakes and blunders, both in a rational and religious point of view, of which we see thousands daily guilty, are owing to their ignorance of themselves. To know myself, had been all along my constant study. I weighed myself alone: I balanced myself with others: I watched every means of information, to see how much ground I occupied as a man and as a poet: I studied assiduously Nature's design in my formation—where the lights and shades in character were intended. I was pretty confident my poems would meet with some applause; but at the worst, the roar of the Atlantic would deafen the voice of censure, and the novelty of West Indian scenes make me forget neglect. I threw off six hundred copies, for which I got subscriptions for about three hundred and fifty.[1]—My vanity was highly gratified by the reception I met with from the public; and besides, I pocketed, all expenses deducted, nearly twenty pounds. This sum came very seasonably, as I was thinking of indenting myself, for want of money to procure my passage. As soon as I was master of nine guineas, the price of wafting me to the torrid zone, I took a steerage passage in the first ship that was to sail from the Clyde; for

> ' Hungry ruin had me in the wind.'

I had been for some days skulking from covert to covert, under all the terrors of a jail; as some ill-advised people had uncoupled the merciless pack of the law at my heels. I had taken the last farewell of my few friends; my chest was on the way to Greenock; I had composed the last song I should ever measure in Caledonia, ' The gloomy night is gathering fast,' when a letter from Dr. Blacklock to a friend of mine, overthrew all my schemes, by opening new prospects to my poetic ambition."

To the above rapid narrative of the poet, we may annex a few details, gathered from his various biographers and from his own letters.

While his sheets were in the press (June—July, 1786), it appears that his friends, Hamilton and Aiken, revolved various schemes for procuring him the means of remaining in Scotland; and having studied some of the practical branches of mathematics, as we have seen, and in particular *gauging*, it occurred to himself that a situation in the Excise might be better suited to him than any other he

---

[1] Gilbert Burns mentions, that a single individual, Mr. William Parker, merchant in Kilmarnock, subscribed for thirty-five copies. [This happens to be another of Gilbert's blunders. Chambers has pointed out that Gilbert set down Parker's name instead of that of " Robert Muir, wine merchant, Kilmarnock."]

was at all likely to obtain by the intervention of such patrons as he possessed.

He appears to have lingered longer after the publication of the poems than one might suppose from his own narrative, in the hope that these gentlemen might at length succeed in their efforts in his behalf. The poems were received with favour, even with rapture, in Ayrshire, and ere long over the adjoining counties. "Old and young," thus speaks Robert Heron, "high and low, grave and gay, learned or ignorant, were alike delighted, agitated, transported. I was at that time resident in Galloway, contiguous to Ayrshire, and I can well remember how even ploughboys and maid-servants would have gladly bestowed the wages they earned the most hardly, and which they wanted to purchase necessary clothing, if they might but procure the works of Burns." The poet soon found that his person also had become an object of general curiosity, and that a lively interest in his personal fortunes was excited among some of the gentry of the district, when the details of his story reached them—a circumstance pretty sure to happen—along with his modest and manly preface.[1]

---

[1] *Preface to the First Edition.*

" The following trifles are not the production of the poet, who, with all the advantages of learned art, and, perhaps, amid the elegancies and idlenesses of upper life, looks down for a rural theme, with an eye to Theocritus or Virgil. To the author of this, these and other celebrated names their countrymen are, in their original languages, *a fountain shut up, and a book sealed.* Unacquainted with the necessary requisites for commencing poet by rule, he sings the sentiments and manners he felt and saw in himself and his rustic compeers around him, in his and their native language. Though a rhymer from his earliest years, at least from the earliest impulses of the softer passions, it was not till very lately that the applause, perhaps the partiality, of friendship, wakened his vanity so far as to make him think any thing of his worth showing; and none of the following works were composed with a view to the press. To amuse himself with the little creations of his own

Among others, the celebrated Professor Dugald Stewart of Edinburgh, and his accomplished lady, then resident at their beautiful seat of Catrine, began to notice him with much

---

fancy, amid the toil and fatigues of a laborious life; to transcribe the various feelings, the loves, the griefs, the hopes, the fears, in his own breast; to find some kind of counterpoise to the struggles of a world, always an alien scene, a task uncouth to the poetical mind—these were his motives for courting the Muses, and in these he found poetry to be its own reward.

"Now that he appears in the public character of an author, he does it with fear and trembling. So dear is fame to the rhyming tribe, that even he, an obscure, nameless bard, shrinks aghast at the thought of being branded as ' an impertinent blockhead, obtruding his nonsense on the world; and, because he can make a shift to jingle a few doggerel Scotch rhymes together, looking upon himself as a poet of no small consequence, forsooth!'

"It is an observation of that celebrated poet, Shenstone, whose divine elegies do honour to our language, our nation, and our species, that ' *Humility* has depressed many a genius to a hermit, but never raised one to fame!' If any critic catches at the word *genius* the author tells him, once for all, that he certainly looks upon himself as possessed of some poetic abilities, otherwise his publishing in the manner he has done, would be a manœuvre below the worst character which, he hopes, his worst enemy will ever give him. But to the genius of a Ramsay, or the glorious dawnings of the poor, unfortunate Fergusson, he, with equal unaffected sincerity, declares that, even in his highest pulse of vanity, he has not the most distant pretensions. These two justly admired Scotch poets he has often had in his eye in the following pieces; but rather with a view to kindle at their flame, than for servile imitation.

"To his subscribers, the author returns his most sincere thanks. Not the mercenary bow over a counter, but the heart-throbbing gratitude of the bard, conscious how much he owes to benevolence and friendship for gratifying him, if he deserves it, in that dearest wish of every poetic bosom—to be distinguished. He begs his readers, particularly the learned and the polite, who may honour him with a perusal, that they will make every allowance for education and circumstances of life; but if, after a fair, candid, and impartial criticism, he shall stand convicted of dullness and nonsense, let him be done by as he would in that case do by others—let him be condemned, without mercy, to contempt and oblivion."

polite and friendly attention.[1] Dr. Hugh Blair, who then
held an eminent place in the literary society of Scotland,
happened to be paying Mr. Stewart a visit, and on reading
"The Holy Fair," at once pronounced it the "work of a
very fine genius;" and Mrs. Stewart, herself a poetess,
flattered him perhaps still more highly by her warm com-
mendations. But, above all, his little volume happened to
attract the notice of Mrs. Dunlop of Dunlop,[2] a lady of
high birth and ample fortune, enthusiastically attached to
her country, and interested in whatever appeared to concern the honour of Scotland. This excellent woman, while
slowly recovering from the languor of an illness, laid her
hands accidentally on the new production of the provincial
press, and opened the volume at the "Cotter's Saturday
Night." "She read it over," says Gilbert, "with the
greatest pleasure and surprise; the poet's description of the
simple cottagers operated on her mind like the charm of a
powerful exorcist, repelling the demon ennui, and restoring
her to her wonted inward harmony and satisfaction." Mrs.
Dunlop instantly sent an express to Mossgiel, distant sixteen miles from her residence, with a very kind letter to
Burns, requesting him to supply her, if he could, with
half-a-dozen copies of the book, and to call at Dunlop as
soon as he could find it convenient. Burns was from home,
but he acknowledged the favour conferred on him in an
interesting letter, still extant; and shortly afterwards commenced a personal acquaintance with one that never after-

---

[1] [Our biographer's imagination is here at work. At this period the
Professor was in a condition worse than that of a widower, his wife
being laid aside by illness, of which she died in 1787. His marriage to
Miss Cranstoun, the "poetess," did not take place till 1790.]

[2] This lady was the daughter of Sir Thomas Wallace, Baronet, of
Craigie, supposed to represent the family of which the great hero of
Scotland was a cadet.

wards ceased to befriend him to the utmost of her power. His letters to Mrs. Dunlop form a very large proportion of all his subsequent correspondence, and addressed as they were to a person, whose sex, age, rank, and benevolence, inspired at once profound respect and a graceful confidence, will ever remain the most pleasing of all the materials of our poet's biography.

At the residences of these new acquaintance, Burns was introduced into society of a class which he had not before approached; and of the manner in which he stood the trial, Mr. Stewart thus writes to Dr. Currie:

" His manners were then, as they continued ever afterwards, simple, manly, and independent; strongly expressive of conscious genius and worth; but without anything that indicated forwardness, arrogance, or vanity. He took his share in conversation, but not more than belonged to him; and listened, with apparent attention and deference, on subjects where his want of education deprived him of the means of information. If there had been a little more of gentleness and accommodation in his temper, he would, I think, have been still more interesting; but he had been accustomed to give law in the circle of his ordinary acquaintance; and his dread of anything approaching to meanness or servility, rendered his manner somewhat decided and hard. Nothing, perhaps, was more remarkable among his various attainments than the fluency and precision, and originality of his language, when he spoke in company, more particularly as he aimed at purity in his turn of expression, and avoided, more successfully than most Scotchmen, the peculiarities of Scottish phraseology. At this time, Burns's prospects in life were so extremely gloomy, that he had seriously formed a plan of going out to Jamaica in a very humble situation, not, however, without lamenting that his want of patronage should force him to think of a project so repugnant to his feelings, when his ambition aimed at no higher an object than the station of an exciseman or gauger in his own country."

The provincial applause of his publication, and the consequent notice of his superiors, however flattering such things must have been, were far from administering any essential relief to the urgent necessities of Burns's situation. Very shortly before his first visit to Catrine, where he met with the young and amiable Basil Lord Daer, whose condescension and kindness on the occasion he celebrates in some well-known verses, we find the poet writing to his friend, Mr. Aiken of Ayr, in the following sad strain :—" I have been feeling all the various rotations and movements within respecting the excise. There are many things plead strongly against it; the uncertainty of getting soon into business, the consequences of my follies, which may perhaps make it impracticable for me to stay at home ; and besides, I have for some time been pining under secret wretchedness, from causes which you pretty well know—the pang of disappointment, the sting of pride, with some wandering stabs of remorse, which never fail to settle on my vitals like vultures, when attention is not called away by the calls of society, or the vagaries of the Muse. Even in the hour of social mirth, my gaiety is the madness of an intoxicated criminal under the hands of the executioner. All these reasons urge me to go abroad ; and to all these reasons I have only one answer—the feelings of a father. This, in the present mood I am in, overbalances everything that can be laid in the scale against it."

He proceeds to say that he claims no right to complain. " The world has in general been kind to me, fully up to my deserts. I was for some time past fast getting into the pining distrustful snarl of the misanthrope. I saw myself alone, unfit for the struggle of life, shrinking at every rising cloud in the chance-directed atmosphere of fortune, while all defenceless, I looked about in vain for a cover.

It never occurred to me, at least never with the force it deserved, that this world is a busy scene, and man a creature destined for a progressive struggle; and that, however, I might possess a warm heart, and inoffensive manners (which last, by the by, was rather more than I could well boast) still, more than these passive qualities, there was something to be *done*. When all my school-fellows and youthful compeers were striking off, with eager hope and earnest intent, on some one or other of the many paths of busy life, I was 'standing idle in the market-place,' or only left the chase of the butterfly from flower to flower, to hunt fancy from whim to whim. You see, sir, that if to *know* one's errors, were a probability of *mending* them, I stand a fair chance; but, according to the reverend Westminster divines, though conviction must precede conversion, it is very far from always implying it."

In the midst of all the distresses of this period of suspense, Burns found time, as he tells Mr. Aiken, for some "vagaries of the muse;" and one or two of these may deserve to be noticed here, as throwing light on his personal demeanour during this first summer of his fame. The poems appeared in July, and one of the first persons of superior condition (Gilbert, indeed, says *the* first) who courted his acquaintance in consequence of having read them, was Mrs. Stewart of Stair, a beautiful and accomplished lady.[1] Burns presented her on this occasion with

---

[1] [The widow of Burns stumbled at this polite epithet applied by the biographer to the very plain-looking old lady thus complimented. Mr. McDiarmid was reading the passage aloud to her, when she interrupted him with the exclamation—"This is egregiously incorrect! She was the reverse of beautiful!" On our own part, we must also correct Mr. L. in regard to his next sentence. On the present occasion, the poet did send her a parcel of his earlier pieces together with two songs newly composed—his "Farewell to the banks of Ayr," and "The lass o' Ballochmyle." But "Afton Water," referred to and quoted in the text, was not

some MS. songs : and among the rest, with one in which her own charms were celebrated, in that warm strain of compliment which our poet seems to have all along considered the most proper to be used whenever fair lady was to be addressed in rhyme.

> " Flow gently, sweet Afton, among thy green braes,
> Flow gently, I'll sing thee a song in thy praise ;
> My Mary's asleep by thy murmuring stream,
> Flow gently, sweet Afton, disturb not her dream.
> How pleasant thy banks and green valleys below,
> Where wild in the woodlands the primroses blow—
> There oft, as mild evening sweeps over the lea,
> The sweet-scented birk shades my Mary and me."

It was in July of the same year, that he had happened, in the course of an evening ramble on the banks of the Ayr, to meet with a young and lovely unmarried lady, of the family of Alexander of Ballochmyle ; and now (Nov. 18, 1786) emboldened, we are to suppose, by the reception his volume had met with, he enclosed to her some verses, which he had written in commemoration of that passing glimpse of her beauty, and conceived in a strain of luxurious

---

composed till several years thereafter, during the poet's latter days in Ellisland ; and it was also presented to Mrs. Stewart along with a choice lot of the poet's then unpublished pieces in the year 1791. The latter collection—named " The Afton MSS."—is now in the poet's monument at Alloway, a gift from the lady's grandson, Mr. Allason Cunninghame of Logan and Afton, in September, 1880.

We know not who invented the absurd piece of mythology—that Mrs. Stewart was the heroine of the admired song Afton Water,—" My Mary's asleep," &c. The lady might have been the poet's grandmother, and her name was " Catherine Gordon." We observe that, in Currie's early editions, that legend is not given as a note to the song ; but in the fourth edition it is inserted, and retained constantly thereafter. There can be little doubt that the story was a little *ruse* got up by Gilbert, to divest Currie's readers of the natural conjecture that " Highland Mary " was here again " the theme of his lays."]

fervour, which certainly, coming from a man of Burns's station and character, must have sounded very strangely in a delicate maiden's ear.

> " Oh, had she been a country maid,
>   And I the happy country swain,
> Though sheltered in the lowest shed,
>   That ever rose on Scotia's plain!
> Through weary winter's wind and rain,
>   With joy, with rapture, I would toil,
> And nightly to my bosom strain
>   The bonie lass of Ballochmyle."

Burns has himself left it on record that he resented the silence in which Miss Alexander received this tribute to her charms. I suppose we may account for his over-tenderness to young ladies in pretty much the same way that Professor Dugald Stewart does, in the letter above quoted, for a certain want of "gentleness and accommodation" in his method of addressing persons of his own sex. His rustic experience among the fair ones of his own circle could have had no tendency to whisper the lesson of reserve.

The autumn of this eventful year was drawing to a close, and Burns, who had already lingered three months in the hope which he now considered vain, of an Excise appointment, perceived that another year must be lost altogether, unless he made up his mind, and secured his passage to the West Indies. The Kilmarnock edition of his poems was, however, nearly exhausted; and his friends encouraged him to produce another at the same place, with the view of equipping himself the better for his voyage. But " Wee Johnie " would not undertake the new impression, unless Burns advanced the price of the paper required for it; and with this demand the poet had no means of complying. Mr. Ballantyne, the chief magistrate of Ayr (the same gentleman to whom the poem on the " Brigs of Ayr " was afterwards inscribed), offered to furnish the money;

and probably his kind offer would have been accepted; but ere this matter could be arranged, the prospects of the poet were, in a very unexpected manner, altered and improved.

Burns went to pay a parting visit to Dr. Lawrie, minister of Loudoun, a gentleman from whom and his accomplished family, he had previously received many kind attentions. After taking farewell of this benevolent circle, the poet proceeded, as the night was setting in, " to convey his chest," as he says, " so far on the road to Greenock, where he was to embark in a few days for America." And it was under these circumstances that he composed the song already referred to, which he meant as his farewell dirge to his native land, and which ends thus :—

> " Farewell, old Coila's hills and dales,
> Her heathy moors and winding vales,
> The scenes where wretched fancy roves,
> Pursuing past unhappy loves.
> Farewell, my friends! farewell, my foes!
> My peace with these—my love with those—
> The bursting tears my heart declare,
> Farewell, the bonie banks of Ayr."

Dr. Lawrie had given Burns much good counsel, and what comfort he could, at parting, but prudently said nothing of an effort which he had previously made in his behalf. He had sent a copy of the poems, with a sketch of the author's history, to his friend Dr. Thomas Blacklock of Edinburgh, with a request that he would introduce both to the notice of those persons whose literary opinions were at the time most listened to in Scotland, in the hope that, by their intervention, Burns might yet be rescued from the necessity of expatriating himself. Dr. Blacklock's answer reached Dr. Lawrie a day or two after Burns had made his visit, and composed his dirge; and it was not yet too late.

Lawrie forwarded it immediately to Gavin Hamilton, who carried it to Burns. It is as follows :—

"Edinburgh, Sep. 4, 1786.

"I ought to have acknowledged your favour long ago, not only as a testimony of your kind remembrance, but as it gave me an opportunity of sharing one of the finest, and perhaps one of the most genuine entertainments of which the human mind is susceptible. A number of avocations retarded my progress in reading the poems; at last, however, I have finished that pleasing perusal. Many instances have I seen of Nature's force or beneficence exerted under numerous and formidable disadvantages; but none equal to that with which you have been kind enough to present me. There is a pathos and delicacy in his serious poems, a vein of wit and humour in those of a more festive turn, which cannot be too much admired, nor too warmly approved; and I think I shall never open the book without feeling my astonishment renewed and increased. It was my wish to have expressed my approbation in verse; but whether from declining life, or a temporary depression of spirits, it is at present out of my power to accomplish that intention.

"Mr. Stewart, Professor of Morals in this University, had formerly read me three of the poems, and I had desired him to get my name inserted among the subscribers; but whether this was done, or not, I never could learn. I have little intercourse with Dr. Blair, but will take care to have the poems communicated to him by the intervention of some mutual friend. It has been told me by a gentleman, to whom I showed the performances, and who sought a copy with diligence and ardour, that the whole impression is already exhausted. It were, therefore, much to be wished, for the sake of the young man, that a second edition, more numerous than the former, could immediately be printed;

as it appears certain that its intrinsic merit, and the exertion
of the author's friends, might give it a more universal circulation than anything of the kind which has been published
in my memory." _(Currie, vol. ii., p. 36.)_

We have already seen with what surprise and delight
Burns read this generous letter. Although he had ere this
conversed with more than one person of established literary
reputation, and received from them attentions, of which
he was ever after grateful,—the despondency of his spirit
appears to have remained as dark as ever, up to the very
hour when his landlord produced Dr. Blacklock's letter;
and one may be pardoned for fancying, that in his " Vision,"
he has himself furnished no unfaithful representation of
the manner in which he was spending what he looked on
as one of the last nights, if not the very last, he was to
pass at Mossgiel, when the friendly Hamilton unexpectedly
entered the melancholy dwelling.

> " There, lanely, by the ingle-cheek
> I sat, and eyed the spewing reek,
> That fill'd, wi' hoast-provoking smeek,
>   The auld clay-biggin',
> And heard the restless rattans squeak
>   About the riggin'.
>
> All in this mottie misty clime,
> I backward mused on wasted time,
> How I had spent my youthfu' prime,
>   An' done nae thing,
> But stringin' blethers up in rhyme
>   For fools to sing.
>
> Had I to gude advice but harkit,
> I might by this hae led a market,
> Or strutted in a bank an' clarkit
>   My cash account.
> While here, half-mad, half-fed, half-sarkit,
>   Is a' the amount."

" Dr. Blacklock," says Burns, " belonged to a set of

critics, for whose *applause* I had not *dared to hope*. His opinion that I would meet with encouragement in Edinburgh, fired me so much, that away I posted for that city, without a single acquaintance, or a single letter of introduction. The baneful star that had so long shed its blasting influence on my zenith, for once made a revolution to the nadir." [1]

---

[1] [In the letter, above given, from Dr. Blacklock to the Rev. Dr. Lawrie, the reader may observe that nothing is said or suggested to encourage Burns to come to Edinburgh : the writer merely urges the immediate issue of a second edition of his poems. Dr. Currie's version of the poet's autobiography here quoted from, certainly implies that Burns read it as an invitation to proceed to that city ; but in the manuscript his words are simply these :—" Dr. Blacklock's idea that I should meet every encouragement for a second edition, fired me so much, that away I posted to Edinburgh," &c. Thus we find that the selecting of the metropolis as the place of his second publication was the result of his own option ; and it certainly does appear that his eagerness to obtain an appointment as an excise-officer formed a strong part of his motive to proceed to Edinburgh. This point, if made out, would infringe a little on the romantic aspect of that brilliant part of the poet's career ; but the truth is very precious. He reached the city on 28th November, and in one of his earliest letters to Ayrshire friends, he says : " My avowed patrons are the Duchess of Gordon, the Countess of Glencairn, with my Lord, and Lady Betty, the Dean of Faculty, and Sir John Whitefoord." Dr. Currie, in his first edition, prints a letter from Sir John Whitefoord to Burns, dated " Edinburgh, Dec. 4, 1786," which, however, was withdrawn from his next issue, and never afterwards restored. The following remarkable passage touches strongly on our present point :—" I received your letter a few days ago. I do not pretend to much interest, but what I have I shall be ready to exert in procuring the attainment of any object you have in view. . . . I have been told you wish to be made a gauger ; I submit it to your consideration whether it would not be more desirable, if a sum could be raised by subscription for a second edition of your poems, to lay it out in the stocking of a farm," &c. The excise scheme was a pet one of the bard's own, and consideration of that fact ought to have checked the indignant utterances of Carlyle and others of smaller note who declaimed against his friendly patrons for finding no better post for him than " a Gaugership ! "]

Two of the biographers of Burns have had the advantage of speaking from personal knowledge of the excellent man whose interposition was thus serviceable. " It was a fortunate circumstance," says Walker, " that the person whom Dr. Lawrie applied to, merely because he was the only one of his literary acquaintances with whom he chose to use that freedom, happened also to be the person best qualified to render the application successful. Dr. Blacklock was an enthusiast in his admiration of an art which he had practised himself with applause. He felt the claims of a poet with a paternal sympathy, and he had in his constitution a tenderness and sensibility that would have engaged his beneficence for a youth in the circumstances of Burns, even though he had not been indebted to him for the delight which he received from his works ; for if the young men were enumerated whom he drew from obscurity, and enabled by education to advance themselves in life, the catalogue would naturally excite surprise. . . . He was not of a disposition to discourage with feeble praise, and to shift off the trouble of future patronage, by bidding him relinquish poetry, and mind his plough."[1]

" There was never, perhaps," thus speaks the unfortunate Heron, whose own unmerited sorrows and sufferings would not have left so dark a stain on the literary history of Scotland, had the kind spirit of Blacklock been common among his lettered countrymen—" There was never, perhaps, one among all mankind whom you might more truly have called *an angel upon earth*, than Dr. Blacklock. He was guileless and innocent as a child, yet endowed with manly sagacity and penetration. His heart was a perpetual

---

[1] Morison, vol. i., p. 9. In the same passage Mr. Walker contrasts Blacklock's conduct to Burns with Walpole's to Chatterton. If the Professor had ever read Walpole's defence of himself, he could not have fallen into this once common, but now exploded, error.

spring of benignity. His feelings were all tremblingly alive to the sense of the sublime, the beautiful, the tender, the pious, the virtuous. Poetry was to him the dear solace of perpetual blindness."

Such was the amiable old man, whose life Mackenzie has written, and on whom Johnson "looked with reverence."[1] The writings of Blacklock are forgotten (though some of his songs in "The Museum" deserve another fate), but the memory of his virtues will not pass away until mankind shall have ceased to sympathize with the fortunes of genius, and to appreciate the poetry of Burns.

---

[1] "This morning I saw at breakfast Dr. Blacklock the blind poet, who does not remember to have seen light, and is read to by a poor scholar in Latin, Greek, and French. He was originally a poor scholar himself. I looked on him with reverence."—Letter to Mrs. Thrale, Edinburgh, August 17, 1773.

CHAPTER V.

" Edina ! Scotia's darling seat !
  All hail thy palaces and towers,
Where once beneath a monarch's feet
  Sat legislation's sovereign powers ;
From marking wildly-scatter'd flow'rs,
  As on the banks of Ayr I stray'd,
And singing, lone, the lingering hours,
  I shelter in thy honour'd shade."

THERE is an old Scottish ballad which begins thus :—

" As I came in by Glenap,
  I met with an aged woman,
And she bade me cheer up my heart,
  For the best of my days was coming."

This stanza was one of Burns's favourite quotations ;
and he told a friend[1] many years afterwards, that he remembered humming it to himself, over and over, on his
way from Mossgiel to Edinburgh.[2] Perhaps the excellent

---

[1] David McCulloch, Esq., brother to the laird of Ardwell [whose
sister Elizabeth was the wife of Sir Walter Scott's younger brother,
Thomas. While a citizen of Dumfries, the poet became intimate with
David].

[2] [Dr. Currie, in his first edition, recorded that this journey was performed on foot in the course of two days. In that particular his informant was Gilbert Burns—so little did the one brother, although
living in the same house together, know the ways and means of the
other. On this occasion the poet was well-mounted and attired—an excellent horse having been lent to him by a brother farmer, who, on
observing the error of fact in Currie's " Memoir," immediately commu-

Blacklock might not have been particularly flattered with the circumstance had it reached his ears.

Although he repaired to the capital with such alertness, solely, as has been alleged, in consequence of Blacklock's letter to Lawrie, it appears that he allowed some weeks to pass ere he presented himself to the Doctor's personal notice.[1] He found several of his old Ayrshire acquaintances established in Edinburgh, and, I suppose, felt himself constrained to give himself up for a brief space to their society. He printed, however, without delay, a prospectus of a second edition of his poems, and being introduced by Mr. Dalrymple of Orangefield to the Earl of Glencairn, that amiable nobleman easily persuaded Creech, then the chief bookseller in Edinburgh (who had once been his own travelling-tutor), to undertake the publication. The honourable Henry Erskine, Dean of the Faculty of Advocates, the most agreeable of companions, and the most benignant of wits, took him also, as the poet expresses it, " under his wing." The kind Blacklock received him with all the warmth of paternal affection when he did wait on him, and introduced him to Dr. Blair, and other eminent *literati ;* his subscription lists were soon filled ; Lord Glencairn made interest with the Caledonian Hunt (an associa-

---

nicated with Gilbert correcting the mistake. Gilbert duly announced the correction to Currie, who, however, took a lazy and ineffectual method of rectifying the gross blunder by merely deleting those six words—" having performed his journey on foot." The consequence was that for half a century thereafter the mistake was perpetuated ; and in a famously annotated edition of Currie produced by Chambers in 1838, we are told, on the alleged authority of John Richmond, the bard's bedfellow, this additional " fact : "—" The poet was so knocked up by his walk from Mauchline to Edinburgh, that he could not leave his room for two days !"]

1 Burns reached Edinburgh before the end of November ; and yet Dr. Lawrie's letter (General Correspondence, p. 37), admonishing him to wait on Blacklock, is dated December 22.

tion of the most distinguished members of the northern aristocracy), to accept the dedication of the forthcoming edition, and to subscribe individually for copies. Several noblemen, especially of the west of Scotland, came forward with subscription-moneys considerably beyond the usual rate. In so small a capital, where everybody knows everybody, that which becomes a favourite topic in one circle of society, soon excites an universal interest; and before Burns had been a fortnight in Edinburgh, we find him writing to his earliest patron, Gavin Hamilton, in these terms:—"For my own affairs, I am in a fair way of becoming as eminent as Thomas à Kempis or John Bunyan; and you may expect henceforth to see my birthday inscribed among the wonderful events in the Poor Robin and Aberdeen Almanacks, along with the Black Monday, and the Battle of Bothwell Bridge." Dec. 7th, 1786.

It will ever be remembered, to the honour of the man who at that period held the highest place in the imaginative literature of Scotland, that he was the first who came forward to avow in print his admiration of the genius, and his warm interest in the fortunes, of the poet. Distinguished as his own writings are by the refinements of classical arts, Mr. Henry Mackenzie was, fortunately for Burns, a man of liberal genius, as well as polished taste; and he, in whose own pages some of the best models of elaborate elegance will ever be recognized, was among the first to feel, and the first to stake his own reputation on the public avowal, that the Ayrshire ploughman belonged to the order of beings whose privilege it is to snatch graces "beyond the reach of art." It is but a melancholy business to trace among the records of literary history, the manner in which most great original geniuses have been greeted on their first appeals to the world, by the contemporary arbiters of taste; coldly and timidly indeed have the sympathies of professional criticism flowed on most such occasions in past times and in the present, but the reception of Burns was worthy of the "Man of Feeling." After alluding to the provincial circulation and reputation of his poems,[1] "I hope," said the "Lounger," "I shall not be thought to assume too much, if I endeavour to place him in a higher point of view, to call for a verdict of his country on the merits of his works, and to claim for him those honours which their excellence appears to deserve. In mentioning the circumstance of his humble station, I mean not to rest his pretensions solely on that title, or to urge the merits of his poetry, when considered in relation to the lowness of his birth, and the little opportunity of improvement which his education could afford. These particulars, indeed, must excite our wonder at his productions; but his poetry, considered abstractedly, and without the apologies arising from his situation, seems to me fully entitled to command our feelings, and to obtain our applause." . . . After quoting various passages, in some of which his readers "must discover a high tone of feeling, and power, and energy of expression, particularly and strongly characteristic of the mind and the voice of the poet," and others as showing "the power of genius, not less admirable in tracing the manners, than in painting the passions, or in drawing the scenery of nature," and "with what uncommon penetration and sagacity this heaven-taught ploughman, from his humble and unlettered condition, had looked on men and manners," the critic concluded with an eloquent appeal in behalf of the poet personally: "To repair," said he, "the wrongs of suffering or neglected merit; to call forth genius from the obscurity in which it had pined indignant, and place it where it may profit or delight the world—these are exertions which give to wealth an enviable superiority, to greatness and to patronage a laudable pride."

---

[1] The "Lounger" for Saturday, December 9, 1786.

We all know how the serious part of this appeal was ultimately attended to; but, in the meantime, whatever gratifications such a mind as his could derive from the blandishments of the fair, the condescension of the noble, and the flattery of the learned, were plentifully administered to " the lion " of the season.

" I was, sir," thus wrote Burns to one of his Ayrshire patrons,[1] a few days after the "Lounger" appeared—" I was, when first honoured with your notice, too obscure; now I tremble lest I should be ruined by being dragged too suddenly into the glare of polite and learned observation; " and he concludes the same letter with an ominous prayer for " better health and more spirits."

Two or three weeks later, we find him writing as follows :—" (January 13, 1787.) I went to a Mason Lodge yesternight, where the M.W. Grand Master Charteris and all the Grand Lodge of Scotland visited. The meeting was numerous and elegant: all the different lodges about town were present in all their pomp. The Grand Master, who presided with great solemnity, among other general toasts gave ' Caledonia and Caledonia's bard, Brother B——,' which rung through the whole assembly with multiplied honours and repeated acclamations. As I had no idea such a thing would happen, I was downright thunderstruck ; and trembling in every nerve, made the best return in my power. Just as I had finished, one of the grand officers said, so loud that I could hear, with a most comforting accent, ' very well indeed,' which set me something to rights again."

And a few weeks later still, he is thus addressed by one of his old associates who was meditating a visit to Edinburgh.[2] " By all accounts, it will be a difficult matter to

---

[1] John Ballantine, Provost of Ayr, Dec. 13, 1786.
[2] [This old associate was Mr. Peter Stuart, editor of " The Star "

get a sight of you at all, unless your company is bespoke a week beforehand. There are great rumours here of your intimacy with the Duchess of Gordon, and other ladies of distinction. I am really told that

           ' Cards to invite, fly by thousands each night;'

and if you had one, there would also, I suppose, be 'bribes for your old secretary.' I observe you are resolved to make hay while the sun shines, and avoid, if possible, the fate of poor Fergusson. *Quærenda pecunia primum est—Virtus post nummos*, is a good maxim to thrive by. You seemed to despise it while in this country; but, probably, some philosophers in Edinburgh have taught you better sense."

In this proud career, however, the popular idol needed no slave to whisper whence he had risen, and whither he was to return in the ebb of the spring-tide of fortune. His "prophetic soul" was probably furnished with a sufficient memento every night—when, from the soft homage of glittering saloons, or the tumultuous applause of convivial assemblies, he made his retreat to the humble garret of a *writer's* apprentice, a native of Mauchline, and as poor as himself, whose only bed "Caledonia's Bard" was fain to partake throughout this triumphant winter.[1]

He bore all his honours in a manner worthy of himself; and of this the testimonies are so numerous, that the only difficulty is that of selection. "The attentions he received," says Mr. Dugald Stewart, "from all ranks and descriptions

---

newspaper in London, but who was originally from Edinburgh, and for some time was resident in Ayrshire.]

[1] "Mr. Richmond of Mauchline told me that Burns spent the first winter of his residence in Edinburgh, in his lodgings. They slept in the same bed, and had only one room, for which they paid three shillings a week. It was in the house of a Mrs. Carfrae, Baxter's Close, Lawnmarket, first scale-stair on the left hand in going down, first door in the stair."— *Cromek's MSS.*

of persons, were such as would have turned any head but his own. I cannot say that I could perceive any unfavourable effect which they left on his mind. He retained the same simplicity of manners and appearance which had struck me so forcibly when I first saw him in the country; nor did he seem to feel any additional self-importance from the number and rank of his new acquaintance."

Professor Walker, who met him for the first time early in the same season, at breakfast in Dr. Blacklock's house, has thus recorded his impressions :—" I was not much struck with his first appearance, as I had previously heard it described. His person, though strong and well knit, and much superior to what might be expected in a ploughman, was still rather coarse in its outline. His stature, from want of setting up, appeared to be only of the middle size, but was rather above it. His motions were firm and decided; and though without any pretensions to grace, were at the same time so free from clownish restraint, as to show that he had not always been confined to the society of his profession. His countenance was not of that elegant cast, which is most frequent among the upper ranks, but it was manly and intelligent, and marked by a thoughtful gravity which shaded at times into sternness. In his large dark eye the most striking index of his genius resided. It was full of mind; and would have been singularly expressive, under the management of one who could employ it with more art, for the purpose of expression.

" He was plainly, but properly dressed, in a style midway between the holiday costume of a farmer, and that of the company with which he now associated. His black hair, without powder, at a time when it was very generally worn, was tied behind, and spread upon his forehead. Upon the whole, from his person, physiognomy, and dress, had I met him near a seaport, and been required to guess his condition, I should have probably conjectured him to be the master of a merchant vessel of the most respectable class.

"In no part of his manner was there the slightest degree of affectation, nor could a stranger have suspected, from anything in his behaviour or conversation, that he had been for some months the favourite of all the fashionable circles of a metropolis.

"In conversation he was powerful. His conceptions and expression were of corresponding vigour, and on all subjects were as remote as possible from commonplace. Though somewhat authoritative, it was in a way which gave little offence, and was readily imputed to his inexperience in those modes of smoothing dissent and softening assertion, which are important characteristics of polished manners. After breakfast I requested him to communicate some of his unpublished pieces, and he recited his farewell song to the 'Banks of Ayr,' introducing it with a description of the circumstances in which it was composed, more striking than the poem itself.

"I paid particular attention to his recitation, which was plain, slow, articulate, and forcible, but without any eloquence or art. He did not always lay the emphasis with propriety, nor did he humour the sentiment by the variations of his voice. He was standing during the time, with his face towards the window, to which, and not to his auditors, he directed his eye—thus depriving himself of any additional effect which the language of his composition might have borrowed from the language of his countenance. In this he resembled the generality of singers in ordinary company, who, to shun any charge of affectation, withdraw all meaning from their features, and lose the advantage by which vocal performers on the stage augment the impression, and give energy to the sentiment of the song. . . .

"The day after my first introduction to Burns, I supped

LIFE OF ROBERT BURNS.

in company with him at Dr. Blair's. The other guests
were very few ; and as each had been invited chiefly to have
an opportunity of meeting with the poet, the Doctor endeavoured to draw him out, and to make him the central
figure of the group. Though he therefore furnished the
greatest proportion of the conversation, he did no more
than what he saw evidently was expected." [1]

To these reminiscences I shall now add those of one who
is likely to be heard unwillingly on no subject; and—young
as he was in 1786—on few subjects, I think, with greater
interest than the personal appearance and conversation of
Robert Burns. The following is an extract from a letter
of Sir Walter Scott:—

" As for Burns, I may truly say, *Virgilium vidi tantum.*
I was a lad of fifteen in 1786-7, when he came first to
Edinburgh, but had sense and feeling enough to be much
interested in his poetry, and would have given the world
to know him ; but I had very little acquaintance with
any literary people, and less with the gentry of the west
country, the two sets that he most frequented. Mr.
Thomas Grierson was at that time a clerk of my father's.
He knew Burns, and promised to ask him to his lodgings
to dinner, but had no opportunity to keep his word, otherwise I might have seen more of this distinguished man.
As it was, I saw him one day at the late venerable Professor Ferguson's, where there were several gentlemen of
literary reputation, among whom I remember the celebrated
Mr. Dugald Stewart. Of course we youngsters sate silent,
looked, and listened. The only thing I remember which
was remarkable in Burns's manner, was the effect produced
upon him by a print of Bunbury's, representing a soldier
lying dead on the snow, his dog sitting in misery on one

---

[1] Morison's " Burns," vol. i., pp. lxxi, lxxii.

side—on the other, his widow, with a child in her arms.
These lines were written beneath :—

> ' Cold on Canadian hills, or Minden's plain,
> Perhaps that parent wept her soldier slain—
> Bent o'er her babe, her eye dissolved in dew,
> The big drops mingling with the milk he drew,
> Gave the sad presage of his future years,
> The child of misery baptised in tears.'

Burns seemed much affected by the print, or rather the
ideas which it suggested to his mind. He actually shed
tears. He asked whose the lines were, and it chanced that
nobody but myself remembered that they occur in a half-
forgotten poem of Langhorne's, called by the unpromising
title of ' The Justice of Peace.' I whispered my information to a friend present, who mentioned it to Burns, who
rewarded me with a look and a word, which, though of
mere civility, I then received, and still recollect, with very
great pleasure.

" His person was strong and robust; his manners rustic,
not clownish ; a sort of dignified plainness and simplicity,
which received part of its effect, perhaps, from one's knowledge of his extraordinary talents. His features are represented in Mr. Nasmyth's picture, but to me it conveys the
idea that they are diminished, as if seen in perspective. I
think his countenance was more massive than it looks in
any of the portraits. I would have taken the poet, had I
not known what he was, for a very sagacious country
farmer of the old Scotch school, *i.e.* none of your modern
agriculturists, who keep labourers for their drudgery, but
the *douce gudeman* who held his own plough. There was a
strong expression of sense and shrewdness in all his linea-
ments ; the eye alone, I think, indicated the poetical character and temperament. It was large, and of a dark cast,
which glowed (I say literally *glowed*) when he spoke with
feeling or interest. I never saw such another eye in a

human head, though I have seen the most distinguished men of my time. His conversation expressed perfect self-confidence, without the slightest presumption. Among the men who were the most learned of their time and country, he expressed himself with perfect firmness, but without the least intrusive forwardness; and when he differed in opinion, he did not hesitate to express it firmly, yet at the same time with modesty. I do not remember any part of his conversation distinctly enough to be quoted, nor did I ever see him again, except in the street, where he did not recognize me, as I could not expect he should. He was much caressed in Edinburgh, but (considering what literary emoluments have been since his day) the efforts made for his relief were extremely trifling.

"I remember on this occasion I mention, I thought Burns's acquaintance with English Poetry was rather limited, and also, that having twenty times the abilities of Allan Ramsay and of Fergusson, he talked of them with too much humility, as his models; there was, doubtless, national predilection in his estimate.

"This is all I can tell you about Burns. I have only to add that his dress corresponded with his manner. He was like a farmer dressed in his best to dine with the Laird. I do not speak *in malam partem*, when I say, I never saw a man in company with his superiors in station and information, more perfectly free from either the reality or the affectation of embarrassment. I was told, but did not observe it, that his address to females was extremely deferential, and always with a turn either to the pathetic or humorous, which engaged their attention particularly. I have heard the late Duchess of Gordon remark this.—I do not know anything I can add to these recollections of forty years since."

Darkly as the career of Burns was destined to terminate, there can be no doubt that he made his first appearance at a period highly favourable for his reception as a British, and especially as a Scottish poet. Nearly forty years had elapsed since the death of Thomson; Collins, Gray, Goldsmith, had successively disappeared; Dr. Johnson had belied the rich promise of his early appearance, and confined himself to prose, and Cowper had hardly begun to be recognized as having any considerable pretensions to fill the long-vacant throne in England. At home—without derogation from the merits either of "Douglas" or the "Minstrel," be it said—men must have gone back at least three centuries to find a Scottish poet at all entitled to be considered as of that high order to which the generous criticism of Mackenzie at once admitted "the Ayrshire Ploughman." Of the form and garb of his composition, much unquestionably and avowedly was derived from his more immediate predecessors, Ramsay and Fergusson; but there was a bold mastery of hand in his picturesque descriptions, to produce anything equal to which it was necessary to recall the days of "Christ's Kirk on the Green," and "Peebles to the Play:" and in his more solemn pieces, a depth of inspiration, and a massive energy of language, to which the dialect of his country had been a stranger, at least since "Dunbar the Mackar."[1] The Muses of Scotland have never indeed been silent; and the ancient minstrelsy of the land, of which a slender portion had as yet been committed to the safeguard of the press, was handed from generation to generation, and preserved, in many a fragment, faithful images of the peculiar tenderness, and peculiar humour, of the national fancy and character—precious representations, which Burns himself never surpassed in his happiest efforts. But these were

---

[1] [It may be necessary here to explain that the phrase "Mackar" is an old Saxon one, applied to poets, equivalent to "Creator." Some have incorrectly supposed it to mean "Magician."]

fragments; and, with a scanty handful of exceptions, the best of them, at least of the serious kind, were very ancient. Among the numberless effusions of the Jacobite Muse, valuable as we now consider them for the record of manners and events, it would be difficult to point out half a dozen strains, worthy, for poetical excellence alone, of a place among the old chivalrous ballads of the Southern, or even of the Highland Border. Generations had passed away since any Scottish poet had appealed to the sympathies of his countrymen in a lofty Scottish strain.

The dialect itself had been hardly dealt with. "It is my opinion," said Dr. Geddes, "that those who, for almost a century past, have written in Scotch, Allan Ramsay not excepted, have not duly discriminated the genuine idiom from its vulgarisms. They seem to have acted a similar part to certain pretended imitators of Spenser and Milton, who fondly imagine that they are copying from those great models, when they only mimic their antique mode of spelling, their obsolete terms, and their irregular constructions." And although I cannot well guess what the Doctor considered as the irregular constructions of Milton, there can be no doubt of the general justice of his observations. Ramsay and Fergusson were both men of humble condition, the latter of the meanest, the former of no very elegant habits; and the dialect which had once pleased the ears of kings, who themselves did not disdain to display its powers and elegancies in verse, did not come untarnished through their hands. Fergusson, who was entirely town-bred, smells more of the Cowgate than of the country; and pleasing as Ramsay's rustics are, he appears rather to have observed the surface of rural manners, in casual excursions to Penicuik and the Hunters' Tryste, than to have expressed the results of intimate knowledge and sympathy. His dialect was a somewhat incongruous mixture of the Upper Ward of Lanarkshire and the Luckenbooths; and he could neither write English verses, nor engraft English phraseology on his Scotch, without betraying a lamentable want of skill in the use of his instruments. It was reserved for Burns to interpret the inmost soul of the Scottish peasant in all its moods, and in verse exquisitely and intensely Scottish, without degrading either his sentiments or his language with one touch of vulgarity. Such is the delicacy of native taste, and the power of a truly masculine genius.

This is the more remarkable, when we consider that the dialect of Burns's native district is, in all mouths but his own, a peculiarly offensive one—far removed from that of the favoured districts in which the ancient minstrelsy appears, with rare exceptions, to have been produced. Even in the elder days, it seems to have been proverbial for its coarseness : [1] and the Covenanters were not likely to mend it. The few poets [2] whom the West of Scotland had produced in the old time, were all men of high condition ; and who, of course, used the language, not of their own villages, but of Holyrood. Their productions, moreover, in so far as they have been preserved, had nothing to do with the peculiar character and feelings of the men of the West. As Burns himself has said,—" It is somewhat singular, that in Lanark, Renfrew, Ayr, &c., there is scarcely an old song or tune, which, from the title, &c.,

---

[1] Dunbar, among other sarcasms on his antagonist Kennedy, says :—

" I haif on me a pair of Lothiane hipps
Sall fairer Inglis mak, and mair perfyte,
Than thou can blabber with thy Carrick lipps."

[2] Such as Kennedy, Shaw, Montgomery, and, more lately, Hamilton of Gilbertfield ;

" Who bade the brakes of Airdrie long resound
The plaintive dirge that mourn'd his favourite hound."

can be guessed to belong to, or be the production of, those counties."

The history of Scottish literature, from the union of the crowns to that of the kingdoms, has not yet been made the subject of any separate work at all worthy of its importance; nay, however much we are indebted to the learned labours of Pinkerton, Irving, and others, enough of the *general* obscurity of which Warton complained still continues, to the no small discredit of so accomplished a nation. But how miserably the *literature* of the country was affected by the loss of the court under whose immediate patronage it had, in almost all preceding times, found a measure of protection that will ever do honour to the memory of the unfortunate house of Stuart, appears to be indicated with sufficient plainness in the single fact, that no man can point out any Scottish author of the first rank in all the long period which intervened between Buchanan and Hume. The removal of the chief nobility and gentry, consequent on the Legislative Union, appeared to destroy our last hopes as a separate nation, possessing a separate literature of our own; nay, for a time to have all but extinguished the flame of intellectual exertion and ambition. Long torn and harassed by religious and political feuds, this people had at last heard, as many believed, the sentence of irremediable degradation prouounced by the lips of their own prince and parliament. The universal spirit of Scotland was humbled; the unhappy insurrections of 1715 and 1745, revealed the full extent of her internal disunion; and England took, in some respects, merciless advantage of the fallen.

Time, however, passed on; and Scotland, recovering at last from the blow which had stunned her energies, began to vindicate her pretensions, in the only departments which had been left open to her, with a zeal and a success which will ever distinguish one of the brightest pages of her history.   Deprived of every national honour and distinction which it was possible to remove—all the high branches of external ambition lopped off—sunk at last, as men thought, effectually into a province, willing to take law with passive submission, in letters as well as polity, from her powerful sister—the old kingdom revived suddenly from her stupor, and once more asserted her name in reclamations, which England was compelled not only to hear, but to applaud, and "wherewith all Europe rung from side to side," at the moment when a national poet came forward to profit by the reflux of a thousand half-forgotten sympathies—amidst the full joy of a national pride, revived and re-established beyond the dream of hope.

It will always reflect honour on the galaxy of eminent men of letters, who, in their various departments, shed lustre at that period on the name of Scotland, that they suffered no pedantic prejudices to interfere with their reception of Burns.   Had he not appeared personally among them, it may be reasonably doubted whether this would have been so.   They were men, generally speaking, of very social habits; living together in a small capital, nay, almost all of them in or about one street; maintaining friendly intercourse continually; not a few of them considerably addicted to the pleasures which have been called, by way of excellence I presume, convivial.   Burns's poetry might have procured him access to these circles; but it was the extraordinary resources he displayed in conversation, the strong vigorous sagacity of his observations on life and manners, the splendour of his wit, and the glowing energy of his eloquence when his feelings were stirred, that made him the object of serious admiration among those practised masters of the art of *talk*.   There were several of them who probably adopted in their hearts the opinion of Newton, that "poetry is ingenious nonsense."   Adam Smith, for one, could have had no very ready respect at the service of such an unproductive labourer as a maker of Scottish ballads; but the stateliest of these philosophers had enough to do to maintain the attitude of equality when brought into personal contact with Burns's gigantic understanding; and every one of them, whose impressions on the subject have been recorded, agrees in pronouncing his conversation to have been the most remarkable thing about him.

And yet it is amusing enough to trace the lingering reluctance of some of those polished scholars, about admitting, even to themselves, in his absence, what it is certain they all felt sufficiently when they were actually in his presence. It is difficult, for example, to read without a smile that letter of Mr. Dugald Stewart, in which he describes himself and Mr. Alison as being surprised to discover that Burns, after reading the latter author's elegant " Essay on Taste," had really been able to form some shrewd enough notion of the general principles of the association of *ideas.*

Burns would probably have been more satisfied with himself in these learned societies, had he been less addicted to giving free utterance in conversation to the very feelings which formed the noblest inspirations of his poetry. His sensibility was as tremblingly exquisite as his sense was masculine and solid; and he seems to have, ere long, suspected that the professional metaphysicians who applauded his rapturous bursts, surveyed them in reality with something of the same feeling which may be supposed to attend a skilful surgeon's inspection of a curious specimen of morbid anatomy. Why should he lay his inmost heart thus open to dissectors, who took special care to keep the knife from their own breasts? The secret blush that overspread his haughty countenance when such suggestions occurred to him in his solitary hours, may be traced in the opening lines of a diary which he began to keep ere he had been long in Edinburgh.

"April 9, 1787.—As I have seen a good deal of human

life in Edinburgh, a great many characters which are new
to one bred up in the shades of life as I have been, I am
determined to take down my remarks on the spot. Gray
observes, in a letter to Mr. Palgrave, that, 'half a word
fixed, upon or near the spot, is worth a cartload of recollection.' I don't know how it is with the world in general,
but with me, making my remarks is by no means a solitary
pleasure. I want some one to laugh with me, some one to
be grave with me, some one to please me and help my dis-
crimination, with his or her own remark, and at times, no
doubt, to admire my acuteness and penetration. The world
is so busied with selfish pursuits, ambition, vanity, interest,
or pleasure, that very few think it worth their while to
make any observation on what passes around them, except
where that observation is a sucker, or branch of the darling
plant they are rearing in their fancy. Nor am I sure, notwithstanding all *the sentimental flights of novel writers*, and
the sage philosophy of moralists, if we are capable of so intimate and cordial a coalition of friendship, *as that one of us
may pour out his bosom, his every thought and floating fancy,
his very inmost soul, with unreserved confidence, to another,
without hazard of losing part of that respect which man demands
from man;* or, from the unavoidable imperfections attending
human nature, of one day repenting his confidence.

" For these reasons, I am determined to make these pages
my confidant. I will sketch every character that any way
strikes me, to the best of my observation, with unshrinking
justice. I will insert anecdotes, and take down remarks,
in the old law phrase, *without feud or favour.*—Where I hit
on anything clever, my own applause will, in some measure,
feast my vanity; and, begging Patroclus' and Achates'
pardon, I think a lock and key a security, at least equal to
the bosom of any friend whatever." [1]

----

[1] [It may be worth noting here that this Edinburgh "diary," or

And the same lurking thorn of suspicion peeps out else-where in this complaint: "I know not how it is; I find I can win *liking*—but not *respect*."[1]

"Burns," says a great living poet, in commenting on the free style, in which Dr. Currie did not hesitate to expose some of the weaker parts of his behaviour, very soon after the grave had closed on him,—"Burns was a man of extra-ordinary genius, whose birth, education, and employments, had placed and kept him in a situation far below that in which the writers and readers of expensive volumes are usually found. Critics upon works of fiction have laid it down as a rule, that remoteness of place, in fixing the choice of a subject, and in prescribing the mode of treating it, is equal in effect to distance of time;—restraints may be thrown off accordingly. Judge then of the delusions which artificial distinctions impose, when to a man like Dr. Currie, writing with views so honourable, the *social condition* of the individual of whom he was treating, could seem to place him at such a distance from the exalted reader, that cere-mony might be discarded with him, and his memory

---

common-place book, still exists in its primitive entireness. Allan Cun-ningham, overlooking the fact that Currie published ample quotations from it, alleged that it had been stolen from the poet's lodgings in the Lawnmarket, and he describes it, in his "hue and cry," as "a clasped volume with lock and key." This description is manufactured out of the poet's remark at the close of the paragraph above quoted. The lock and key of his travelling-desk or trunk is what Burns here talks of.]

[1] [Our biographer does not make his quotation here with his customary accuracy, neither does he seem sure where he found the poet's remark. It is taken from Cromek's "Reliques," p. 339, and reads thus:—"I don't well know what is the reason of it, but some how or other though I am, when I have a mind, pretty generally beloved; yet, I never could get the art of commanding respect. ... N.B. To try if I can discover the causes of this wretched infirmity."]

sacrificed, as it were, almost without compunction. This is indeed to be *crushed beneath the furrow's weight*." [1]

It would be idle to suppose that the feelings here ascribed, and justly, no question, to the amiable and benevolent Currie, did not often find their way into the bosoms of those persons of superior condition and attainments, with whom Burns associated at the period when he first emerged into the blaze of reputation ; and what found its way into men's bosoms, was not likely to avoid betraying itself to the perspicacious glance of the proud peasant. How perpetually he was alive to the dread of being looked down upon as a man, even by those who most zealously applauded the works of his genius, might perhaps be traced through the whole sequence of his letters. When writing to *men* of high station, at least, he preserves, in every instance, the attitude of self-defence. But it is only in his own secret tables that we have the fibres of his heart laid bare, and the cancer of this jealousy is seen distinctly at its painful work : *habemus reum et confitentem.*

" There are few of the sore evils under the sun give me more uneasiness and chagrin than the comparison how a man of genius, nay of avowed worth, is received everywhere, with the reception which a mere ordinary character, decorated with the trappings and futile distinctions of fortune, meets. I imagine a man of abilities, his breast glowing with honest pride, conscious that men are born equal, still giving *honour to whom honour is due ;* he meets, at a great man's table, a Squire Something, or a Sir Somebody ; he knows the *noble* landlord, at heart, gives the Bard, or whatever he is, a share of his good wishes, beyond, perhaps, any one at table ; yet how will it mortify him to see a fellow, whose abilities would scarcely have made an *eightpenny tailor*, and whose heart is not worth three farthings, meet

---

[1] Mr. Wordsworth's letter to a friend of Burns, p. 12.

with attention and notice that are withheld from the son of genius and poverty?

"The noble Glencairn has wounded me to the soul here, because I dearly esteem, respect, and love him. He showed so much attention—engrossing attention—one day, to the only blockhead at table (the whole company consisted of his lordship, dunderplate, and myself), that I was within half a point of throwing down my gage of contemptuous defiance; but he shook my hand, and looked so benevolently good at parting—God bless him! though I should never see him more, I shall love him until my dying day! I am pleased to think I am so capable of the throes of gratitude, as I am miserably deficient in some other virtues.

"With Dr. Blair I am more at my ease. I never respect him with humble veneration; but when he kindly interests himself in my welfare, or still more, when he descends from his pinnacle, and meets me on equal ground in conversation, my heart overflows with what is called *liking*. When he neglects me for the mere carcass of greatness, or when his eye measures the difference of our points of elevation, I say to myself, with scarcely any emotion, what do I care for him, or his pomp either?"

"It is not easy," says Burns, attempting to be more philosophical—"It is not easy forming an exact judgment of any one; but, in my opinion, Dr. Blair is merely an astonishing proof of what industry and application can do. Natural parts like his are frequently to be met with; his vanity is proverbially known among his own acquaintances; but he is justly at the head of what may be called fine writing, and a critic of the first, the very first rank, in prose; even in poetry, *a bard of Nature's making can alone take the pas of him*. He has a heart, not of the very finest water, but far from being an ordinary one. In short, he is a truly worthy and most respectable character."

"Once," says a nice speculator on the "follies of the

wise," [1]—" once we were nearly receiving from the hand of genius the most curious sketches of the temper, the irascible humours, the delicacy of soul, even to its shadowiness, from the warm *sbozzos* of Burns, when he began a diary of his heart—a narrative of characters and events, and a chronology of his emotions. It was natural for such a creature of sensation and passion to project such a regular task, but quite impossible to get through it." This most curious document, it is to be observed, has not yet been printed entire. Another generation will, no doubt, see the whole of the confession; [2] however, what has already been given, it may be surmised, indicates sufficiently the complexion of Burns's prevailing moods, during his moments of retirement, at this interesting period of his history. It was in such a mood (they recurred often enough) that he thus reproached " Nature—partial nature : "—

> " Thou giv'st the ass his hide, the snail his shell,
> The envenom'd wasp victorious guards his cell :
> But, oh ! thou bitter stepmother, and hard,
> To thy poor fenceless naked child, the bard. . . .
> *In naked feeling and in aching pride,*
> He bears the unbroken blast from every side." [3]

There was probably no blast that pierced this haughty soul so sharply as the contumely of condescension.

" One of the poet's remarks," as Cromek tells us, " when he first came to Edinburgh, was, that between the men of

---

[1] D'Israeli on the Literary Character, vol. i., p. 136.

[2] [With the exception of a very inconsiderable portion printed in Alexander Smith's (" Golden Treasury," 1865) edition of the poems of Burns, the remainder of this Edinburgh diary was not made public till 1879, when the present possessor of the precious MS. produced it in " Macmillan's Magazine" of that year, simultaneously permitting its publication in Vol. VI. of William Paterson's library edition of the poet's works, where it may be seen.]

[3] First Epistle to Graham of Fintry, 1788.

rustic life and the polite world he observed little difference
—that in the former, though unpolished by fashion and
unenlightened by science, he had found much observation,
and much intelligence—but a refined and accomplished
woman was a thing almost new to him, and of which he
had formed but a very inadequate idea." [1] To be pleased, is
the old and the best receipt how to please; and there is
abundant evidence that Burns's success among the high-
born ladies of Edinburgh, was much greater than among the
" stately patricians," as he calls them, of his own sex. The
vivid expression of one of them has become proverbial—
that she never met with a man, " whose conversation so completely set her off her feet; " and Sir Walter Scott, in his
reference to the testimony of the late Duchess of Gordon,
has no doubt indicated the twofold source of the fascination.
But even here, he was destined to feel ere long something
of the fickleness of fashion. He confessed to one of his old
friends, before the season was over, that some who had

---

[1] [This is quoted from page 68 of the " Reliques," where it is given in
a footnote by way of corollary to the poet's expression of his adoring admiration of Miss Lesley Bailie and her sister, thus :—" I declare, one day
I had the honour of dining at Mr. Bailie's, I was almost in the predica-
ment of the children of Israel, when they could not look on Moses's face
for the glory that shone in it, when he descended from the Mount! " It is
questionable if Cromek had any better authority than his own surmise for
putting that remark into the lips of Burns when he first approached the
higher-class dames of Edinburgh. But the poet made use of similar remarks
in one of his letters to Mrs. Dunlop. Speaking of rustic beauties and their
peculiar merits, he adds :—" We cannot hope for that highly polished
mind, that charming delicacy of soul which is found among the female
world in the more elevated stations of life, and which is certainly by far
the most bewitching charm in the famous *cestus* of Venus. It is indeed
such an inestimable treasure that, where it can be had in its native purity,
unstained by shades of affectation, and unalloyed by caprice, I declare to
Heaven, I should think it cheaply purchased at the expense of every other
earthly good ! "]

caressed him the most zealously, no longer seemed to know him, when he bowed in passing their carriages, and many more acknowledged his salute but coldly.

It is but too true, that ere this season was over Burns had formed connections in Edinburgh which could not have been regarded with much approbation by the eminent literati in whose society his *début* had made so powerful an impression. But how much of the blame (if serious blame indeed there was in the matter) ought to attach to his own fastidious jealousy—how much to the mere caprice of human favour, we have scanty means of ascertaining: no doubt, both had their share; and it is also sufficiently apparent that there were many points in Burns's conversational habits, which men, accustomed to the delicate observances of refined society, might be more willing to tolerate under the first excitement of personal curiosity, than from any very deliberate estimate of the claims of such a genius, under such circumstances developed. He by no means restricted his sarcastic observations on those whom he encountered in the world to the confidence of his note-book; but startled polite ears with the utterance of audacious epigrams, far too witty not to obtain general circulation in so small a society as that of the Northern capital, far too bitter not to produce deep resentment, far too numerous not to spread fear almost as widely as admiration. Even when nothing was farther from his thoughts than to inflict pain, his ardour often carried him headlong into sad scrapes. Witness, for example, the anecdote given by Professor Walker, of his entering into a long discussion of the merits of the popular preachers of the day, at the table of Dr. Blair, and enthusiastically avowing his low opinion of all the rest in comparison with Dr. Blair's own colleague and most formidable rival[1]—a man, certainly en-

---

[1] [The biographer here, in a footnote, gives " The Rev. Robert

dowed with extraordinary graces of voice and manner, a
generous and amiable strain of feeling, and a copious flow

Walker's" name as that of the colleague of Dr. Hugh Blair at this time.
But a very little inquiry on his part would have saved him from the
commission of such a blunder. The Rev. Robert Walker, who at one
time was Dr. Blair's colleague in the High Church, died in 1783, long
before Burns ever dreamed of visiting Edinburgh. Professor Walker,
who first published the anecdote, took special care to withhold the name
of the minister to whom our poet thus awarded the palm for pulpit
oratory; and if Mr. Lockhart was really so ignorant of the preacher's
name as his erroneous footnote pronounces him to have been, how in the
name of common honesty, did he thus venture to describe his voice, his
style, and peculiarities; ending by assuring his reader that Burns's
favourite declaimer was no more to be compared to Dr. Blair "than I to
Hercules?" A mystery has long hung over this little matter, which
now, through the natural operation of the law of prescription, is easily
solved. The same "favourite preacher" of Burns is again and again
referred to in the Clarinda Correspondence (authorized edition, 1842), but
unnamed—nay, falsely named by the editor, who does not, however,
adopt the pseudonyme chosen by Mr. Lockhart—he calls him "the
Rev. Mr. Gould," although such a name was never on the roll of established ministers of Edinburgh. It is no longer reckoned a scandal to
utter the name of Burns's favourite divine—the Rev. William Greenfield,
who, besides being Dr. Blair's colleague, was Professor of Rhetoric in the
University of Edinburgh. The poet mentions him in his letter to Robert
Muir, Dec. 15, 1786, among the "noblesse and literati who had taken
him under their patronage;" and there still exists in the poet's holograph
a noble letter which Burns addressed to the "Rev. Mr. Greenfield" (on
5th December, 1786), within a week after arriving in Edinburgh. The
poet's private diary, above referred to, contains, alongside of his sketch
of Dr. Blair, a highly favourable picture of Greenfield, and in his
humorous epistle to Creech, he refers to "Greenfield's modest grace."
That gentleman, it is sad to tell, after achieving the highest honours of
his class, suddenly lost his position, shortly after the death of Burns, but
prior to the death of Dr. Blair, through the commission of some unpar-
donable social enormity, which caused him to flee from Scotland to escape
criminal proceedings, and he died in private exile in 1827. Under an
assumed name, his son greatly distinguished himself at the Scottish Bar,
and was a Lord of Session in high repute at the time of his decease in
1852.]

of language; but having no pretensions either to the general accomplishments for which Blair was honoured in a most accomplished society, or to the polished elegance which he first introduced into the eloquence of the Scottish pulpit. Professor Walker well describes the unpleasing effects of such an *escapade;* the conversation during the rest of the evening, "labouring under that compulsory effort which was unavoidable, while the thoughts of all were full of the only subject on which it was improper to speak." Burns showed his good sense by making no effort to repair this blunder; but years afterwards, he confessed that he could never recall it without exquisite pain. Mr. Walker properly says, it did honour to Dr. Blair that his kindness remained totally unaltered by this occurrence: but the Professor would have found nothing to admire in that circumstance, had he not been well aware of the rarity of such good-nature among the *genus irritabile* of authors, orators, and wits.

A specimen (which some will think worse, some better) is thus recorded by Cromek—"Reliques," p. 80:—"At a private breakfast, in a literary circle of Edinburgh, the conversation turned on the poetical merit and pathos of Gray's 'Elegy,' a poem of which he was enthusiastically fond. A clergyman present, remarkable for his love of paradox, and for his eccentric notions upon every subject, distinguished himself by an injudicious and ill-timed attack on this exquisite poem, which Burns, with generous warmth for the reputation of Gray, manfully defended. As the gentleman's remarks were rather general than specific, Burns urged him to bring forward the passages which he thought exceptionable. He made several attempts to quote the poem, but always in a blundering, inaccurate manner. Burns bore all this for a good while with his usual good-natured forbearance, till at length, goaded by the fastidious criticisms and wretched quibblings of his opponent, he roused himself, and with an eye flashing contempt and indignation, and with great vehemence of gesticulation, he thus addressed the old critic : ' Sir, I now perceive a man may be an excellent judge of poetry by square and rule, and after all be a d—d blockhead ;'"—so far, Mr. Cromek ; and all this was to a clergyman, and at *breakfast*. Even to the ladies, when he suspected them of wishing to make a show of him, he could not help administering a little of his village discipline. A certain stately peeress sent to invite him, without, as he fancied, having sufficiently cultivated his acquaintance beforehand, to her assembly. "Mr. Burns," answered the bard, " will do himself the honour of waiting on the ——— of ———, provided her ladyship will invite also the learned pig."—Such an animal was then exhibiting in the Grass-market.

While the second edition of poems was passing through the press, Burns was favoured with many critical suggestions and amendments ; to one of which only he attended. Blair, reading over with him, or hearing him recite (which he delighted at all times in doing) his "Holy Fair," stopped him at the stanza—

> " Now a' the congregation o'er
> Is silent expectation,
> For Moodie speels the holy door
> Wi' tidings o' *Salvation*."

"Nay," said the Doctor, " read *damnation*." Burns improved the wit of the verse, undoubtedly, by adopting the emendation ; but he gave another strange specimen of want of *tact*, when he insisted that Dr. Blair, one of the most scrupulous observers of clerical propriety, should permit him to acknowledge the obligation in a note.

But to pass from these trifles—it needs no effort of imagination to conceive what the sensations of an isolated set of scholars (almost all either clergymen or professors) must have been in the presence of this big-boned, black-browed, brawny stranger, with his great flashing eyes, who, having forced his way among them from the plough-tail at a single stride, manifested in the whole strain of his bearing and conversation, a most thorough conviction that, in a society of the most eminent men of his nation, he was exactly where he was entitled to be; hardly deigned to flatter them by exhibiting even an occasional symptom of being flattered by their notice: by turns calmly measured himself against the most cultivated understandings of his time in discussion; overpowered the *bon mots* of the most celebrated convivialists by broad floods of merriment, impregnated with all the burning life of genius; astounded bosoms habitually enveloped in the thrice-piled folds of social reserve, by compelling them to tremble—nay, to tremble visibly—beneath the fearless touch of natural pathos; and all this without indicating the smallest willingness to be ranked among those professional ministers of excitement, who are content to be paid in money and smiles for doing what the spectators and auditors would be ashamed of doing in their own persons, even if they had the power of doing it; and,—last and probably worst of all,—who was known to be in the habit of enlivening societies which they would have scorned to approach, still more frequently than their own, with eloquence no less magnificent; with wit in all likelihood still more daring; often enough, as the superiors whom he fronted without alarm might have guessed from the beginning, and had, ere long, no occasion to guess, with wit pointed at themselves.

The lawyers of Edinburgh, in whose wider circles Burns figured at his outset, with at least as much success as among the professional literati, were a very different race of men from these; they would neither, I take it, have pardoned rudeness, nor been alarmed by wit. But being, in those days, with scarcely an exception, members of the landed aristocracy of the country, and forming by

far the most influential body (as indeed they still do) in
the society of Scotland, they were, perhaps, as proud a set
of men as ever enjoyed the tranquil pleasures of unques-
tioned superiority.   What their haughtiness, as a body,
was, may be guessed, when we know that inferior birth
was reckoned a fair and legitimate ground for excluding
any man from the bar.   In one remarkable instance, about
this very time, a man of very extraordinary talents and
accomplishments was chiefly opposed in a long and painful
struggle for admission, and, in reality, for no reasons but
those I have been alluding to, by gentlemen who, in the
sequel, stood at the very head of the Whig party in Edinburgh; and the same aristocratical prejudice has, within
the memory of the present generation, kept more persons
of eminent qualifications in the background, for a season,
than any English reader would easily believe.   To this
body belonged nineteen out of twenty of those " patricians,"
whose stateliness Burns so long remembered and so bitterly
resented.   It might, perhaps, have been well for him had
stateliness been the worst fault of their manners.   Wine-
bibbing appears to be in most regions a favourite indulgence
with those whose brains and lungs are subjected to the
severe exercises of legal study and forensic practice.   To
this day, more traces of these old habits linger about the
inns of court than in any other section of London.   In
Dublin and Edinburgh, the barristers are even now eminently convivial bodies of men ; but among the Scotch
lawyers of the time of Burns, the principle of jollity was
indeed in its " high and palmy state."   He partook largely
in those tavern scenes of audacious hilarity, which then
soothed, as a matter of course, the arid labours of the
northern *noblesse de la robe* (so they are well called in " Red-
gauntlet "), and of which we are favoured with a specimen
in the " High Jinks " chapter of " Guy Mannering."

The tavern-life is now-a-days nearly extinct everywhere ;

but it was then in full vigour in Edinburgh, and there can be no doubt that Burns rapidly familiarized himself with it during his residence. He had, after all, tasted but rarely of such excesses while in Ayrshire. So little are we to consider his " Scotch Drink," and other jovial strains of the early period, as conveying anything like a fair notion of his actual course of life, that " Auld Nanse Tinnock," the Mauchline landlady, is known to have expressed, amusingly enough, her surprise at the style in which she found her name celebrated in the Kilmarnock edition, saying, " that Robert Burns might be a very clever lad, but he certainly was *regardless*, as, to the best of her belief, he had never taken three half mutchkins in her house in all his life." [1] And in addition to Gilbert's testimony to the same purpose, we have on record that Mr. Archibald Bruce (qualified by Heron, " a gentleman of great worth and discernment "), had observed Burns closely during that period of his life, and seen him " steadily resist such solicitations and allure-ments to convivial enjoyments, as hardly any other person could have withstood."

The unfortunate Heron knew Burns well; and himself mingled largely [2] in some of the scenes to which he adverts in the following strong passage:—" The enticements of pleasure too often unman our virtuous resolution, even while we wear the air of rejecting them with a stern brow. We resist, and resist, and resist; but, at last, suddenly turn, and passionately embrace the enchantress. The *bucks* of Edinburgh accomplished, in regard to Burns, that in which the *boors* of Ayrshire had failed. After residing some months in Edinburgh, he began to estrange himself,

---

[1] Mr. R. Chambers's MS. notes, taken during a tour in Ayrshire, in the summer of 1826.

[2] See Burns's allusion to Heron's own habits, in a poetical Epistle to Blacklock.

not altogether, but in some measure, from graver friends. Too many of his hours were now spent at the tables of persons who delighted to urge conviviality to drunkenness —in the tavern and in the brothel." (Heron, p. 27).

It would be idle *now* to attempt passing over these things in silence ; but it could serve no good purpose to dwell on them.

During the *winter*, Burns continued as has been mentioned, to lodge with John Richmond ; and we have the authority of this early friend of the poet for the statement, that while he did so, " he kept good hours." He removed afterwards to the house of Mr. William Nicol (one of the teachers of the High School of Edinburgh), in Buccleugh Pend, and this change is, I suppose, to be considered as a symptom that the keeping of good hours was beginning to be irksome.[1] Nicol was a man of quick parts and considerable learning, who had risen from a rank as humble as that of Burns : from the beginning an enthusiastic admirer, and, ere long, a constant associate of the poet, and a most dangerous associate ; for, with a warm heart, the man united a fierce irascible temper, a scorn of many of the decencies of life, a noisy contempt of religion, at least of the religious institutions of his country, and a violent propensity for the bottle. He was one of those who would

---

[1] [Chambers has left on record a protest against this random inference, thus :—" Mr. Lockhart draws an unfavourable inference from the poet's residing with Mr. Nicol for a short time when he returned to the city in August ; but for this change Mr. Richmond supplies a reason which exculpates the bard. During Burns's absence on his Border tour, Mr. Richmond took in another fellow-lodger ; so that when the poet came back, and applied for re-admission to Mrs. Carfrae's humble menage, he found the place filled up, and was compelled to go elsewhere." Moreover, the stay in Nicol's house was only from the 7th to the 25th of August, when, according to previous arrangement, the two friends started together on their famous tour to the Highlands.]

fain believe themselves to be men of genius; and that
genius is a sufficient apology for trampling under foot all
the old vulgar rules of prudence and sobriety,—being on
both points equally mistaken. Of Nicol's letters to Burns,
and about him, I have seen many that have never been,
and probable that never will be, printed—cumbrous and
pedantic effusions, exhibiting nothing that one can imagine
to have been pleasing to the poet, except what was probable
enough to redeem all imperfections—namely, a rapturous
admiration of his genius. This man, nevertheless, was, I
suspect, very far from being an unfavourable specimen of
the society to whom Heron thus alludes (p. 28):—" He
(the poet) *suffered* himself to be surrounded by a race of
miserable beings, who were proud to tell that they had
been in company with BURNS, and had seen Burns as loose
and as foolish as themselves. He was not yet irrecoverably
lost to temperance and moderation; but he was already
almost too much captivated with these wanton revels, to
be ever more won back to a faithful attachment to *their*
more sober charms." Heron adds—" He now also began
to contract something of new arrogance in conversation.
Accustomed to be, among his favourite associates, what is
vulgarly, but expressively, called the cock of the company,
he could scarcely refrain from indulging in similar freedom
and dictatorial decision of talk, even in the presence of
persons who could less patiently endure his presumption; "
an account *ex facie* probable, and which sufficiently tallies
with some hints in Mr. Dugald Stewart's description of
the poet's manners, as he first observed him at Catrine, and
with one or two anecdotes already cited from Walker and
Cromek.

Of these failings, and indeed of all Burns's failings, it
may be safely asserted, that there was more in his history
to account and apologize for them, than can be alleged in
regard to almost any other great man's imperfections. We

have seen, how, even in his earliest days, the strong thirst
of distinction glowed within him—how in his first and rudest
rhymes he sung

"——— to be great is charming;"

and we have also seen that the display of talent in conversation was the first means of distinction that occurred to
him. It was by that talent that he first attracted notice
among his fellow peasants, and after he mingled with the
first Scotchmen of his time, this talent was still that which
appeared the most astonishing of all he possessed. What
wonder that he should delight in exerting it where he could
exert it the most freely—where there was no check upon a
tongue that had been accustomed to revel in the licence of
village-mastery? where every sally, however bold, was sure
to be received with triumphant applause—where there were
no claims to rival his—no proud brows to convey rebuke,
above all, perhaps, no grave eyes to convey regret? "Nonsense," says Cumberland, "talked by men of wit and
understanding in the hours of relaxation, is of the very
finest essence of conviviality; but it implies a trust in the
company not always to be risked." It was little in Burns's
character to submit to nice and scrupulous rules, when he
knew, that by crossing the street, he could find society who
would applaud him the more, the more heroically all such
rules were disregarded; and he who had passed from the
company of the jolly *bachelors* of Tarbolton and Mauchline,
to that of the eminent Scotchmen whose names were
honoured all over the civilized world, without discovering
any difference that appeared worthy of much consideration,
was well prepared to say, with the prince of all free-speakers
and free-livers, "I will take mine ease in mine inn!"

But these, assuredly, were not the only feelings that
influenced Burns; in his own letters, written during his
stay in Edinburgh, we have the best evidence to the con-

trary. He shrewdly suspected, from the very beginning, that the personal notice of the great and the illustrious was not to be as lasting as it was eager : he foresaw, that sooner or later he was destined to revert to societies less elevated above the pretensions of his birth ; and, though his jealous pride might induce him to record his suspicions, in language rather too strong than too weak, it is quite impossible to read what he wrote without believing that a sincere distrust lay rankling at the roots of his heart, all the while that he appeared to be surrounded with an atmosphere of joy and hope.

On the 15th of January, 1787, we find him thus addressing his kind patroness, Mrs. Dunlop :—

" You are afraid I shall grow intoxicated with my prosperity as a poet. Alas ! madam, I know myself and the world too well. I do not mean any airs of affected modesty I am willing to believe that my abilities deserved some notice ; but in a most enlightened, informed age and nation, when poetry is and has been the study of men of the first natural genius, aided with all the powers of polite learning, polite books, and polite company—to be dragged forth to the full glare of learned and polite observation, with all my imperfections of awkward rusticity, and crude unpolished ideas on my head, I assure you, madam, I do not dissemble when I tell you I tremble for the consequences. The novelty of a poet in my obscure situation, without any of those advantages which are reckoned necessary for that character, at least at this time of day, has raised a partial tide of public notice, which has borne me to a height where I am absolutely, feelingly certain, my abilities are inadequate to support me ; and too surely do I see that time, when the same tide will leave me, and recede, perhaps as far below the mark of truth. . . . I mention this once for all, to disburthen my mind, and I do not wish to hear or say more about it. But, ' when proud fortune's ebbing tide recedes' you will bear me witness, that when my bubble of fame was at the highest, I stood unintoxicated with the inebriating cup in my hand, *looking forward with rueful resolve* to the hastening time when the blow of Calumny should dash it to the ground with all the eagerness of vengeful triumph."[1]

And about the same time (Jan. 20, 1787), to Dr.

---

1 [The foregoing eloquent passage is quoted from p. 49, Currie, vol. ii. The present annotator more than suspects that these words were never addressed by Burns to Mrs. Dunlop, but have been extracted from a letter of prior date, addressed by the poet to his friend the Rev. William Greenfield (of whom some account has been given in a former note), and interpolated so as to seem a paragraph of the printed letter to Mrs. Dunlop, dated 15th January, 1787. An inspection of that letter as it still stands in the printed correspondence, will satisfy any penetrating reader, that if the paragraph referred to were eliminated, the letter would make a more consistent *whole*, and that some patchwork has been perpetrated there. The reader may well ask—" What was the motive for such a hocus-pocus manœuvre as this ? " The answer is, that strange cooking of correspondence was practised in Dr. Currie's establishment when Gilbert Burns and Mrs. Dunlop were at the head of the culinary department. The passage was too fine to be denied a place in Currie's volume, but the words were addresed to one of the bard's correspondents who had now (1800) lost *caste* in polite society, and the bare mention of his name would have been deemed a blemish to the work on which this triumvirate were engaged. Excision of the passage in question from the genuine letter, and the transplanting thereof to another not impro- bable situation, was an easy operation. The only change required in its language was the substitution of " Dear Madam" for " Dear Sir."

The bard's own veritable letter, dated December 5, 1786, and addressed as already stated, is now to be seen in a bound volume of *Burnsiana*, preserved in the Library of the University of Edinburgh—part of a bequest to that Library by the late David Laing. The manuscript bears markings indicating that it had passed through Dr. Currie's hands, and the general contents of the volume prove that Lockhart must also have had access to it; for we find there the various letters addressed by Burns to the Earl of Glencairn, his sister Lady Harriet Don, Lady Betty Cunningham, and Lady Winifred Maxwell, referred to or quoted throughout the present Biography.]

Moore:—"The hope to be admired for ages is, in by far the greater part of those even who are authors of repute, an unsubstantial dream. For my part, my first ambition was, and still my strongest wish is, to please my compeers, the rustic inmates of the hamlet, while ever-changing language and manners shall allow me to be relished and understood. I am very willing to admit that I have some poetical abilities; and as few if any writers, either moral or poetical, are intimately acquainted with the classes of mankind among whom I have chiefly mingled, I may have seen men and manners in a different phasis from what is common, which may assist originality of thought." To the same (Feb. 15), "I scorn the affectation of seeming modesty to cover self-conceit. That I have some merit, I do not deny; but I see, with frequent wringings of heart, that the novelty of my character, and the honest national prejudice of my countrymen, have borne me to a height altogether untenable to my abilities."—And lastly, April the 23rd, 1787, we have the following passage in a letter also to Dr. Moore:—" I leave Edinburgh in the course of ten days or a fortnight . . . . I shall return to my rural shades, *in all likelihood never more to quit them.* I have formed many intimacies and friendships here, *but I am afraid they are all of too tender a construction to bear carriage a hundred and fifty miles.*"

One word more on the subject which introduced these quotations:—Mr. Dugald Stewart, no doubt, hints at what was a common enough complaint among the elegant literati of Edinburgh, when he alludes, in his letter to Currie, to the "not very select society" in which Burns indulged himself. But two points still remain somewhat doubtful; namely, whether, show and marvel of the season as he was, the "Ayrshire ploughman" really had it in his power to live *always* in society which Mr. Stewart would have considered as "very select;" and secondly, whether, in so

doing, he could have failed to chill the affection of those
humble Ayrshire friends who, having shared with him all
that they possessed on his first arrival in the metropolis,
faithfully and fondly adhered to him, after the spring-tide
of fashionable favour did, as he foresaw it would do,
"recede;" and, moreover, perhaps to provoke, among the
higher circles themselves, criticisms more distasteful to his
proud stomach than any probable consequences of the course
of conduct which he actually pursued.

The second edition of Burns's poems was published near
the end of April, by Creech; there were no less than
1,500 subscribers, engaging for 2,800 copies. Although for
these the final settlement with the bookseller did not take
place till more than a year after, Burns now found himself
in possession of a considerable sum of ready money; and
the first impulse of his mind was to visit some of the classic
scenes of Scottish history and romance.[1] He had as yet
seen but a small part of his own country, and this by no
means among the most interesting of her districts—until,
indeed, his own poetry made it equal, on that score, to any
other.

The magnificent scenery of the capital itself had filled
him with extraordinary delight. In the spring mornings,
he walked sometimes to the top of Arthur's Seat, and lying
prostrate on the turf, surveyed the rising of the sun out of

---

[1] "The appellation of a Scottish bard is by far my highest pride ; to
continue to deserve it is my most exalted ambition. Scottish scenes,
and Scottish story, are the themes I could wish to sing. I have no dearer
aim than to have it in my power, unplagued with the routine of business,
for which Heaven knows I am unfit enough, to make leisurely pilgrim-
ages through Caledonia ; to sit on the fields of her battles, to wander on
the romantic banks of her rivers, and to muse by the stately towers or
venerable ruins, once the honoured abodes of her heroes. But these are
Utopian thoughts."—*Letter to Mrs. Dunlop, Edinburgh, 22nd March*,
1787.

the sea, in silent admiration; his chosen companion on such occasions being that ardent lover of nature, and learned artist, Mr. Alexander Nasmyth.[1] The Braid Hills, to the south of Edinburgh, were also among his favourite morning walks; and it was in some of these that Mr, Dugald Stewart tells us "he charmed him still more by his private conversation, than he had ever done in company." "He was," adds the Professor, "passionately fond of the beauties of nature; and I recollect once he told me, when I was admiring a distant prospect in one of our morning walks, that the sight of so many smoking cottages gave a pleasure to his mind which none could understand who had not witnessed, like himself, the happiness and the worth which they contained."

Burns was far too busy with society and observation to find time for poetical composition during this first residence in Edinburgh. Creech's edition included some pieces of great merit, which had not been previously printed; but, with the exception of the "Address to Edinburgh," which is chiefly remarkable for the grand stanzas on the Castle and Holyrood, with which it concludes, all of these appear to have been written before he left Ayrshire. Several of

---

1 It was to this venerable artist that Burns sat for the portrait engraved in Creech's edition, and since repeated so often, that it must be familiar to all readers. Mr. Nasmyth also kindly prepared a vignette sketch of the poet at full-length as he appeare l in Edinburgh in the first hey-day of his reputation; dressed in tight jockey boots, with very tight buckskin breeches, according to the fashion of the day, in what was called the "Fox-livery," viz., a blue coat and buff waistcoat, with broad blue stripes. An engraving from that sketch formed a title-page illustration to the first edition of this Memoir in "Constable's Miscellany," vol. xxiii. The surviving friends of Burns who have seen it are unanimous in opinion that it furnishes a very lively representation of the bard as he first attracted public notice on the streets of Edinburgh. The scenery of the background is very nearly that of Burns's native spot—the Kirk of Alloway, and the old bridge of Doon.

them, indeed, were very early productions. The most important additions were, " Death and Doctor Hornbook," " The Brigs of Ayr," " The Ordination," and the " Address to the Unco Gude." [1] In this edition also, " When Guildford good our Pilot stood," made its first appearance, on reading which, Dr. Blair uttered his pithy criticism, "Burns's politics always smell of the smithy."

It ought not to be omitted, that our poet bestowed some of the first fruits of this edition in the erection of a decent tombstone over the hitherto neglected remains of his unfortunate predecessor, Robert Fergusson, in the Canongate churchyard.

The evening before he quitted Edinburgh, the poet addressed a letter to Dr. Blair, in which, taking a most respectful farewell of him, and expressing, in lively terms, his sense of gratitude for the kindness he had shown him, he thus recurs to his own views of his own past and future condition :—" I have often felt the embarrassment of my singular situation. However the meteor-like novelty of my appearance in the world might attract notice, I knew very well that my utmost merit was far unequal to the task of preserving that character when once the novelty was over. I have made up my mind, that abuse, or almost even neglect, will not surprise me in my quarters." To this touching letter the amiable Blair replied in a truly paternal strain of consolation and advice :—" Your situation," says he, " was indeed very singular ; you have had to stand a severe trial. I am happy that you have stood it so well. . . . You are now, I presume, to retire to a more private walk of life. . . . You have laid the foundation for just public esteem. In the midst of those employ-

---

[1] [This remarkable poem, " Address to the Unco Gude," is believed, on good grounds, to have been composed in Edinburgh, while the printing of the new edition was in progress."]

ments, which your situation will render proper, you will not, I hope, neglect to promote that esteem, by cultivating your genius, and attending to such productions of it as may raise your character still higher. At the same time, be not in too great a haste to come forward. Take time and leisure to improve and mature your talents; for, on any second production you give the world, your fate as a poet will very much depend. There is, no doubt, a gloss of novelty which time wears off. As you very properly hint yourself, you are not to be surprised if, in your rural retreat, you do not find yourself surrounded with that glare of notice and applause which here shone upon you. No man can be a good poet without being somewhat of a philosopher. He must lay his account, that any one who exposes himself to public observation, will occasionally meet with the attacks of illiberal censure, which it is always best to overlook and despise. He will be inclined sometimes to court retreat, and to disappear from public view. He will not affect to shine always, that he may at proper seasons come forth with more advantage and energy. He will not think himself neglected if he be not always praised." Such were Blair's admonitions.

" And part was heard, and part was lost in air." [1]

Burns had one object of worldly business in his journey;

---

[1] On the same occasion, the poet addressed Lord Glencairn in these terms; the letter is here first made public :—

" My Lord,—I go away to-morrow morning early; and allow me to vent the fulness of my heart in thanking your Lordship for all that patronage, that benevolence, and that friendship, with which you have honoured me. With brimful eyes I pray, that you may find in that Great Being, whose image you so nobly bear, that Friend which I have found in you. My gratitude is not selfish design—that I disdain—it is not dodging after the heels of greatness—that is an offering you disdain. It is a feeling of the same kind with my devotion.—R. B."

namely, to examine the estate of Dalswinton, near Dumfries, the proprietor of which had, on learning that the poet designed to return to his original calling, expressed a strong wish to have him for his tenant.

CHAPTER VI.

"Ramsay and famous Fergusson,
    Gied Forth and Tay a lift aboon;
Yarrow and Tweed to mony a tune
        Thro' Scotland rings,
While Irvine, Lugar, Ayr, and Doon,
        Naebody sings."

ON the 6th of May, Burns left Edinburgh, in company with Mr. Robert Ainslie,[1] son to Mr. Ainslie of Berrywell, in Berwickshire, with the design of perambulating the picturesque scenery of the southern border, and in particular of visiting the localities celebrated by the old minstrels, of whose works he was a passionate admirer; and of whom, by the way, one of the last appears to have been all but a namesake of his own.[2]

---

[1] Afterwards Clerk to the Signet. Among other changes "which fleeting time procureth," this amiable gentleman, whose youthful gaiety made him a chosen associate of Burns, is chiefly known as the author of an Essay on the Evidences of Christianity, and some devotional tracts. [He survived till April, 1838, when he had reached the age of seventy-one. He married about two years after the death of Burns.]

[2] [Nicol Burne lived about the middle of the sixteenth century. Bred a priest in connection with the Abbeys of Dryburgh and Melrose, he pretended to side with the Reformers in 1558, and was appointed Professor of Philosophy at St. Leonard's College, St. Andrew's; but he afterwards recanted and rejoined his Mother Church. At Paris in 1581 he published "Ane admonition to the antichristian ministers of the Deformit Kirk of Scotland." Lockhart here supposes "Priest Burne" to have been the author of a song preserved in the Tea-table Miscellany of Allan Ramsay, called "Leaderhaughs and Yarrow," in the last verse

This was long before the time when those fields of Scottish romance were to be made accessible to the curiosity of citizens by stage-coaches ; and Burns and his friend performed their tour on horseback, the former being mounted on a favourite mare, whom he had named Jenny Geddes, in honour of the zealous virago who threw her stool at the Dean of Edinburgh's head, on the 23rd of July, 1637, when the attempt was made to introduce a Scottish Liturgy into the service of St. Giles's ; the same trusty animal whose merits have been recorded by Burns, in a letter which must have been puzzling to most modern Scotsmen, before the days of Dr. Jamieson.[1]

Burns passed from Edinburgh to Berrywell, the residence of Mr. Ainslie's family, and visited successively Dunse,

---

of which he designs himself " Minstrel Burne," and seems to lament the ravages in his youthful neighbourhood caused by the violence of those times, thus :—

> " The bird that flees thro' Reedpath trees,
>   And Gledswood banks ilk morrow,
> May chant their joys on Leaderhaughs
>   And bonie howms o' Yarrow ;
> But Minstrel Burne can not assuage
>   His grief while life endureth,
> To see the changes of this age,
>   That fleeting time procureth ;
> For mony a place stands in hard case,
>   Where blythe folk kenn'd nae sorrow,
> With Homes that dwelt on Leader side,
>   And Scotts that dwelt on Yarrow."]

[1] " My auld ga'd gleyde o' a meere has huchyall'd up hill and down brae, as teuch and birnie as a vera deevil wi' me. It's true she's as poor's a sangmaker, and as hard's a kirk, and tipper-taipers when she taks the gate, like a lady's gentlewoman in a minuwae, or a hen on a het girdle ; but she's a yauld poutherie girran for a' that. When ance her ringbanes and spavies, her cruiks and cramps, are fairly soupled, she beets to, beets to, and ay the hindmost hour the lightest," &c. &c.—*Letter to William Nicol, Reliques*, p. 28.

Coldstream, Kelso, Fleurs, and the ruins of Roxburgh
Castle, where a holly bush still marks the spot on which
James II. of Scotland was killed by the bursting of a
cannon; Jedburgh, where he admired the "charming
romantic situation of the town, with gardens and orchards
intermingled among the houses of a once magnificent
cathedral (abbey) ;" and was struck (as in the other towns
of the same district) with the appearance of "old rude
grandeur," and the idleness of decay; Melrose, "that far-
famed glorious ruin," Selkirk, Ettrick, and the Braes of
Yarrow. Having spent three weeks in this district, of
which it has been justly said, that "every field has its
battle, and every rivulet its song," Burns passed the Border,
and visited Alnwick, Warkworth, Morpeth, Newcastle,
Hexham, Wardrue, and Carlisle. He then turned north-
wards, and rode by Annan and Dumfries to Dalswinston,
where he examined Mr. Miller's property, and was so much
pleased with the soil, and the terms on which the landlord
was willing to grant him a lease, that he resolved to return
again in the course of the summer.

Dr. Currie has published some extracts from the journal
which Burns kept during this excursion, but they are mostly
very trivial. He was struck with the superiority of soil,
climate, and cultivation, in Berwick and Roxburghshires,
as compared with his native county; and not a little surprised when he dined at a Farmers' Club at Kelso, with the
apparent wealth of that order of men. "All gentlemen,
talking of high matters—each of them keeps a hunter from
£30 to £50 value, and attends the Fox-hunting Club in the
county." The farms in the west of Scotland are, to this
day, very small for the most part, and the farmers little
distinguished from their labourers in their modes of life ;
the contrast was doubtless stronger, forty years ago, between them and their brethren of the Lothians and the
Merse.

The Magistrates of Jedburgh presented Burns with the freedom of their town : he was unprepared for the compliment, and jealous of obligations, stept out of the room, and made an effort (of course an ineffectual one) to pay beforehand the landlord's bill for the " riddle of claret," which is usually presented on such occasions in a Scotch burgh.[1]

The poet visited, in the course of his tour, Sir James Hall of Dunglass, author of the well-known " Essay on Gothic Architecture," &c.; Sir Alexander, and Lady Harriet Don (the charming sister of his patron, Lord Glencairn), at Newton-Don; Mr. Brydone, the author of " Travels in Sicily ; " the amiable and learned Dr. Somerville of Jedburgh, the historian of Queen Anne, &c.; and, as usual, recorded in his journal his impressions as to their manners and characters. His reception was everywhere most flattering.

He wrote no verses, as far as is known, during this tour, except a humorous Epistle to his bookseller, Creech, dated Selkirk, 13th May. In this he makes complimentary allusions to some of the men of letters who were used to meet at breakfast in Creech's apartments in those days— whence the name of *Creech's levee;* and touches, too briefly, on some of the scenery he had visited.

> " Up wimpling stately Tweed I've sped,
> And Eden scenes on crystal Jed,
> And Ettrick banks now roaring red,
>   While tempests blaw." [2]

---

[1] Chambers' " Picture of Scotland," 1827, vol. i., p. 96. [The author of that work mentions the public entertainment of Burns by the magistrates, but says nothing about the conferring of " the freedom of the town." Neither is there any minute of that event in the Town-clerk's books. But our poet himself has made this entry in his journal of the tour,—" was waited on by the magistrates, and presented with the freedom of the burgh."]

[2] [The editor has been privileged to inspect, in the hands of Mr.

Burns returned to Mauchline on the 8th of June. It is pleasing to imagine the delight with which he must have been received by his family after the absence of six months, in which his fortunes and prospects had undergone so wonderful a change. He left them comparatively unknown, his tenderest feelings torn and wounded by the behaviour of the Armours, and so miserably poor, that he had been for some weeks obliged to skulk from the sheriff's officers, to avoid the payment of a paltry debt. He returned, his poetical fame established, the whole country ringing with his praises, from a capital in which he was known to have formed the wonder and delight of the polite and the learned, if not rich ; yet with more money already than any of his kindred had ever hoped to see him possess, and with prospects of future patronage and permanent elevation in the scale of society, which might have dazzled steadier eyes than those of maternal and fraternal affection. The prophet had at last honour in his own country : but the haughty spirit that had preserved its balance in Edinburgh, was not likely to lose it at Mauchline ; and we have him writing from the *auld clay biggin'* on the 18th of June, in terms as strongly expressive as any that ever came from his pen, of that jealous pride which formed the groundwork of his character ; that dark suspiciousness of fortune, which the subsequent course of his history too well justified ; that nervous intolerance of condescension, and consummate scorn of meanness, which attended him through life, and made the study of his species, for which nature had given him such extraordinary qualifications, the source of more pain than was ever counterbalanced by the exquisite

Creech's representatives, the poet's MS. of this communication in verse and prose, and, curiously enough, the one stanza of landscape painting here singled out, is wanting in the original. Its introduction must have been an after-thought!]

capacity for enjoyment with which he was also endowed. There are few of his letters in which more of the dark places of his spirit come to light:—"I never, my friend, thought mankind capable of anything very generous; but the stateliness of the patricians of Edinburgh, and the servility of my plebeian brethren (who, perhaps, formerly eyed me askance), since I returned home, have nearly put me out of conceit altogether with my species. I have bought a pocket Milton, which I carry perpetually about me, in order to study the sentiments, the dauntless magnanimity, the intrepid unyielding independence, the desperate daring, and noble defiance of hardship, in that great personage— Satan. . . The many ties of acquaintance and friendship I have, or think I have, in life— I have felt along the lines, and, d——n them, they are almost all of them of such frail texture, that I am sure they would not stand the breath of the least adverse breeze of fortune." (To Wm. Nicol, 18 June.)

Among those who, having formerly "eyed him askance," now appeared sufficiently ready to court his society, were the family of Jean Armour. Burns's affection for this young woman had outlived his resentment of her compliance with her father's commands in the preceding summer; and from the time of this reconciliation, it is probable he always looked forward to a permanent union with the mother of his children.

Burns at least fancied himself to be busy with serious plans for his future establishment; and was very naturally disposed to avail himself, as far as he could, of the opportunities of travel and observation, which an interval of leisure, destined probably to be a short one, might present. Moreover, in spite of his gloomy language, a specimen of which has just been quoted, we are not to doubt that he derived much pleasure from witnessing the extensive popularity of his writings, and from the flattering homage he was sure to receive in his own person in the various districts of his native country; nor can any one wonder, that after the state of high excitement in which he had spent the winter and spring, he, fond as he was of his family, and eager to make them partakers in all his good fortune, should have, just at this time, found himself incapable of sitting down contentedly for any considerable period together in so humble and quiet a circle as that of Mossgiel.

His appetite for wandering appears to have been only sharpened by his Border excursion. After remaining a few days at home, he [proceeded (so far as can be gathered from incidental allusions), by way of Greenock and Loch Long, to Inverary; and back again by Loch Lomond, Dumbarton and Glasgow to Mauchline. The journey was performed on horseback, and some little management would be involved in getting "Jenny Geddes" across occasional ferries].[1] Of this second excursion no journal has been

---

[1] With the exception of the latter part of the return journey, this trip appears to have been a solitary one, and one of his objects in undertaking it may have been to visit the relatives of the deceased "Highland Mary." There is an entry in continuation of his journal, begun in April preceding, which irresistibly suggests his musings on the present occasion in the west churchyard of Greenock, where the remains of Mary had been laid in October of the past year. He heads it, "Elegy on Stella," and here are three of its stanzas:—

> "From thy loved friends, where first thy breath
>   Was taught by Heaven to flow,
> Far, far removed, the ruthless stroke
>   Surpris'd, and laid thee low.
>
> "At the last limit of our isle,
>   Wash'd by the western wave,
> Touch'd by thy fate, a thoughtful bard
>   Sits lonely by thy grave.
>
> "Him too the stern impulse of fate.
>   Resistless bears along;
> And the same rapid tide shall whelm
>   The Poet and the song."

discovered ; nor do the extracts from his correspondence, printed by Dr. Currie, appear to be worthy of much notice. In one, he briefly describes the West Highlands as a country " where savage streams tumble over savage mountains, thinly overspread with savage flocks, which starvingly support as savage inhabitants ; " and in another, he gives an account of Jenny Geddes running a race *after dinner* with a Highlander's pony—of dancing and drinking till sunrise at a gentleman's house on Loch Lomond ; and of other similar matters.—" I have as yet," says he, " fixed on nothing with respect to the serious business of life. I am, just as usual, a rhyming, mason-making, raking, aimless, idle fellow. However, I shall somewhere have a farm soon."

Burns spent the month of July at Mossgiel, and Mr. Dugald Stewart, in a letter to Currie, gives some recollections of him as he then appeared :—" Notwithstanding the various reports I heard during the preceding winter, of Burns's predilection for convivial, and not very select, society, I should have concluded in favour of his habits of sobriety from all of him that ever fell under my own observation. He told me himself, indeed, that the weakness of his stomach was such as to deprive him entirely of any merit in his temperance. I was, however, somewhat alarmed about the effect of his now comparatively sedentary and luxurious life, when he confessed to me, the first night he spent in my house after his winter's campaign in town, that he had been much disturbed when in bed by a palpitation at his heart—a complaint to which he said he had of late become subject.

" In the course of the same season, I was led by some curiosity to attend, for an hour or two, a masonic lodge in Mauchline, where Burns presided. He had occasion to make some short unpremeditated compliments to different individuals, from whom he had no reason to expect a visit, and everything he said was happily conceived, and forcibly as well as fluently expressed. His manner of speaking in public had evidently the marks of some practice in extempore elocution."

[The masonic meeting thus referred to was held on 25th July, 1787, and is duly recorded in the poet's own hand in a minute of the lodge, from which we learn that besides the Depute-master (Burns) and the Professor, the following gentlemen were in attendance, viz., "Claude Alexander of Ballochmyle; Claude Neilson, from Paisley; Dr. George Grierson, of Glasgow; John Farquhar Gray, of Gilmiscroft; and Alexander Allison, of Barnmuir."]

It was probably at this time that Burns indited a lively copy of verses which have not as yet (1829) been printed, and which I find introduced with the following memorandum in a small collection of MSS., sent by the poet to Lady H. Don (obligingly communicated to me by Sir Walter Scott for use in the present work) :—"Mr. Chalmers, a gentleman in Ayrshire, a particular friend of mine, asked me to write a poetical epistle to a young lady, his dulcinea. I had seen her, but was scarcely acquainted with her, and wrote as follows :—

> " Madam,
>
>> " Wi' braw new branks in mickle pride,
>>   And eke a braw new brechan,
>> My Pegasus I'm got astride,
>>   And up Parnassus pechin';
>> Whiles owre a bush wi' downward crush,
>>   The doited beastie stammers;
>> Then up he gets, and off he sets,
>>   For sake o' *Willie Chalmers.*
>
>> " I doubt na, lass, that weel kenn'd name
>>   May cost a pair o' blushes;
>> I am nae stranger to your fame,
>>   Nor his warm-urgèd wishes.
>> Your bonie face, sae mild and sweet,
>>   His honest heart enamours,
>> And faith ye'll no be lost a whit,
>>   Tho' wair'd on *Willie Chalmers.*

" Auld Truth hersel' might swear ye're fair,
    And Honour safely back her,
And Modesty assume your air,
    And ne'er a ane mistak' her :
And sic twa love-inspiring e'en,
    Might fire even holy palmers ;
Nae wonder then they've fatal been
    To honest *Willie Chalmers*.

" I doubt na Fortune may you shore
    Some mim-mou'd pouthered priestie,
Fu' lifted up wi' Hebrew lore,
    And band upon his breastie ;
But oh ! what signifies to you
    His lexicons and grammars ;
The feeling heart's the royal blue,
    And that's wi' *Willie Chalmers*.

" Some gapin' glowrin' countra laird,
    May warsle for your favour ;
May claw his lug and straik his beard,
    And host up some palaver.
My bonie maid, before ye wed
    Sic clumsy-witted hammers,
Seek Heaven for help, and barefit skelp
    Awa' wi' *Willie Chalmers*.

" Forgive the Bard ! my fond regard
    For ane that shares my bosom,
Inspires my muse to gie 'm his dues,
    For de'il a hair I roose him.
May powers aboon unite you soon,
    And fructify your amours,—
And every year come in mair dear
    To you and *Willie Chalmers*."

[At this period, besides composing his " Elegy on Sir
James Hunter Blair," Bart., who died suddenly on 1st of
July, the poet scrolled and extended his famous Autobio-
graphic letter to Moore, which bears date 2nd August,
1787. That document is closed by this announcement in
a postscript :—" My presence is required in Edinburgh for

a week or so, and I set off to-morrow." Accordingly, he is found in that city for the next fortnight or three weeks, inditing humorous letters to his Ayrshire friends from the house of Nicol—the attic portion of a tenement in Buccleuch Street, entered from a pend leading to what is now St. Patrick's Square.

On 23rd of that month he writes to Robert Ainslie (then enjoying his summer vacation at Innerleithen) in these terms:—"I have but the time to write this, that Mr. Nicol on the opposite side of the table takes to correct a proof-sheet of a thesis. They are gabbling Latin so loud that I cannot hear what my own soul is saying in my own skull. . . To-morrow I leave Edinburgh in a chaise; Nicol thinks it more comfortable than horseback, to which I say, Amen; so Jenny Geddes goes home to Ayrshire—to use a phrase of my mother's—' wi' her finger in her mouth.' "]

Some fragments of the poet's journal of this, his most important tour of that season, have recently been discovered, and are now in my hands; so that I may hope to add some particulars to the account of Dr. Currie. The travellers hired a post-chaise for their expedition—the High School master being, probably, no very skilful equestrian.

"August 25th, 1787.—This day," says Burns, " I leave Edinburgh for a tour, in company with my good friend, Mr. Nicol, whose originality of humour promises me much entertainment.—*Linlithgow*—A fertile improved country is West Lothian. The more elegance and luxury among the farmers, I always observe, in equal proportion, the rudeness and stupidity of the peasantry. This remark I have made all over the Lothians, Merse, Roxburgh, &c.; and for this, among other reasons, I think that a man of romantic taste, ' a man of feeling,' will be better pleased with the poverty, but intelligent minds, of the peasantry of Ayrshire (peasantry they are all below the justice of peace), than the opulence of a club of Merse farmers, when he, at the same time, considers the Vandalism of their plough-folks, &c. I carry this idea so far, that an unenclosed, unimproved country, is to me actually more agreeable as a prospect, than a country cultivated like a garden."

It was hardly to be expected that Robert Burns should have estimated the wealth of nations entirely on the principles of a political economist.

Of Linlithgow, he says, "the town carries the appearance of rude, decayed, idle grandeur—charmingly rural retired situation—the old Royal Palace a tolerably fine, but melancholy ruin—sweetly situated by the brink of a loch. Shown the room where the beautiful injured Mary Queen of Scots was born. A pretty good old Gothic church—the infamous stool of repentance, in the old Romish way, on a lofty situation. What a poor pimping business is a Presbyterian place of worship ! dirty, narrow, and squalid, stuck in a corner of old Popish grandeur, such as Linlithgow, and much more, Melrose ! Ceremony and show, if judiciously thrown in, are absolutely necessary for the bulk of mankind, both in religious and civil matters."

At Bannockburn he writes as follows :—" Here no Scot can pass uninterested. I fancy to myself that I see my gallant countrymen coming over the hill, and down upon the plunderers of their country, the murderers of their fathers, noble revenge and just hate glowing in every vein, striding more and more eagerly as they approach the oppressive, insulting, blood-thirsty foe. I see them meet in glorious triumphant congratulation on the victorious field, exulting in their heroic royal leader, and rescued liberty and independence."[1] Here we have the germ of Burns's famous " Ode on the Battle of Bannockburn."

---

[1] In the last words of Burns's note above quoted, he perhaps glances at a beautiful trait of old Barbour, where he describes Bruce's soldiers

It was on this expedition, that having been visited with a high flow of Jacobite indignation while viewing the neglected palace at Stirling, he was imprudent enough to write some verses, bitterly vituperative of the reigning family, on the window of his inn. The verses were copied and talked of; and although, the next time Burns passed through Stirling, he himself broke the pane of glass containing them, they were remembered years afterwards to his disadvantage, and even danger. The last couplet, alluding, in the coarsest style, to the melancholy state of the King's health at the time,[1] was indeed an outrage of which no political prejudice could have made a gentleman approve: but he, in all probability, composed his verses after dinner; and surely what Burns would fain have undone, others should have been not unwilling to forget. In this case, too, the poetry "smells of the smith's shop," as well as the sentiment.

Mr. Dugald Stewart has pronounced Burns's epigrams to be, of all his writings, the least worthy of his talents. Those which he composed in the course of his tour, on being refused admittance to see the iron-works at Carron, and on finding himself ill-served at the inn at Inverary, in consequence of the Duke of Argyle's having a large party at the Castle, form no exceptions to the rule. He had

---

as crowding round him at the conclusion of one of his hard-fought days, with as much curiosity as if they had never seen his person before.

> " Sic words spak they of their king ;
> And for his hie undertaking
> Ferleyit and yernit him for to see,
> That with him ay was wont to be."

[1] [The biographer might here have considered that the mental eclipse with which the King was afflicted at intervals during his long reign did not become manifest to the outside world till more than a year after the " Stirling lines " were inscribed.]

never, we may suppose, met with the famous recipe of the Jelly-bag Club; and was addicted to beginning with the point.

[It was on the afternoon of Sunday, the 26th of August, that the excursionists reached Stirling, and on the following morning, Burns, leaving Nicol at the inn to contemplate the rash inscription above criticized so unmercifully, proceeded by himself on his first visit to Harvieston and the banks of the Devon. He has described that little by-tour, with some interesting details, in his published letter to Gavin Hamilton, of 28th August. The entries in his journal are simply these :—"Monday, 27th—Go to Harvieston—Mr. Hamilton and family—Mrs. Chalmers—Mrs. Shields—Go to see Cauldron linn, and Rumbling-brig, and the Deils-mill. Return in the evening to Stirling.

" Tuesday, 28th—Breakfast with Capt. Forrester—leave Stirling—Ochil Hills—Forth; Teith; Devon—Allan river; Strathallan, a fine country but little improven—Ardoch Camp—Cross the Earn to Crieff—Dine, and go to Arbruchil; cold reception at Arbruchil—Sup at Crieff.

"Wednesday, 29th—Leave Crieff—Glen Almond, Glenquaich; landlord and landlady remarkable characters— Taymouth—described in rhyme—Meet the Hon. Charles Townshend."]

This Taymouth entry alludes to the " verses written with a pencil over the mantel-piece of the parlour in the inn at Kenmore," some of which are among his best purely English heroics—

> " The meeting cliffs each deep-sunk glen divides,
> The woods, wild-scattered, clothe their ample sides;
> The outstretching lake, embosom'd among hills,
> The eye with pleasure and amazement fills;
> The Tay meand'ring sweet in infant pride,
> The palace rising on his verdant side,
> The lawns wood-fring'd in Nature's native taste,
> The hillocks dropt in Nature's careless haste,

The arches striding o'er the new-born stream,
The village glittering in the noon-tide beam,—

*   *   *   *

Lone wand'ring by the hermit's mossy cell,
Poetic ardours in my bosom swell,—
Here Poesy might wake her heaven-taught lyre,
And look through Nature with creative fire;
Here, to the wrongs of Fate half reconciled,
Misfortune's lighten'd steps might wander wild;
And Disappointment, in these lonely bounds,
Find balm to soothe her bitter rankling wounds;
Here heart-struck Grief might heav'nward stretch her scan,
And injured Worth forget—and pardon Man." [1]

Of Glenlyon we have this memorandum :—" Druids'
temple, three circles of stones, the outermost sunk; the
second has thirteen stones remaining; the innermost eight;
two large detached ones like a gate to the south-east—*say
prayers in it.*"

His notes on Dunkeld and Blair of Athol are as follow :—
" *Dunkeld*—Breakfast with Dr. Stuart—Neil Gow plays;

---

[1] As an act of justice to Lockhart as well as to Burns, we give a
fuller quotation from these impromptu verses than that formerly presented. Principal Shairp, in 1879, went out of his way a little to sneer
at Lockhart for having expressed himself pleased with these lines, and
with the poet's " vigorous couplets" on the " roaring Fyers." The
latter he pronounces to be " stilted, forced, and artificial," and of the
former he says, " If these lines are among the best of Burns's purely
English heroics," we can but say " how poor are the best! What is to
be thought of such lines as

' Poetic ardours in my bosom swell,
Lone wand'ring by the hermit's mossy cell,' &c. ? "

What is to be thought of them ? Why, the first ten lines above quoted
are a perfect photograph of the locality described; while the poetic and
humane reflections in the closing ten lines are as truthful as they are
beautiful. Can Professor Shairp match these twenty lines by any
example from Thomson or other descriptive poet?

a short, stout-built, Highland figure, with his greyish hair
shed on his honest social brow—an interesting face, marking
strong sense, kind openheartedness, mixed with unmistrusting simplicity—visit his house—Margaret Gow.—
Friday—ride up Tummel river to Blair. Fascally, a beautiful romantic nest—wild grandeur of the pass of Killi-
krankie—visit the gallant Lord Dundee's stone.[1] *Blair*—
sup with the Duchess—easy and happy, from the manners
of that family—confirmed in my good opinion of my friend
Walker.—*Saturday*—visit the scenes round Blair—fine, but
spoilt with bad taste."

Professor Walker, who, as we have seen, formed Burns's
acquaintance in Edinburgh, through Blacklock, was at this
period tutor in the family of Athole, and from him the
following particulars of Burns's reception at the seat of his
noble patron are derived. "I had often, like others, experienced the pleasures which arise from the sublime or
elegant landscape, but I never saw those feelings so intense
as in Burns. When we reached a rustic hut on the river
Tilt, where it is overhung by a woody precipice, from which
there is a noble waterfall, he threw himself on the heathy
seat, and gave himself up to a tender, abstracted, and voluptuous enthusiasm of imagination. It was with much
difficulty I prevailed on him to quit this spot, and to be
introduced in proper time to supper.

"He seemed at once to perceive and to appreciate what
was due to the company and to himself, and never to forget
a proper respect for the separate species of dignity belonging
to each. He did not arrogate conversation ; but when led
into it, he spoke with ease, propriety, and manliness. He
tried to exert his abilities, because he knew it was ability

---

[1] It is *not* true that this stone marks the spot where Dundee received
his death-wound. The stone is certainly very ancient.

alone gave him a title to be there. The Duke's fine young family attracted much of his admiration; he drank their healths as *honest men and bonny lasses*, an idea which was much applauded by the company, and with which he has very felicitously closed his poem.

"Next day I took a ride with him through some of the most remarkable parts of that neighbourhood, and was highly gratified by his conversation. As a specimen of his happiness of conception, and strength of expression, I will mention a remark which he made on his fellow-traveller, who was walking at the time a few paces before us. He was a man of a robust, but clumsy person; and, while Burns was expressing to me the value he entertained for him, on account of his vigorous talents, although they were clouded at times by coarseness of manners; 'in short,' he added, 'his mind is like his body, he has a confounded strong in-knee'd sort of a soul.'[1]

"Much attention was paid to Burns, both before and after the Duke's return, of which he was perfectly sensible, without being vain; and at his departure I recommended to him, as the most appropriate return he could make, to write some descriptive verses on any of the scenes with which he had been so much delighted. After leaving Blair, he, by the Duke's advice, visited the Falls of Bruar; and in a few days I received a letter from Inverness with the verses enclosed."[2]

At Blair, Burns first met with Mr. Graham of Fintray,

---

[1] [Professor Walker, who afterwards (1811) produced a memoir of Burns, narrates how cleverly he managed to keep Nicol in temper, apart from the poet, on this occasion, by furnishing him with a rod and tackle; and the angling sport, of which the dominie was very fond, quite absorbed his attention and allayed his jealousy, while the poet was made a pet of in the mansion.]

[2] The Banks of the Bruar, whose naked condition called forth "the humble petition," to which Mr. Walker thus refers, have, since those

a gentleman to whose kindness he was afterwards indebted on more than one important occasion; and Mr. Walker expresses great regret that he did not remain a day or two more, in which case he must have been introduced to Mr. Dundas, afterwards Viscount Melville, who was then Treasurer of the Navy, and had the chief management of the affairs of Scotland. This eminent statesman was, though little addicted to literature, a warm lover of his country, and in general, of whatever redounded to her honour; he was, moreover, very especially qualified to appreciate Burns as a companion; and, had such an introduction taken place, he might not improbably have been induced to bestow that consideration on the claims of the poet, which, in the absence of any personal acquaintance, Burns's works ought to have received at his hands.[1]

From Blair, Burns passed "many miles through a wild country, among cliffs grey with eternal snows, and gloomy savage glens," till he crossed Spey, and went down the stream through Strathspey (so famous in Scottish music), Badenoch, &c., to Grant Castle, where he spent half a day with Sir James Grant; crossed the country to Fort George,

---

days, been well cared for, and the river in its present state could have no pretext for the prayer—

> " Let lofty firs, and ashes cool,
>   My lowly banks o'erspread,
> And view, deep-bending in the pool,
>   Their shadows' watery bed;
> Let fragrant birks, in woodbines drest,
>   My craggy cliffs adorn,
> And for the little songster's nest,
>   The close embowering thorn."

[1] [The stay of Burns and his companion at Blair was from the evening of Friday, 31st August, to Sunday, 2nd September. Nicol could not be employed in angling on Sunday, and as the poet would not trust to his conduct indoors, he made the excuse of headache, and begged to be suffered to resume his journey after breakfast.]

but called by the way at Cawdor, the ancient seat of Macbeth, where he "saw the identical bed in which, *tradition says*, King Duncan was murdered"; lastly, from Fort George to Inverness.[1]

From Inverness, Burns went along the Moray Frith to Fochabers, taking Culloden-Muir and Brodie-house in his way.[2]

"Cross Spey to Fochabers—fine palace, worthy of the noble, the polite, and generous proprietor.—The Duke makes me happier than ever great man did ; noble, princely, yet mild, condescending, and affable—gay and kind. The Duchess charming, witty, kind, and sensible—God bless them ! "

Burns, who had been much noticed by this noble family when in Edinburgh, happened to present himself at Gordon Castle just at the dinner hour, and being invited to take his place at the table, did so, without for a moment adverting to the circumstance that his travelling companion

---

[1] Letter to Gilbert Burns, Edinburgh, 17th December, 1787.

[2] (Extract from *Journal.*)—*Thursday*, Came over Culloden-Muir—reflection on the field of battle—breakfast at Kilraick *—old Mrs. Rose—sterling sense, warm heart, strong passion, honest pride—all to an uncommon degree—a true chieftain's wife—daughter of Clephane—Mrs. Rose, jun., a little milder than the mother, perhaps owing to her being younger—Mrs. Rose and Rev. Mr. Grant accompany us to Kildrummie—two young ladies, a Miss Ross, who sang two Gaelic songs—beautiful and lovely—Miss Sophie Brodie, not very beautiful, but most agreeable and amiable—both of them them the gentlest, mildest, sweetest creatures on earth, and happiness be with them ! Brodie-house to lie—Mr. B. truly polite, but not quite the Highland cordiality.—*Friday*, cross the Findhorn to Forres—famous stone at Forres—Mr. Brodie tells me the muir where Shakespeare has laid Macbeth's witch-meeting is still haunted—that the country folks won't pass through it at night.—*Elgin*—venerable ruins of the abbey, a grander effect at first glance than Melrose, but nothing near so beautiful.

---

* Commonly spelt Kilravock, the seat of an ancient family.

had been left alone at the inn, in the adjacent village. On remembering this soon after dinner, he begged to be allowed to rejoin his friend; and the Duke of Gordon, who now for the first time learned that he was not journeying alone, immediately proposed to send an invitation to Mr. Nicol to come to the Castle. His Grace's messenger found the haughty schoolmaster striding up and down before the inn door in a state of high wrath and indignation, at what he considered Burns's neglect, and no apologies could soften his mood. He had already ordered horses, and the poet finding that he must choose between the ducal circle and his irritable associate, at once left Gordon Castle, and repaired to the inn, whence Nicol and he, in silence and mutual displeasure, pursued their journey along the coast of the Moray Frith.[1] This incident may serve to suggest some of the annoyances to which persons moving, like our poet, on the debateable land between two different ranks of society, must ever be subjected. To play the lion under such circumstances, must be difficult at the best; but a delicate business indeed, when the jackals are presumptuous. This pedant could not stomach the superior success of his friend—and yet, alas for human nature! he certainly was one of the most enthusiastic of his admirers, and one of the most affectionate of all his intimates. The abridgment of Burns's visit to Gordon Castle, " was not only," says Mr. Walker, " a mortifying disappointment, but in all probability a serious misfortune; as a longer stay among persons of such influence, might have begot a permanent intimacy, and on their parts, an active concern for his future advancement." [2] But this touches on a subject which we cannot at present pause to consider.

---

[1] [Burns very happily compared himself during that excursion to " a man travelling with a loaded blunderbuss at full cock."]

[2] Morison, vol. i., p. 89.

A few days after leaving Fochabers, Burns transmitted
to Gordon Castle his acknowledgment of the hospitality he
had received from the noble family, in the stanzas—

> " Streams that glide on orient plains,
> Never bound by winter's chains," &c.

The Duchess, on hearing them read, said she supposed they
were Dr. Beattie's, and on learning whose they really were,
expressed her wish that Burns had celebrated Gordon Castle
in his own dialect. The verses are, in quality, below the
usual standard of his productions.

Pursuing his journey along the coast, the poet visited
successively Nairn, Forres, Aberdeen, and Stonehaven,
where his cousin, James Burness, writer in Montrose, met
him by appointment, and conducted him into the circle of
his paternal kindred, among whom he spent two or three
days. When the poet's father, Wm. Burnes, abandoned his
native district, never to revisit it, he (as he used to tell
his children) took a sorrowful farewell of his brother on the
summit of the last hill from which the roof of their lowly
home could be descried; and the old man ever after kept up
an affectionate correspondence with his family. It fell to
the poet's lot, as we have seen, to communicate his father's
last illness and death to the Kincardineshire kindred; and
of his subsequent correspondence with Mr. James Burness,
some specimens have already been given, by the favour of
his son. Burns now formed a personal acquaintance with
these good people; and in a letter to his brother Gilbert, we
find him describing them in terms which show the lively
interest he took in all their concerns.

" The rest of my stages," says he, " are not worth re-
hearsing; warm as I was from Ossian's country, where I
had seen his grave, what cared I for fishing-towns and
fertile carses?" He arrived once more in Edinburgh, on
the 16th of September, having travelled about six hundred

miles in two-and-twenty days—greatly extended his acquaintance with his own country, and visited some of its most classical scenery—observed something of Highland manners, which must have been as interesting as they were novel to him—and strengthened considerably among the sturdy Jacobites of the North those political opinions which he at this period avowed.

Of the few poems composed during this Highland tour, we have already mentioned two or three. While standing by the Fall of Fyers, near Loch Ness, he wrote with his pencil the vigorous couplets—

> "Among the heathy hills and rugged woods,
> The roaring Fyers pours his mossy floods," &c.

[The journal of this great Highland tour closes with these entries :—"Sat., Sep. 15—Come to Kinrose to lie—reflections in a fit of the colic. Sunday, Sep. 16—Come through a cold, barren country to Queensferry—dine—cross the ferry, and arrive in Edinburgh."]

[But the bard's country rambles were not yet over for that season. His hasty spurt of revolutionary rodomontade inscribed on the window-pane of his inn at Stirling seems to have given him some uneasiness, and perhaps he longed for an opportunity of effacing it. Mr. James McKittrick Adair, a young gentleman of the medical profession—a relative of Mrs. Dunlop—about this time applied to him expressing an earnest wish to be introduced to the group of ladies at Harvieston. Perhaps the poet's glowing conversational raptures about the charms of Charlotte Hamilton had given birth to this desire, and her eulogist soon proved himself in no way loth to gratify it. Mr. Crawfurd Tait, of Harvieston, a Writer to the Signet, who practised his profession in Edinburgh, was a widower, and his household affairs in the country were superintended by Mrs. Hamilton, the widowed stepmother of Mr. Gavin Hamilton, of

Mauchline, assisted by Mrs. Chalmers, also a widow, both of whom were sisters of the deceased Mrs. Tait. Mrs. Chalmers had, residing along with her, two daughters, the one a young widow—Lady Mackenzie—and the other an engaging and accomplished spinster, who about a year after this period married Mr. Lewis Hay, of Sir Wm. Forbes and Company's Bank. Burns had been introduced to the latter lady, Miss Peggy Chalmers, in course of the preceding winter, but had few opportunities of intimacy with her at that time. When he visited Harvieston in August he failed to enjoy the pleasure of meeting her there, because she had been left behind in the city, and now he was informed of her return to the banks of the Devon. Another inducement to revisit Harvieston lay in the circumstance that he had, while at Athole House, met Sir Wm. Murray, who extracted a promise that the bard would visit him at his seat, Ochtertyre, in Strathearn, at no great distance from Mr. Tait's country retreat. A similar promise to visit the residence of Mr. Ramsay, at Auchtertyre on the Teith, near Stirling, would help to confirm the poet's resolution to travel again in that direction.]

[Early in October,[1] accordingly, Burns revisited Stirling and its neighbourhood, in company with Mr. Adair (who not long thereafter settled as a medical practitioner in Harrowgate, with the rosy Charlotte Hamilton as his helpmate); and he had the satisfaction of smashing the offensive pane of glass with the butt-end of his riding-whip.] The young ladies of Harvieston were, according to Dr. Currie, surprised with the calm manner in which Burns contemplated their fine scenery on Devon Water; and the Doctor enters into a little dissertation on the subject, showing that

---

[1] [Owing to a slip of memory on the part of Dr. Adair, who communicated to Currie in 1799 many of the details of this excursion, the date of it was erroneously set down, "August," instead of October.]

a man of Burns's lively imagination might probably have formed anticipations which the realities of the prospect might rather disappoint. This is probable enough ; but I suppose few will take it for granted that Burns surveyed any scenes, either of beauty or grandeur, without emotion, merely because he did not choose to be ecstatic for the benefit of a company of young ladies. He was very impatient of interruption on such occasions ; I have heard that, riding one dark night near Carron, his companion teased him with noisy exclamations of delight and wonder, whenever an opening in the wood permitted them to see the magnificent glare of the furnaces: " Look ! Burns, Good heaven ! look ! look ! what a glorious sight ! " " Sir," said Burns, clapping spurs to his horse, " I would not *look* —*look* at your bidding, if it were the mouth of hell."

On this occasion, Burns continued about ten days at Harvieston, in the immediate neighbourhood of the magnificent scenery of Castle Campbell,[1] and the Vale of the Devon.

In compliment to Adair's sweetheart, and in testimony of his own admiration, our poet celebrated her charms in a song, which, in opposition to his usual custom, is characterized only by the respectfulness of admiration—

" How pleasant the banks of the clear winding Devon," &c.

He was especially fascinated with Charlotte's cousin, Miss Peggy Chalmers (afterwards Mrs. Hay), and not only com-

---

[1] Castle Campbell, called otherwise " The Castle of Gloom," is situated very grandly in a gorge of the Ochils, commanding an extensive view of the plain of Stirling. This ancient possession of the Argyle family was, in some sort, a town residence for those chieftains in the days when the Court was usually held at Stirling, Linlithgow, or Falkland. The castle was burnt by Montrose, and has never been repaired. The " cauldron linn" and " rumbling brigg " of the Devon lie near Castle Campbell, on the verge of the plain.

posed two or three fine songs[1] under that inspiration, but
addressed to her, in course of the following ten months, one
of the most interesting series of his letters. Indeed, with the
exception of his letters to Mrs. Dunlop, there is perhaps no
part of his correspondence which may be quoted so uniformly
to his honour.

He was received with particular kindness at Auchtertyre,
on the Teith, by Mr. Ramsay (a friend of Blacklock), whose
beautiful retreat he enthusiastically admired. His host was
among the last of that old Scottish line of Latinists, which
began with Buchanan, and, I fear, may be said to have
ended with Gregory. Mr. Ramsay, among other eccentri-
cities, had sprinkled the walls of his house with Latin inscriptions, some of them highly elegant; and those particularly interested Burns, who asked and obtained copies and
translations of them. This amiable man (whose manners
and residence were not, I take it, out of the novelist's recollection when he painted Monkbarns) was deeply read in
Scottish antiquities, and the author of some learned essays
on the elder poetry of his country. His conversation must
have delighted any man of talents; and Burns and he were
mutually charmed with each other. Ramsay advised him
strongly to turn his attention to the romantic drama, and
proposed the "Gentle Shepherd" as a model: he also
urged him to write "Scottish Georgics," observing, that
Thomson had by no means exhausted that field. He appears
to have relished both hints. "But," says Mr. R., "to have
executed either plan, steadiness and abstraction from company were wanting."

"I have been in the company of many men of genius
(writes Mr. Ramsay), some of them poets; but I never
witnessed such flashes of intellectual brightness as from him,

---

[1] See songs:—"My Peggy's face, My Peggy's form," and "Where,
braving angry winter's storms."

the impulse of the moment, sparks of celestial fire. I never was more delighted, therefore, than with his company two days *tête-à-tête*. In a mixed company I should have made little of him : for, to use a gamester's phrase, he did not always know ' when to play off and when to play on.'

" When I asked him whether the Edinburgh literati had mended his poems by their criticisms—' Sir,' said he, ' those gentlemen remind me of some spinsters in my country, who spin their thread so fine, that it is neither fit for weft nor woof.'"

At Clackmannan Tower, the poet's Jacobitism procured him a hearty welcome from the ancient lady of the place, who gloried in considering herself as a lineal descendant of Robert Bruce. She bestowed on Burns what knighthood the touch of the hero's sword could confer; delighted him by giving as her toast after dinner, *Hoohi uncos !*—" away strangers ! " and when he would have kissed her hand at parting, insisted on a warmer salute, saying, " What ails thee at my lips, Robin ? " At Dunfermline the poet betrayed deep emotion, Dr. Adair tells us, on seeing the grave of the Bruce ; but passing to another mood on entering the adjoining church, he mounted the pulpit and addressed his companion, who had, at his desire, ascended the *cutty-stool*, in a parody of the *rebuke* which he had himself undergone some time before at Mauchline.

When at Sir William Murray's of Ochtertyre, he celebrated Miss Murray of Lintrose, commonly called " The Flower of Strathmore," in the song—

> " Blythe, blythe, and merry was she,
> Blythe was she but and ben," &c. ;

and the verses, " On scaring some wildfowl on Loch Turit," [1] were composed while under the same roof. These

---

[1]   " Why, ye tenants of the lake,
        For me your wat'ry haunts forsake," &c.

last, except, perhaps, "Bruar Water," are the best that he added to his collection during the wanderings of the summer. But in Burns's subsequent productions, we find many traces of the delight with which he had contemplated Nature in these alpine regions.

The poet once more visited his family at Mossgiel, and Mr. Miller at Dalswinton, ere the winter set in; and on more leisurely examination of that gentleman's estate, we find him writing as if he had all but decided to become his tenant on the farm of Elliesland. It was not, however, until he had for the third time visited Dumfriesshire, in March, 1788, that a bargain was actually concluded.

More than half of the intervening months were spent in Edinburgh, where Burns found, or fancied, that his presence was necessary for the satisfactory completion of his affairs with the booksellers. It seems to be clear enough, that one great object was the society of his jovial intimates in the capital. Nor was he without the amusement of a little romance to fill up what vacant hours they left him. He formed, about this time, his acquaintance with a lady, distinguished, I believe, for taste and talents, as well as for personal beauty, and the purity of whose character was always above suspicion—the same to whom he addressed the song,

> "Clarinda, mistress of my soul," &c.,

and a series of prose epistles, a few of which have been separately published, and which, if they present more instances of bombastic language and fulsome sentiment than could be produced from all his writings besides, contain also, it must be acknowledged, passages of deep and noble feeling, which no one but Burns could have penned. One sentence, as strongly illustrative of the poet's character, I may venture to transcribe: "People of nice sensibility and generous minds have a certain intrinsic dignity, which fires at being trifled with, or lowered, *or even too closely approached.*" [1]

At this time the publication called " Johnson's Museum of Scottish Song," was going on in Edinburgh ; and its projector appears to have early prevailed on Burns to give him his assistance in the arrangement of his materials. Though the song on Miss Peggy Kennedy, commencing

> " Young Peggy blooms, our boniest lass,"

is the only hitherto unpublished one of his which appears in the first volume, issued in 1787, many of the old ballads included in it bear traces of his hand ; but in the second volume, which appeared in March, 1788, we find no fewer than five songs by Burns ; two that have been already mentioned,[2] and three far better than these, viz. :—" Theniel Menzies' bonie Mary," that grand lyric,

> " Farewell, ye dungeons dark and strong,
>   The wretch's destiny,
> Macpherson's time will not be long
>   On yonder gallows tree ; "

both of which performances bespeak the recent impressions of his Highland visit ; and, lastly, " Whistle and I'll come to you, my lad." Burns had been, from his youth upwards, an enthusiastic lover of the old minstrelsy and music of his country ; but he now studied both subjects with far better opportunities and appliances than he could have commanded previously ; and it is from this time that we must date his ambition to transmit his own poetry to posterity, in eternal association with those exquisite airs which had hitherto, in

---

[1] It is proper to note, that the " Letters to Clarinda " were printed by one who had no right to do so, and that the Court of Session granted an interdict against their circulation. [In 1843, her grandson published an authorized edition of the correspondence.]

[2] [" Clarinda," and " How pleasant the banks of the clear winding Devon."]

far too many instances, been married to verses that did not deserve to be immortal. It is well known, that from this time Burns composed very few pieces but songs; and whether we ought or ought not to regret that such was the case, must depend on the estimate we make of his songs as compared with his other poems; a point on which critics are to this hour divided, and on which their descendants are not very likely to agree. Mr. Walker, who is one of those that lament Burns's comparative dereliction of the species of composition which he most cultivated in the early days of his inspiration, suggests very sensibly, that if Burns had not taken to song-writing, he would probably have written little or nothing, amidst the various temptations to company and dissipation which now and henceforth surrounded him—to say nothing of the active duties of life in which he was at length about to be engaged.

Burns, although not present, on the 31st of December, at a dinner to celebrate the birthday of the unfortunate Charles Edward Stuart, produced for the occasion an ode, part of which Dr. Currie has preserved. The specimen will not induce any regret that the remainder of the piece has been suppressed. It appears to be a mouthing rhapsody —far, far different indeed from the " Chevalier's Lament," which the poet composed some months afterwards, with probably the tithe of the effort, while riding alone "through a tract of melancholy muirs between Galloway and Ayrshire, it being Sunday." [1]

For six weeks of the time that Burns spent this year in Edinburgh, he was confined to his room, in consequence of an overturn in a hackney coach. "Here I am," he writes, " under the care of a surgeon, with a bruised limb extended on a cushion, and the tints of my mind vying with the

---

[1] Letter to Robert Cleghorn, March 31, 1788.

livid horrors preceding a midnight thunder-storm. A drunken coachman was the cause of the first, and incomparably the lightest evil; misfortune, bodily constitution, hell, and myself, have formed a *quadruple alliance* to guarantee the other. I have taken tooth and nail to the Bible, and have got through the five books of Moses, and half way in Joshua. It is really a glorious book. I sent for my bookbinder to-day, and ordered him to get an 8vo Bible in sheets, the best paper and print in town, and bind it with all the elegance of his craft."[1]

In another letter to the same lady (Dec. 19), which opens gaily enough, we find him reverting to the same prevailing darkness of mood. "I can't say I am altogether at my ease when I see anywhere in my path that meagre, squalid, famine-faced spectre, Poverty, attended, as he always is, by iron-fisted Oppression and leering Contempt. But I have sturdily withstood his buffetings many a hard-laboured day, and still my motto is, I DARE. My worst enemy is *moi-même*. There are just two creatures that I would envy—a horse in his wild state traversing the forests of Asia, or an oyster on some of the desert shores of Europe. The one has not a wish without enjoyment; the other has neither wish nor fear."

One more specimen of this magnificent hypochondriacism addressed to Mrs. Dunlop (Jan. 21, 1788), may be sufficient. "These have been six horrible weeks. Anguish and low spirits have made me unfit to read, write, or think. I have a hundred times wished that one could resign life as an officer does a commission; for I would not *take in* any poor ignorant wretch by *selling out*. Lately, I was a sixpenny private; and, God knows, a miserable soldier enough: now I march to the campaign a starving cadet, a little more conspicuously wretched. I am ashamed of all this; for, though I do not want bravery for the warfare of life, I could

---

[1] Letter to Miss Chalmers, Dec. 12, 1787.

wish, like some other soldiers, to have as much fortitude or cunning as to dissemble or conceal my cowardice."

It seems impossible to doubt that Burns had, in fact, lingered in Edinburgh, in the hope that, to use a vague but sufficiently expressive phrase, "something would be done for him." He visited and revisited a farm,—talked and wrote scholarly and wisely about "having a fortune at the plough-tail," and so forth; but all the while nourished, and assuredly it would have been most strange if he had not, the fond dream, that the admiration of his country would ere long present itself in some solid and tangible shape. His illness and confinement gave him leisure to concentrate his imagination on the darker side of his prospects; and the letters which we have quoted, may teach those who may envy the powers and the fame of genius, to pause for a moment over the annals of literature, and think what superior capabilities of misery have been, in the great majority of cases, interwoven with the possession of those very talents, from which all but their possessors derive unmingled gratification.

Burns's distresses, however, were to be still farther aggravated. While still under the hands of his surgeon, he received intelligence from Mauchline that his intimacy with Jean Armour had once more exposed her to the reproaches of her family. The father sternly and at once turned her out of doors; and Burns, unable to walk across his room, had to write to his friends in Mauchline, to procure shelter for his children, and for her whom he considered as—all but his wife.[1] In a letter to Miss Chalmers (Jan. 22, 1788), written on hearing of this new misfortune, he says, "*I wish I were*

---

[1] [This is not quite correctly stated. Jean's only living child, Robert, born Sep. 3, 1786, was well cared for by the poet's mother at Mossgiel. All that Burns required to do at present—and which he did—was to screen Miss Armour from the effects of her father's wrath, by getting

dead, but I'm no like to die. I fear I am something like—
undone; but I hope for the best. You must not desert me.
Your friendship I think I can count on, though I should
date my letters from a marching regiment. Early in life,
and all my life, I reckoned on a recruiting drum as my
forlorn hope. Seriously though, life at present presents
me with but a melancholy path ; but—my limb will soon
be sound, and I shall struggle on."

It seems to have been *now* that Burns at last (Jan. 29,
1788) screwed up his courage to solicit the active interference in his behalf of the Earl of Glencairn. The letter is
a brief one. Burns could ill endure this novel attitude, and
he rushed at once to his request. " I wish," says he, " to
get into the Excise. I am told your lordship will easily
procure me the grant from the commissioners; and your
lordship's patronage and kindness, which have already
rescued me from obscurity, wretchedness, and exile, em-
bolden me to ask that interest. You have likewise put it
in my power to save the little tie of *home* that sheltered an
aged mother, two brothers, and three sisters, from destruction. There, my lord, you have bound me over to the
highest gratitude. My heart sinks within me at the idea
of applying to any other of The Great who have honoured
me with their countenance. I am ill qualified to dog the
heels of greatness with the impertinence of solicitation ; and
tremble nearly as much at the thought of the cold promise
as of the cold denial."

It would be hard to think that this letter was coldly or
negligently received; on the contrary, we know that Burns's
gratitude to Lord Glencairn lasted as long as his life. But

---

her lodged for a time with his friend Muir at Tarbolton Mill. By-and-
by, when near her expected confinement, he took for her an empty room
in Mauchline which he furnished, and her mother was induced to wait on
her, in secret, as a nurse.]

the excise appointment which he coveted was not procured by any exertion of this noble patron's influence. Mr. Alexander Wood, surgeon (still affectionately remembered in Scotland as "kind old Sandy Wood"), happening to hear Burns, while his patient, mention the object of his wishes, went immediately, without dropping any hint of his intention, and communicated the state of the poet's case to Mr. Graham of Fintry, one of the Commissioners of Excise, who had met Burns at the Duke of Athole's in the autumn, and who immediately had the poet's name put on the roll.

" I have chosen this, my dear friend, (thus wrote Burns to Miss Chalmers, Feb. 17, 1788) after mature deliberation. The question is not at what door of Fortune's palace shall we enter in; but which of her doors does she open to us? I was not likely to get anything to do. I wanted *un but*, which is a dangerous, an unhappy situation. I got this without any hanging on, or mortifying solicitation. It is immediate bread, and, though poor in comparison of the last eighteen months of my existence, 'tis luxury in comparison of all my preceding life. *Besides, the Commissioners are some of them my acquaintances, and all of them my firm friends.*"

Our poet seems to have kept up an angry correspondence, during his confinement, with his bookseller, Mr. Creech, whom he also abuses very heartily in his letters to his friends in Ayrshire. The publisher's accounts, however, when they were at last made up, must have given the impatient author a very agreeable surprise; for in his letter above quoted, to Lord Glencairn, we find him expressing his hopes that the gross profits of his book might amount to " better than £200," whereas, on the day of settling with Mr. Creech, he found himself in possession of £500, if not of £600.[1]

---

[1] Mr. Nicol, the most intimate friend Burns had at this time, writes to Mr. John Lewars, excise-officer at Dumfries, immediately on hearing

This supply came truly in the hour of need ; and it seems to have elevated his spirits greatly, and given him for the time a new stock of confidence; for he now resumed immediately his purpose of taking Mr. Miller's farm, retaining his Excise Commission in his pocket as a *dernier ressort*, to be made use of only should some reverse of fortune come upon him.   His first act,[1] however, was to relieve his brother from his difficulties, by advancing £180, or £200, to assist him in the management of Mossgiel.   " I give myself no airs on this," he generously says in a letter to Dr. Moore (Jan. 4, 1789), "for it was mere selfishness on my part. I was conscious that the wrong scale of the balance was pretty heavily charged, and I thought that the throwing a little filial piety and fraternal affection into the scale in my favour, might help to smooth matters at the *grand reckoning.*"

---

of the poet's death,—" He certainly told me that he received £600 for the first Edinburgh edition, and £100 afterwards for the copyright " (MS. in my possession). Dr. Currie states the gross product of Creech's edition at £500, and Burns himself, in one of his printed letters, at £400 only. Nicol hints, in the letter already referred to, that Burns had contracted debts while in Edinburgh, which he might not wish to avow on all occasions ; and if we are to believe this, and, as is probable, the expense of printing the subscription edition, should, moreover, be deducted from the £700 stated by Mr. Nicol—the apparent contradictions in these stories may be pretty nearly reconciled. Currie states at the end of his Memoir that Burns realized " nearly nine hundred pounds in all by his poems ? "

[1] [In the poet's letter to the Earl of Glencairn, dated Jan. 29, 1788, before quoted, he thus refers to this particular act as already performed :—" Your lordship's patronage and kindness have likewise put it in my power to save the little tie of home that sheltered an aged mother, two brothers, and three sisters, from destruction."]

CHAPTER VII.

" To make a happy fireside clime
        For weans and wife,
That's the true pathos and sublime
        Of human life."

BURNS, as soon as his bruised limb was able for a
journey, rode to Mossgiel, and went through the
ceremony of a Justice-of-Peace marriage with Jean Armour, in the writing-chambers of his friend Gavin Hamilton.[1] He then crossed the country to Dalswinton, and

---

[1] [Not quite so fast as here indicated did the poet make up his mind
to commit himself to this course. He was enabled to quit Edinburgh
(but only for three weeks) on 18th February, 1788. Having arranged
matters for Jean's present emergency at Mauchline, as described in a
previous note, he proceeded to Dumfries along with his father's old friend,
John Tennant, and, guided by his advice, resolved to take a lease of the
farm of Elliesland. Meanwhile he continued his madcap, and perhaps
not very hearty, correspondence with Clarinda, whom he had found to
be somewhat exacting in her demands on his time and attention. He
returned to the city about the 10th of March, where the lease of Elliesland was executed on the 13th, and completed his arrangements for
entering into the service of the Excise. After some further dalliance
with Clarinda, in course of which intelligence must have reached him of
Jean's delivery of twins (for the second time) who, however, died shortly
after birth, he finally left Edinburgh on 24th of March. Between his
sense of duty to Jean Armour, and his infatuated entanglement with
Clarinda—not to mention his more excusable aspirations towards Peggy
Chalmers—he had (to use his own words) " to face a dilemma which
damned him with only a choice of different species of error and imprudence." Happily for his own peace, and the peace of two or three more

concluded his bargain with Mr. Miller as to the farm of Elliesland, on terms which must undoubtedly have been considered by both parties as highly favourable to the poet; they were indeed fixed by two of Burns's old friends, who accompanied him for that purpose from Ayrshire. The lease was for four successive terms, of nineteen years each, —in all seventy-six years ; the rent for the first three years and crops fifty pounds ; during the remainder of the period £70. Mr. Miller bound himself to defray the expense of any plantations which Burns might please to make on the banks of the river ; and the farm-house and offices being in a dilapidated condition, the new tenant was to receive £300 from the proprietor, for the erection of suitable buildings. "The land," says Allan Cunningham, "was good, the rent moderate, and the markets were rising."

Burns entered on possession of his farm at Whitsuntide 1788, but the necessary rebuilding of the house prevented his removing Mrs. Burns thither until the season was far advanced. He had, moreover, to qualify himself for holding his excise commission by six weeks' attendance on the business of that profession in Tarbolton. From these circumstances, he led this summer a wandering and unsettled life, and Dr. Currie mentions this as one of his chief misfortunes. "The poet," as he says, "was continually riding between Ayrshire and Dumfriesshire ; and, often spending a night on the road, sometimes fell into company, and forgot the resolutions he had formed."

What these resolutions were, the poet himself shall tell us. On the third day of his residence at Elliesland, he thus writes to Mr. Ainslie : "I have all along hitherto, in

---

innocent souls, his final resolve was to cast in his lot for life with his own Jean. On 28th April we find him writing to James Smith, ordering "a new shawl for Mrs. Burns—'Tis my first present to her," he writes, "since I have irrevocably called her mine."]

the warfare of life, been bred to arms, among the light-
horse, the piquet guards of fancy, a kind of hussars and
Highlanders of the brain; but I am firmly resolved to sell
out of these giddy battalions.   Cost what it will, I am determined to buy in among the grave squadrons of heavy-
armed thought, or the artillery-corps of plodding contri-
vance. . . .   Were it not for the terrors of my ticklish
situation respecting a family of children, I am decidedly
of opinion that the step I have taken is vastly for my
happiness."

To all his friends, he expresses himself in terms of
similar satisfaction in regard to his marriage.   " Your
surmise, madam," he writes to Mrs. Dunlop (July 10), "is
just.   I am indeed a husband.   I found a once much-loved,
and still much-loved female, literally and truly cast out to
the mercy of the naked elements, but as I enabled her to
purchase a shelter; and there is no sporting with a fellow-
creature's happiness or misery.   The most placid good-
nature and sweetness of disposition; a warm heart, gratefully devoted with all its powers to love me; vigorous
health and sprightly cheerfulness, set off to the best advantage by a more than commonly handsome figure; these,
I think, in a woman, may make a good wife, though she
should never have read a page but the Scriptures of the
Old and New Testament, nor danced in a brighter assembly
than a penny-pay wedding. . . . .   To jealousy or infidelity I am an equal stranger; my preservative from the
first, is the most thorough consciousness of her sentiments
of honour, and her attachment to me; my antidote against
the last, is my long and deep-rooted affection for her.   In
housewife matters, of aptness to learn, and activity to execute, she is eminently mistress, and during my absence in
Nithsdale, she is regularly and constantly an apprentice to
my mother and sisters in their dairy, and other rural
business. . . . .   You are right, that a bachelor state

would have ensured me more friends; but from a cause you will easily guess, conscious peace in the enjoyment of my own mind, and unmistrusting confidence in approaching my God, would seldom have been of the number."

Some months later he tells Miss Chalmers that his marriage "was not, perhaps, in consequence of the attachment of romance,"—he is addressing a young lady—"but," he continues, "I have no cause to repent it. If I have not got polite tattle, modish manners, and fashionable dress, I am not sickened and disgusted with the multiform curse of boarding-school affectation; and I have got the handsomest figure, the sweetest temper, the soundest constitution, and the kindest heart in the country. Mrs. Burns believes as firmly as her creed, that I am *le plus bel esprit et le plus honnête homme* in the universe; although she scarcely ever, in her life, except the Scriptures and the Psalms of David in metre, spent five minutes together on either prose or verse—I must except also a certain late publication of Scotch Poems, which she has perused very devoutly, and all the ballads of the country, as she has (O the partial lover! you will say) the finest woodnote - wild I ever heard." [1]

It was during this honeymoon, as he calls it, while chiefly resident in a miserable hovel at Elliesland, and only occasionally spending a day or two in Ayrshire, that he wrote the beautiful song—

> " Of a' the airts the wind can blaw,
>   I dearly like the west ;
> For there the bonie lassie lives,
>   The lassie I lo'e best ;

---

[1] A letter of Burns to Mrs. Dunlop, dated 10th July, 1788, contains a passage strongly marked with his haughtiness of character. " I have escaped," says he, " the fantastic caprice, the apish affectation, with all the other blessed boarding-school acquirements which are *sometimes* to be found among females of the upper ranks, but almost universally pervade the misses of the would-be-gentry."

> There's wildwoods' growe, and rivers' rowe,
>   And mony a hill between ; [1]
> But day and night my fancy's flight
>   Is ever wi' my Jean.

> "I see her in the dewy flowers,
>   I see her sweet and fair ;
> I hear her in the tunefu' birds,
>   I hear her charm the air :
> There's not a bonie flower that springs
>   By fountain, shaw, or green ;
> There's not a bonie bird that sings,
>   But 'minds me o' my Jean."

"A discerning reader," says Mr. Walker, "will perceive that the letters in which he announces his marriage to some of his most respected correspondents, are written in that state when the mind is pained by reflecting on an unwelcome step, and finds relief to itself in seeking arguments to justify the deed, and lessen its disadvantages in the opinion of others."[2] I confess I am not able to discern any traces of this kind of feeling in any of Burns's letters on this interesting and important occasion. Mr. Walker seems to take it for granted, that because Burns admired the superior manners and accomplishments of women of the higher ranks of society, he must necessarily, whenever he discovered "the interest which he had the power of creating" in such persons, have aspired to find a wife among them.[3]

---

[1] [This peculiar mode of expression would require to be paraphrased to make it intelligible to the English reader :—" There is the *growe* of wildwoods, and the *rowe* of rivers, and the height of many a hill between us."]

[2] Morison, vol. i., p. lxxxvii. 1811.

[3] [Mr. Walker had perfect knowledge of the fact (communicated to him by the lady herself, although he did not then see his way to publish it) that Burns had made a formal offer of marriage to Miss Peggy Chalmers. She also revealed the circumstance to Campbell the poet, with whom she was intimate during her long widowhood. She became a widow in 1800, and survived till 1843.]

But it is, to say the least of the matter, extremely doubtful, that Burns, if he had had a mind, could have found any high-born maiden willing to partake such fortunes as his were likely to be, and yet possessed of such qualifications for making him a happy man, as he had ready for his acceptance in his " Bonie Jean." The proud heart of the poet could never have stooped itself to woo for gold ; and birth and high breeding could only have been introduced into a farm-house to embitter, in the upshot, the whole existence of its inmates. It is very easy to say, that had Burns married an accomplished woman, he *might* have found domestic evenings sufficient to satisfy all the cravings of his mind—abandoned tavern haunts and jollities for ever—and settled down into a regular pattern-character. But it is at least as possible, that consequences of an exactly opposite nature might have ensued. Any marriage, such as Professor Walker alludes to, would, in his case, have been more unequal, than either of those that made Dryden and Addison miserable for life.

Sir Walter Scott, in his Life of Dryden (p. 90) has well described the difficult situation of her who has " to endure the apparently causeless fluctuation of spirits incident to one doomed to labour incessantly in the feverish exercise of the imagination." " Unintentional neglect," says he, "and the inevitable relaxation, or rather sinking of spirit, which follows violent mental exertion, are easily misconstrued into capricious rudeness, or intentional offence ; and life is embittered by mutual accusation, not the less intolerable because reciprocally unjust." Such were the difficulties under which the domestic peace both of Addison and Dryden went to wreck ; and yet, to say nothing of manners and habits of the highest elegance and polish in either case, they were both of them men of strictly pure and correct conduct in their conjugal capacities ; and who can doubt that all these difficulties must have been enhanced tenfold, had any woman of superior condition linked her fortunes with Robert Burns, a man at once of the very warmest animal temperament, and the most wayward and moody of all his melancholy and irritable tribe, who had little vanity that could have been gratified by a species of connection, which, unless he had found a human angel, must have been continually wounding his pride ? But, in truth, these speculations are all worse than worthless. Burns, with all his faults, was an honest and high-spirited man, and he loved the mother of his children ; and had he hesitated to make her his wife, he must have sunk into the callousness of a ruffian, or that misery of miseries, the remorse of a poet.

The Reverend Hamilton Paul ("Life of Burns," p. 45) takes an original view of this business : "Much praise," says he, "has been lavished on Burns for renewing his engagement with Jean when in the blaze of his fame. . . . The praise is misplaced. We do not think a man entitled to credit or commendation for doing what the law could compel him to perform. Burns was in reality a married man, and it is truly ludicrous to hear him, aware as he must have been, of the indissoluble power of the obligation, though every document was destroyed, talking of himself as a bachelor."[1]

---

[1] I am bound to say that, from some criticisms on the first edition of this narrative, published in Scotland, and evidently by Scotch lawyers, it appears that the case, "*Armour* versus *Burns*," had there ever been such a lawsuit, would have been more difficult of decision than I had previously supposed. One thing, however, is quite clear : Burns himself had no notion, that, in acknowledging his *Jean* as his wife, he was but yielding what legal measures could have extorted from him. Let any one consider, for example, the language of the letter in which he announces his marriage and establishment at Elliesland, to Mr. Burness of Montrose—

"(*Elliesland*, *9th Feb.*, 1789.)—Why I did not write you long ago, is what, even on the rack, I could not answer. If you can in your mind form an idea of indolence, dissipation, hurry, cares, change of country, entering on untried scenes of life—all combined—you will save me the trouble of

To return to our story. Burns complains sadly of his solitary condition, when living in the only hovel that he found extant on his farm. "I am," says he (September 9th), "busy with my harvest; but for all that most pleasurable part of life called social intercourse, I am here at the very elbow of existence. The only things that are to be found in this country in any degree of perfection, are

---

a blushing apology. It could not be want of regard for a man for whom I had a high esteem before I knew him—an esteem which has much increased since I did know him; and this caveat entered, I shall plead guilty to any other indictment with which you shall please to charge me.

"After I parted from you, for many months my life was one continued scene of dissipation. Here, at last, I have become stationary, and have taken a farm, and—a wife. The farm lies beautifully situated on the banks of the Nith, a large river that runs by Dumfries, and falls into the Solway Frith. I have gotten a lease of my farm as long as I please; but how it may turn out, is just a guess, as it is yet to improve and enclose, &c.; however, I have good hopes of my bargain on the whole.

"My wife is my Jean, with whose story you are partly acquainted. I found I had a much-loved fellow-creature's happiness or misery among my hands, and I durst not trifle with so sacred a deposit. Indeed, I have not any reason to repent the step I have taken, as I have attached myself to a very good wife, and have shaken myself loose of a very bad failing.

"I have found my book a very profitable business, and with the profits of it have begun life very decently. Should Fortune not favour me in farming, as I have no great faith in her fickle ladyship, I have provided myself in another resource, which, however some folks may affect to despise it, is still a comfortable shift in the day of misfortune. In the heyday of my fame, a gentleman, whose name at least I daresay you know, as his estate lies somewhere near Dundee, Mr. Graham of Fintry, one of the Commissioners of Excise, offered me the commission of an Excise-officer. I thought it prudent to accept the offer; and accordingly, I took my instructions, and have my commission by me. Whether I may ever do duty, or be a penny the better for it, is what I do not know; but I have the comfortable assurance, that, come whatever ill fate will, I can, on my simple petition to the Excise-Board, get into employ."

stupidity and canting. Prose they only know in graces, &c., and the value of these they estimate as they do their plaiding webs, by the ell. As for the Muses, they have as much idea of a rhinoceros as of a poet."[1] And in a letter to Miss Chalmers (Sep. 16, 1788) he says : " This hovel that I shelter in while occasionally here is pervious to every blast that blows, and every shower that falls, and I am only preserved from being chilled to death by being suffocated by smoke. You will be pleased to hear that I have laid aside idle *éclat*, and bind every day after my reapers."

His house, however, did not take much time in building, nor had he reason to complain of want of society long ; nor, it must be added, did Burns bind every day after the reapers.

He brought his wife home to Elliesland about the end of November; and few housekeepers start with a larger provision of young mouths to feed than did this couple. Mrs. Burns had lain in this autumn, for the second time, of twins, and I suppose "sonsy, smirking, dear-bought Bess," accompanied her younger brothers and sisters from Mossgiel. From that quarter also Burns brought a whole establishment of servants, male and female, who, of course, as was then the universal custom amongst the small farmers, both of the west and south of Scotland, partook, at the same table, of the same fare with their master and mistress.[2]

---

[1] Letter to John Beugo, Sept. 9, 1788.

[2] [The reader has already seen that Mrs. Burns did *not* " lie in this autumn"—the mistake is transferred from Currie's Memoir—and she had no " young mouths to feed" during the first year at Elliesland. The boy Robert was not brought to that farm till August, 1789, when he came along with the poet's mother, on the occasion of Jean's confinement with her first-born *in wedlock*—Frank Wallace Burns. The other child—" dear-bought Bess "—continued at Mossgiel till her womanhood. The widow of the poet was alive when the passage in the text was published, and expressed some indignation when it was read to her. She

Elliesland is beautifully situated on the banks of the Nith, about six miles above Dumfries, exactly opposite to the house of Dalswinton, and those noble woods and gardens amidst which Burns's landlord, the ingenious Mr. Patrick Miller, found relaxation from the scientific studies and researches in which he so greatly excelled. On the Dalswinton side, the river washes lawns and groves; but over against these the bank rises into a long red *scaur*, of considerable height, along the verge of which, where the bare shingle of the precipice all but overhangs the stream, Burns had his favourite walk, and might now be seen striding alone, early and late, especially when the winds were loud, and the waters below him swollen and turbulent. For he was one of those that enjoy nature most in the more serious and severe of her aspects; and throughout his poetry, for one allusion to the liveliness of spring, or the splendour of summer, it would be easy to point out twenty in which he records the solemn delight with which he contemplated the melancholy grandeur of autumn, or the savage gloom of winter. Indeed, I cannot but think, that the result of an exact inquiry into the composition of Burns's poems, would be, that "his vein," like that of Milton, flowed most happily, "from the autumnal equinox to the vernal." Of Lord Byron, we know that his vein flowed best at midnight; and Burns has himself told us, that it was his custom "to take a gloamin' shot at the Muses."

The poet was accustomed to say, that the most happy period of his life was the first winter he spent at Elliesland,

---

said, " The whole establishment consisted of two women-assistants, one of whom was the poet's own sister, Nannie. The servants did not partake at the same table, of the same fare with the master and mistress, excepting only on New-year's morning, when, according to ancient custom in the house of William Burnes, the whole household breakfasted together. At every other time Burns and his wife ate alone, with the addition of his sister when she lived at the farm."]

for the first time under a roof of his own, with his wife and children about him ; and in spite of occasional lapses into the melancholy which had haunted his youth, looking forward to a life of well-regulated, and not ill-rewarded, industry. It is known that he welcomed his wife to her roof-tree at Elliesland in the song,

> " I hae a Wife o' my ain, I'll partake wi' naebody ;
> I'll tak cuckold frae nane, I'll gie cuckold to naebody ;
> I hae a penny to spend—there, thanks to naebody ;
> I hae naething to lend—I'll borrow frae naebody."

In commenting on this " little lively lucky song," as he well calls it, Mr. Allan Cunningham says : " Burns had built his house,—he had committed his seed-corn to the ground,—he was in the prime, nay, the morning of life,—health, and strength, and agricultural skill (?) were on his side,—his genius had been acknowledged by his country, and rewarded by a subscription more extensive than any Scottish poet ever received before ; no wonder, therefore, that he broke out into voluntary song, expressive of his sense of importance and independence." [1] Another song was composed in honour of Mrs. Burns, during the happy weeks that followed her arrival at Elliesland : [2]

> " O, were I on Parnassus hill,
>   Or had of Helicon my fill,
>   That I might catch poetic skill,
>   To sing how dear I love thee!
>
> " But Nith maun be my muse's well,
>   My muse maun be thy bonny sel',
>   On Corsincon I'll glowre and spell,
>   And write how dear I love thee !"

---

[1] Cunningham's " Scottish Songs," vol. iv., p. 86.

[2] [This is a mistake : it was composed, as indeed may be inferred from the words, on the same occasion as " Of a' the airts "—a companion tribute of love to an absent wife. " On Corsincon I'll glowre and spell," *i.e.*, my eyes are fixed on the only Ayrshire object that can be seen from Elliesland—a high conical-shaped hill far away in the west.]

In the next stanza, the poet rather transgresses the limits of connubial decorum; but on the whole these tributes to domestic affection are among the last of his performances that one would wish to lose.

The "Mother's Lament for her Son," and two several versions of "Inscription in an Hermitage in Nithsdale," were also written this year. In his letters of the year 1789, Burns makes many apologies for doing but little in his poetical vocation; his farm, without doubt, occupied much of his attention, but the want of social intercourse, of which he complained on his first arrival at Nithsdale, had by this time totally disappeared. On the contrary, his company was courted eagerly, not only by his brother farmers, but by the neighbouring gentry of all classes; and now too for the first time, he began to be visited continually in his own house by curious travellers of all sorts, who did not consider, any more than the generous poet himself, that an extensive practice of hospitality must cost more time than he ought to have had, and far more money than he ever had, at his disposal. Meantime, he was not wholly regardless of the Muses; for, in addition to some pieces which we have already had occasion to notice, he contributed to this year's "Museum," "The Thames flows proudly to the Sea;" "The lazy mist hangs," &c.; "The day returns, my bosom burns;" "Tam Glen," (one of the best of his humorous songs): the splendid lyrics, "Go fetch to me a pint of wine," and "My heart's in the Hielands" (in both of which, however, he adopted some lines of ancient songs to the same tunes), "John Anderson," in part also a *rifacciamento;* the best of all his Bacchanalian pieces, "Willie brewed a peck o' maut," written in celebration of a festive meeting at the country lodgings, near Moffat, of his friend Mr. Nicol, of the High School; and lastly, that noblest of all his ballads, "To Mary in Heaven."

This celebrated poem was, it is on all hands admitted, composed by Burns in 1789, on the anniversary day of the death of his early love, Mary Campbell. Mrs. Burns, the only person who could appeal to personal recollection on this occasion, and whose recollections of all circumstances connected with the history of her husband's poems are represented as being remarkably distinct and vivid, gave the following account to Mr. M'Diarmid concerning the composition of this remarkable production :—Burns spent that day, though labouring under a cold, in the usual work of his harvest, and apparently in excellent spirits. But as the twilight deepened, he appeared to grow "very sad about something," and at length wandered out into the barn-yard, to which his wife, in her anxiety for his health, followed him, entreating him in vain to observe that frost had set in, and to return to the fireside. On being again and again requested to do so, he always promised compliance—but still remained where he was, striding up and down slowly, and contemplating the sky, which was singularly clear and starry. At last Mrs. Burns found him stretched on a mass of straw, with his eyes fixed on a beautiful planet "that shone like another moon ;" and prevailed on him to come in. He immediately, on entering the house, called for his desk, and wrote, exactly as they now stand, with all the ease of one copying from memory, the sublime and pathetic verses :—

> " Thou lingering star, with lessening ray,
>   That lov'st to greet the early morn,
> Again thou usher'st in the day
>   My Mary from my soul was torn.
> O, Mary ! dear departed shade,
>   Where is thy place of blissful rest ?
> See'st thou thy lover lowly laid,
>   Hear'st thou the groans that rend his breast ?" &c.[1]

---

[1] [With all respect for the memory of the poet's widow, and her talented interviewer, Mr. John M'Diarmid, the editor is constrained

From the time when Burns settled himself in Dumfries-
shire, he appears to have conducted with much care the

---

honestly to confess that he is possessed by a spirit of unbelief in the
details of this reminiscence of Mrs. Burns.   Three years after the date
of this composition, the poet, sitting in his little writing-closet in the
" Wee Vennel" of Dumfries, produced another set of verses on the same
subject, equally pathetic and unapproachably artistic as the performance
now under notice ; and yet Mrs. Burns never was asked a question, nor
had a word to say, concerning her husband's abstraction and mys-
teriously sudden " sadness about something," when the " fit" came upon
him to create the immortal ballad—" Ye banks and braes, and streams
around the castle o' Montgomery."

The " harvest work " spoken of in the above narrative is inconsistent
with a day far on in October, when, as is now known, poor Mary Campbell died.   Neither do the other incidents of the legend in any way har-
monize with the facts to be inferred from an intelligent reading of the
opening stanza.   The author does not, at midnight, address a planet that
" shines like another moon." *His* time is " early morn," and *his* star is in
the act of melting into the prevailing dawn, away from the speaker's
gaze : it " lingers " as if poetically loth to " usher in " a day—to him, of
bitter remembrance.   Indeed, so far as can be gathered from the poem,
the author may have been restlessly musing all night in bed, until the
glimmer of a fading star, seen through the window-pane of his chamber,
arrests his attention as the bitter day is being ushered in.   His first
invocation is to that object, and then he addresses the " dear departed
shade " of one who now dwells amid the stars, putting to her the
agonizing question—

> " See'st thou thy lover lowly laid,
>   Hear'st thou the groans that rend his breast ?"

This expression, " lowly laid " (for aught the reader can see to the contrary), may simply mean—laid by the side of Mary's rival and predecessor—the " perfidious Jean " of 1786 !

The closing part of Mrs. Burns's account is even more incredulous—
her shivering, supperless husband is prevailed on to come within doors :
he, " immediately on entering the house, called for his desk, and wrote
with all the ease of one copying from memory, the words exactly as they
now stand " of his sublime address, " To Mary in Heaven ! "   Honest
Sir Harris Nicolas, in his Memoir of Burns, 1830, made the natural

extensive correspondence in which his celebrity had engaged him; it is, however, very necessary, in judging of the letters, and drawing inferences from their language as to the real sentiments and opinions of the writer, to take into consideration the rank and character of the persons to whom they are severally addressed, and the measure of intimacy which really subsisted between them and the poet. In his letters, as in his conversation, Burns, in spite of all his pride, did something to accommodate himself to his company; and he who did write the series of letters addressed to Mrs. Dunlop, Dr. Moore, Mr. Dugald Stewart, Miss Chalmers, and others, eminently distinguished as these are by purity and nobleness of feeling, and perfect propriety of language, presents himself, in other effusions of the same class, in colours which it would be rash to call his own. In a word, whatever of grossness of thought, or rant, extravagance, and fustian in expression, may be found in his correspondence, ought, I cannot doubt, to be mainly ascribed to his desire of accommodating himself for the moment to the habits and taste of certain buckish tradesmen of Edinburgh, and other such-like persons, whom, from circumstances already sufficiently noticed, he numbered among his associates and friends. That he should have condescended to any such compliances must be regretted; but in most cases, it would probably be quite unjust to push our censure further than this.

The letters that passed between him and his brother Gilbert are among the most precious of the collection; for

---

observation that "if evidence be wanting that Mrs. Burns did not entirely possess her husband's heart, it is to be found in the fact that, after a fit of melancholy abstraction one evening, he was induced by her tenderness to return home, when, calling for writing materials, the source of his depression became apparent in a beautiful Ode to a woman he had once loved, of whose death that day (or the day following) happened to be the anniversary!"]

there, there could be no disguise. That the brothers had entire knowledge of, and confidence in each other, no one can doubt; and the plain, manly, affectionate language in which they both write, is truly honourable to them and to the parents that reared them.

"Dear Brother," writes Gilbert, January 1, 1789, "I have just finished my New-year's day breakfast in the usual form, which naturally makes me call to mind the days of former years, and the society in which we used to begin them; and when I look at our family vicissitudes, 'through the dark postern of time long elapsed,' I cannot help remarking to you, my dear brother, how good the God of seasons is to us; and that, however some clouds may seem to lour over the portion of time before us, we have great reason to hope that all will turn out well."

It was on the same New-year's day that Burns himself addressed to Mrs. Dunlop a letter, part of which is here transcribed—it certainly cannot be read too often :—

"ELLIESLAND, *New-Year's-Day Morning,* 1789.

"This, dear madam, is a morning of wishes, and would to God that I came under the apostle James's description! —*the prayer of a righteous man availeth much.* In that case, madam, you should welcome in a year full of blessings; everything that obstructs or disturbs tranquillity and self-enjoyment should be removed, and every pleasure that frail humanity can taste, should be yours. I own myself so little a Presbyterian, that I approve of set times and seasons of more than ordinary acts of devotion, for breaking in on that habituated routine of life and thought, which is so apt to reduce our existence to a kind of instinct, or even sometimes, and with some minds, to a state very little superior to mere machinery.

"This day,—the first Sunday of May,—a breezy, blue-skyed noon sometime about the beginning, and a hoary

o

morning and calm sunny day about the end, of autumn; these, time out of mind, have been with me a kind of holiday. I believe I owe this to that glorious paper in the ' Spectator,' ' The Vision of Mirza,' a piece that struck my young fancy before I was capable of fixing an idea to a word of three syllables : ' On the 5th day of the moon, which, according to the custom of my forefathers, I always *keep holy*, after having washed myself and offered up my morning devotions, I ascended the high hill of Bagdat, in order to pass the rest of the day in meditation and prayer.'

" We know nothing, or next to nothing, of the substance or structure of our souls, so cannot account for those seeming caprices in them, that one should be particularly pleased with this thing, or struck with that, which, on minds of a different cast, makes no extraordinary impression. I have some favourite flowers in spring, among which are the mountain-daisy, the harebell, the fox-glove, the wild brier-rose, the budding birch, and the hoary hawthorn, that I view and hang over with particular delight. I never hear the loud solitary whistle of the curlew, in a summer noon, or the wild mixing cadence of a troop of grey plover, in an autumnal morning, without feeling an elevation of soul like the enthusiasm of devotion or poetry. Tell me, my dear friend, to what can this be owing ? Are we a piece of machinery, which, like the Æolian harp, passive, takes the impression of the passing accident ? Or do these workings argue something within us above the trodden clod ? I own myself partial to such proofs of those awful and important realities—a God that made all things—man's immaterial and immortal nature—and a world of weal or woe beyond death and the grave."

Few, it is to be hoped, can read such things as these without delight; none, surely, that taste the elevated pleasure they are calculated to inspire, can turn from them to the well-known issue of Burns's history, without being afflicted. It is difficult to imagine anything more beautiful, more noble, than what such a person as Mrs. Dunlop might at this period be supposed to contemplate as the probable tenor of his future life. What fame can bring of happiness he had already tasted: he had overleaped, by the force of his genius, all the painful barriers of society; and there was probably not a man in Scotland who would not have thought himself honoured by seeing Burns under his roof. He had it in his power to place his poetical reputation on a level with the very highest names, by proceeding in the same course of study and exertion which had originally raised him into public notice and admiration. Surrounded by an affectionate family, occupied, but not engrossed, by the agricultural labours in which his youth and early manhood had delighted, communing with nature in one of the loveliest districts of his native land, and, from time to time, producing to the world some immortal addition to his verse —thus advancing in years and in fame, with what respect would not Burns have been thought of; how venerable in the eyes of his contemporaries—how hallowed in those of after generations, would have been the roof of Elliesland, the field on which he " bound every day after his reapers," the solemn river by which he delighted to wander! The plain of Bannockburn would hardly have been holier ground.

The "golden days" of Elliesland, as Dr. Currie justly calls them, were not destined to be many. Burns's farming speculations were again fated to failure; and he himself seems to have been aware that such was likely to be the case before he had given the business many months' trial. So early as 10th September, 1788, he applied to his patron, Mr. Graham, of Fintray, to make arrangements for his actual employment as an exciseman; and was accordingly, a year thereafter, appointed to do duty in that capacity, in the district where his lands were situated. His income as a revenue officer was at first only £35; it by-and-by rose to £50;[1] and sometimes was £70.

These pounds were hardly earned, since the duties of his new calling necessarily withdrew him very often from the farm, which needed his utmost attention, and exposed him, which was still worse, to innumerable temptations of the kind he was least likely to resist.

I have now the satisfaction of presenting the reader with some particulars of this part of Burns's history, derived from a source which every lover of Scotland and Scottish poetry must be prepared to hear mentioned with respect. It happened that at the time when our poet went to Niths-dale, the father of Mr. Allan Cunningham was steward on the estate of Dalswinton : he was, as all who have read the writings of his sons will readily believe, a man of remark-able talents and attainments : he was a wise and good man ; a fervid admirer of Burns's genius; and one of those sober neighbours who in vain strove, by advice and warn-ing, to arrest the poet in the downhill path, towards which a thousand seductions were perpetually drawing him. Allan Cunningham was, of course, almost a child when he first saw Burns; but he was no common child ; and, besides, in what he has to say on this subject, we may be sure we are hearing the substance of his benevolent and sagacious father's observations and reflections. His own boyish recollections of the poet's personal appearance and demeanour will, however, be read with interest.

"I was very young," says Mr. Cunningham, "when I first saw Burns. He came to see my father, and their con-versation turned partly on farming, partly on poetry, in both of which my father had taste and skill. Burns had

---

Burns thus wrote to Lady H. Don on January 22, 1789 : "My Excise salary would pay half my rent, and I could manage the whole business of the Division without five guineas of additional expense."

just come to Nithsdale ; and I think he appeared a shade more swarthy than he does in Nasmyth's picture, and at least ten years older than he really was at the time. His face was deeply marked by thought, and the habitual expression intensely melancholy. His frame was very muscular and well proportioned, though he had a short neck, and something of a ploughman's stoop : he was strong, and proud of his strength. I saw him one evening match himself with a number of masons ; and, out of five-and-twenty practised hands, the most vigorous young men in the parish, there was only one that could lift the same weight as Burns.

" He had a very manly face, and a very melancholy look, but on the coming of those he esteemed, his looks brightened up, and his whole face beamed with affection and genius. His voice was very musical. I once heard him read ' Tam o' Shanter,'—I think I hear him now. His fine manly voice followed all the undulations of the sense, and expressed as well as his genius had done, the pathos and humour, the horrible and the awful, of that wonderful performance. As a man feels, so will he write ; and in proportion as he sympathizes with his author, so will he read him with grace and effect.

" I said that Burns and my father conversed about poetry and farming. The poet had newly taken possession of his farm of Elliesland,—the masons were busy building his house,—the applause of the world was with him, and a little of its money in his pocket,—in short, he had found a resting-place at last. He spoke with great delight about the excellence of his farm, and particularly about the beauty of its situation. ' Yes,' my father said, ' the walks on the river banks are fine, and you will see from your windows some miles of the Nith ; but you will also see several farms of fine rich holm,[1] any one of which you might have

---

[1] *Holm* is flat, rich, meadow-land, intervening between a stream and the general elevation of the adjoining country.

had. You have made a poet's choice rather than a farmer's.'[1]

"If Burns had much of a farmer's skill, he had little of a farmer's prudence and economy. I once inquired of James Corrie, a sagacious old farmer, whose ground marched with Elliesland, the cause of the poet's failure. 'Faith,' said he, 'how could he miss but fail, when his servants ate the bread as fast as it was baked? I don't mean figuratively, I mean literally. Consider a little. At that time close economy was necessary to have enabled a man to clear twenty pounds a year by Elliesland. Now, Burns's own handywork was out of the question; he neither ploughed, nor sowed, nor reaped, at least, like a hard-working farmer; and then he had a bevy of servants from Ayrshire. The lasses did nothing but bake bread, and the lads sat by the fireside, and ate it warm, with ale. Waste of time and consumption of food would soon reach to twenty pounds a year.'

"The truth of the case," says Mr. Cunningham, in another letter with which he has favoured me, "the truth is, that if Robert Burns liked his farm, it was more for the beauty of its situation than for the labours which it demanded. He was too wayward to attend to the stated

---

[1] [Allan Cunningham, who furnished the narrative that occupies this and several succeeding pages, was born December 7, 1784, consequently he must have been somewhat under four years old when he thus overheard Burns and his father "conversing about poetry and farming;" and he may have been six years old when (as he alleges) he heard the poet recite "Tam o' Shanter." He tells us that the voice of Burns was "very musical." Cunningham must have been, as Mr. Lockhart observes, "no ordinary child." Robert Chambers had an opportunity of conversing with Mr. Stobie, the kind exciseman who performed gratuitously the duties of Burns, when laid on his death-bed, thus entitling the poet to his full salary. On being questioned regarding Burns's voice, he said, "Burns sang as readily as a nightingale, but he had the voice of a boar."]

duties of a husbandman, and too impatient to wait till the ground returned in gain the cultivation he bestowed upon it.

"The condition of a farmer, a Nithsdale one I mean, was then very humble. His one-story house had a covering of straw, and a clay floor; the furniture was from the hands of a country carpenter; and, between the roof and floor, there seldom intervened a smoother ceiling than of rough rods and grassy turf—while a huge lang-settle of black oak for himself, and a carved armchair for his wife, were the only matters out of keeping with the homely looks of his residence. He took all his meals in his own kitchen, and presided regularly among his children and domestics. He performed family worship every evening—except during the hurry of harvest, when that duty was perhaps limited to Saturday night. A few religious books, two or three favourite poets, the history of his country, and his Bible, aided him in forming the minds and manners of the family. To domestic education, Scotland owes as much as to the care of her clergy, and the excellence of her parish-schools.

"The picture out of doors was less interesting. The ground from which the farmer sought support, was generally in a very moderate state of cultivation. The implements with which he tilled his land were primitive and clumsy, and his own knowledge of the management of crops exceedingly limited. He plodded on in the regular slothful routine of his ancestors; he rooted out no bushes, he dug up no stones; he drained not, neither did he enclose; and weeds obtained their full share of the dung and the lime, which he bestowed more like a medicine than a meal on his soil. His plough was the rude old Scotch one; his harrows had as often teeth of wood as of iron; his carts were heavy and low-wheeled, or were, more properly speaking, tumbler-cars, so called to distinguish them from trail-cars, both of which were in common use. On these rude carriages his manure was taken to the field and his crop brought home. The farmer himself corresponded in all respects with his imperfect instruments. His poverty secured him from risking costly experiments; and his hatred of innovation made him intrench himself behind a breastwork of old maxims and rustic saws, which he interpreted as oracles delivered against *improvement*. With ground in such condition, with tools so unfit, and with knowledge so imperfect, he sometimes succeeded in wringing a few hundred pounds *Scots* from the farm he occupied. Such was generally the state of agriculture when Burns came to Nithsdale. I know not how far his own skill was equal to the task of improvement—his trial was short and unfortunate. An important change soon took place, by which he was not fated to profit; he had not the foresight to see its approach, nor, probably, the fortitude to await its coming.

"In the year 1790, much of the ground in Nithsdale was leased at seven, and ten, and fifteen shillings per acre; and the farmer, in his person and his house, differed little from the peasants and mechanics around him. He would have thought his daughter wedded in her degree, had she married a joiner or a mason; and at kirk or market, all men beneath the rank of a 'portioner' of the soil mingled together, equals in appearance and importance. But the war which soon commenced, gave a decided impulse to agriculture; the army and navy consumed largely; corn rose in demand; the price augmented; more land was called into cultivation; and, as leases expired, the proprietors improved the grounds, built better houses, enlarged the rents; and the farmer was soon borne on the wings of sudden wealth above his original condition. His house obtained a slated roof, sash-windows, carpeted floors, plastered walls, and even began to exchange the hanks of yarn with which it was formerly hung, for paintings and pianofortes. He laid aside his coat of home-made cloth; he retired from his seat among his servants; he—I am grieved to mention it—gave up family worship as a thing unfashionable, and became a kind of *rustic gentleman*, who rode a blood-horse, and galloped home on market-nights at the peril of his own neck, and to the terror of every modest pedestrian.[1] His daughters, too, no longer prided themselves in well-bleached linen and home-made webs; they changed their linsey-wolsey gowns for silk; and so ungracefully did their new state sit upon them, that I have seen their lovers coming in iron-shod clogs to their carpeted floors, and two of the proudest young women in the parish *skaling* dung to their father's potato-field in silk stockings.

"When a change like this took place, and a farmer could, with a dozen years' industry, be able to purchase the land he rented—which many were, and many did—the same, or a still more profitable change might have happened with respect to Elliesland; and Burns, had he stuck by his lease and his plough, would, in all human probability, have found the independence which he sought, and sought in vain from the coldness and parsimony of mankind."

Mr. Cunningham sums up his reminiscences of Burns at Elliesland, in these terms:—

"During the prosperity of his farm, my father often said that Burns conducted himself wisely, and like one anxious for his name as a man, and his fame as a poet. He went to Dunscore Kirk on Sunday, though he expressed oftener than once his dislike to the stern Calvinism of that strict old divine, Mr. Kirkpatrick; he assisted in forming a reading-club; and at weddings, and house-heatings, and

---

[1] Mr. Cunningham's description accords with the lines of Crabbe:

"Who rides his hunter, who his house adorns,
Who drinks his wine, and his disbursement scorns,
Who freely lives, and loves to show he can—
This is the farmer made the gentleman."

kirns,[1] and other scenes of festivity, he was a welcome
guest, universally liked by the young and the old. But the
failure of his farming projects, and the limited income
with which he was compelled to support an increasing
family and an expensive station in life, preyed upon his
spirits; and, during these fits of despair, he was willing
too often to become the companion of the thoughtless and
the gross. I am grieved to say, that besides leaving the
book too much for the bowl, and grave and wise friends for
lewd and reckless companions, he was also in the occasional
practice of composing songs, in which he surpassed the
licentiousness, as well as the wit and humour, of the old
Scottish muse. These have unfortunately found their way
to the press, and I am afraid they cannot be recalled.[2]

"In conclusion, I may say, that few men have had so
much of the poet about them, and few poets so much of
the man—the man was probably less pure than he ought
to have been, but the poet was pure and bright to the
last."

The reader must be sufficiently prepared to hear, that
from the time when he entered on his Excise duties, the
poet more and more neglected the concerns of his farm.[3]

---

[1] *Kirns.*—The harvest-home dances are so called in Scotland. Such
entertainments were universally given by the landlords in those days;
but this good old fashion is fast wearing out in too many districts. It
belonged to a more prudent, as well as humane style of manners, than
now finds favour.

[2] [The reference here is to an ugly little book which, not long after the
poet's death, was published anonymously, and without any *imprimatur*
of authority. It was long hawked about the country under the title of
"The Merry Muses of Caledonia." On this subject, see Appendix D.]

[3] [Burns, on 10th August, 1789, acknowledged receipt of an intimation
from Mr. Graham, of Fintry, that the Commissioners of Excise had
appointed him to active service in the district for which he had made
application, viz., a large circuit embracing ten parishes, with his own
farm in the centre. But the first intimation in his correspondence of

Occasionally, he might be seen holding the plough, an exercise in which he excelled, and was proud of excelling, or stalking down his furrows, with the white sheet of grain wrapt about him, a "tenty seedsman;" but he was more commonly occupied in far different pursuits. "I am now," says he, in one of his letters, "a poor rascally gauger, condemned to gallop two hundred miles every week, to inspect dirty ponds and yeasty barrels."

Both in verse and in prose he has recorded the feelings with which he first followed his new vocation. His jests on the subject are uniformly bitter. "I have the same consolation," he tells Mr. Ainslie, "which I once heard a recruiting sergeant give to his audience in the streets of Kilmarnock: 'Gentlemen, for your farther encouragement, I can assure you that ours is the most blackguard corps under the crown, and, consequently, with us an honest fellow has the surest chance of preferment.'" He winds up almost all his statements of his feelings on this matter, in the same strain—

> "I hae a wife and twa wee laddies,
> They maun hae brose and brats o' duddies.
> Ye ken yoursel, my heart right proud is,
>   I needna vaunt;
> But I'll sned besoms—thraw saugh-woodies,
>   Before they want."

On one occasion, however, he takes a higher tone. "There is a certain stigma," says he to Bishop Geddes, "in the name of Exciseman; but I do not intend to borrow honour from any profession"—which may perhaps remind the reader of Gibbon's lofty language, on finally quitting the

---

his actually having commenced operations is found in a letter to Ainslie, dated 1st November of that year, just after the incident of "The Whistle"-contest at Friar's Carse, and after the more memorable circumstance which led to the composition of his address to "Mary in Heaven."]

learned and polished circles of London and Paris, for his Swiss retirement; " I am too modest, or too proud, to rate my value by that of my associates."

Burns, in his perpetual perambulations over the moors of Dumfries-shire, had every temptation to encounter, which bodily fatigue, the blandishments of hosts and hostesses, and the habitual manners of those who acted along with him in the duties of the Excise, could present. He was, moreover, wherever he went, exposed to perils of his own, by the reputation which he had earned as a poet, and by his extraordinary powers of entertainment in conversation; and he pleased himself with thinking, in the words of one of his letters to the Lady Harriet Don, that " one advantage he had in this new business was, the knowledge it gave him of the various shades of character in man—consequently assisting him in his trade as a poet." [1] From the castle to the cottage, every door flew open at his approach; and the old system of hospitality, then flourishing, rendered it difficult for the most soberly inclined guest to rise from any man's board in the same trim that he sat down to it. The farmer, if Burns were seen passing, left his reapers, and trotted by the side of Jenny Geddes, until he could persuade the bard that the day was hot enough to demand an extra libation. If he entered an inn at midnight, after all the inmates were in bed, the news of his arrival circulated from the cellar to the garret; and ere ten minutes had elapsed, the landlord and all his guests were assembled round the ingle; the largest punch-bowl was produced; and

" Be ours this night—who knows what comes to-morrow ? "

was the language of every eye in the circle that welcomed him. [2] The stateliest gentry of the county, whenever they

---

[1] Letter (unpublished), dated Elliesland, 23rd Dec., 1789.

[2] These particulars are from a letter of David Macculloch, Esq., who

had especial merriment in view, called in the wit and eloquence of Burns to enliven their carousals. The famous
song of " The Whistle of worth," commemorates a scene
of this kind, more picturesque in some of its circumstances
than every day occurred, yet strictly in character with the
usual tenor of life among this jovial *squirearchy*. Three
gentlemen of ancient descent, had met to determine, by a
solemn drinking-match, who should possess *the Whistle*,
which a common ancestor of them all had earned ages
before, in a Bacchanalian contest of the same sort with a
noble toper from Denmark; and the poet was summoned to
watch over and celebrate the issue of the debate.

> " Then up rose our bard, like a prophet in drink,
> Craigdarroch ! thou'lt soar when creation shall sink !
> But if thou would flourish immortal in rhyme,
> Come, one bottle more, and have at the sublime." [1]

Nor, as has already been hinted, was he safe from tempta-

---

being at this period a very young gentleman, a passionate admirer of
Burns, and a capital singer of many of his serious songs, used often, in his
enthusiasm, to accompany the poet on his professional excursions. See
a reference to M'Culloch at p. 103 *ante*, and likewise at p. 224 *postea*.

[1] [This affair of the contest for the Whistle which, since the year 1840,
has engaged the attention of several controversialists, was passed over
in these pages with scarcely a comment from Mr. Lockhart. He simply
repeats Currie's statement that the ballad " celebrates a Bacchanalian
contest among three gentlemen of Nithsdale, where Burns appears as
umpire." Burns certainly, *in the song*, under the artistic licence of a
ballad-writer, " appears as umpire ; " but his letter to Mr. Riddell on
the morning of the day of contest (first published by Cromek in
1808), distinctly shows that Burns had been merely appointed " poet-
laureat " of the occasion, and not a witness of " the mighty claret-shed
of the day." " For me," he writes, "I shall ' hear astonished and
astonished sing.' " He enclosed to Riddell two letters to get franked
by Sir Robert Laurie, one of the champions, adding, " I shall send a
servant again for them in the evening. Wishing that your head may
be crowned with laurels to-night, and free from aches to-morrow, I
have the honour to be, Sir," &c.]

tions of this kind, even when he was at home, and most disposed to enjoy in quiet the society of his wife and children. Lion-gazers from all quarters beset him; they ate and drank at his cost, and often went away to criticize him and his fare, as if they had done Burns and his *black-bowl*[1] great honour in condescending to be entertained for a single evening, with such company and such liquor.

We have on record various glimpses of him, as he appeared while he was half-farmer, half-exciseman; and some of these present him in attitudes and aspects on which it would be pleasing to dwell.[2] For example, the circumstances under

---

[1] Burns's famous black punch-bowl, of Inverary marble, was the nuptial gift of his father-in-law, Mr. Armour, who himself fashioned it. After passing through many hands, it is now (1829) in excellent keeping, that of Archibald Hastie, Esq., of London. [This punch-bowl did not pass through very many hands before it got into Mr. Hastie's possession. Shortly after the poet's death, Mrs. Burns presented it to Mr. Alex. Cunningham, of Edinburgh, who mounted it with silver, and had it inscribed in a tasteful manner. Cunningham died in 1812, while his son, the late James Cunningham, W.S., was yet a boy, and the deceased's executor ordered it to be sold in 1815. John Ballantyne was the salesman, and it was knocked down at eighty guineas to an unknown purchaser, who afterwards turned out to be a London publican. That person soon fell into pecuniary difficulties, the consequence of which was that the relic passed into Mr. Hastie's hands. At his death it went, in terms of his testament, to the British Museum, London.]

[2] A writer in the "Edinburgh Literary Journal," vol. i., p. 82, has just furnished (1829) the following little anecdote:—"It may be readily guessed with what interest I heard, one Thornhill fair-day, that Burns was to visit the market. Boy as I then was, an interest was awakened in me respecting this extraordinary man, which was sufficient, in addition to the ordinary attraction of a village fair, to command my presence in the market. Burns actually entered the fair about twelve; and man, wife, and lass, were all on the outlook for a peep of the Ayrshire ploughman. I carefully dogged him from stand to stand, and from door to door. An information had been lodged against a poor widow of the name of Kate Watson, who had ventured to serve a few of her old country friends with a draught of unlicensed ale, and a lacing of

which the verses on " The Wounded Hare," were written, are mentioned generally by the poet himself. James Thomson, son of the occupier of a farm adjoining Ellies-land, told Allan Cunningham that it was he who wounded the animal. " Burns " (said this person) " was in the custom, when at home, of strolling by himself in the twi-light every evening, along the Nith, and by the *march* between his land and ours. The hares often came and nibbled our wheat-*braird;* and once, in the gloaming, it was in April, I got a shot at one and wounded her; she ran bleeding by Burns, who was pacing up and down by himself, not far from me. He started, and with a bitter curse, ordered me out of his sight, or he would throw me instantly into the Nith ; and had I stayed, I'll warrant he would have been as good as his word, though I was both young and strong."

Among other curious travellers who found their way about this time to Elliesland, was Captain Grose, the cele-brated antiquarian, whom Burns briefly described as

> " A fine fat fodgel wight—
> Of stature short, but genius bright ;"

and who has painted his own portrait, both with pen and pencil, at full length, in his " Olio." This gentleman's tastes

---

whisky, on this village jubilee. I saw him enter her door, and antici-pated nothing short of an immediate seizure of a certain grey-beard and barrel, which, to my personal knowledge, contained the contraband commodities our bard was in quest of. A nod, accompanied by a signi-ficant movement of the forefinger, brought Kate to the doorway or trance, and I was near enough to hear the following words distinctly uttered :
—' Kate, are ye mad ? D'ye no ken that the supervisor and I will be in upon you in the course of forty minutes ? Guid-by t'ye at present.'
Burns was in the street and in the midst of the crowd in an instant, and I had access to know that his friendly hint was not neglected. It saved a poor widow from a fine of several pounds." [It was Prof. Gillespie, of St. Andrew's, who communicated this anecdote.]

and pursuits are ludicrously set forth in the copy of verses—

> " Hear, Land o' Cakes and brither Scots,
> Frae Maidenkirk to John o' Groats,
> A chield's amang ye takin' notes," &c.

and, *inter alia*, his love of port is not forgotten. Grose and Burns had too much in common not to become great friends. The poet's accurate knowledge of Scottish phraseology and customs was of much use to the researches of the humorous antiquarian; and, above all, it is to their acquaintance that we owe " Tam o' Shanter." Burns told the story as he had heard it in Ayrshire, in a letter to the Captain, and was easily persuaded to versify it. The poem is said to have been the work of one day; and Mrs. Burns well remembers the circumstances. He spent most of the day on his favourite walk by the river, where, in the afternoon, she joined him with some of her children. " He was busily engaged *crooning to himsel;* and Mrs. Burns, perceiving that her presence was an interruption, loitered behind with her little ones among the broom. Her attention was presently attracted by the strange and wild gesticulations of the bard, who now, at some distance, was agonized with an ungovernable access of joy. He was reciting very loud, and with the tears rolling down his cheeks, those animated verses which he had just conceived :

> ' Now Tam ! O Tam ! had thae been queans
> A' plump and strappin in their teens ;
> Their sarks, instead of creeshie flannen,
> Been snaw-white seventeen-hunder [1] linen,—
> Thir breeks o' mine, my only pair,
> That ance were plush, o' good blue hair,
> I wad hae gien them aff my hurdies,
> For ae blink o' the bonie burdies.' " [2]

---

[1] The manufacturer's term for fine linen woven on a reed of 1,700 divisions.—*Cromek.*

[2] The above is quoted from a MS. journal of Cromek.   Mr. M'Diar-

To the last, Burns was of opinion that " Tam o' Shanter " was the best of his productions ; and although it does not often happen that poet and public come to the same conclusion on such points, I believe the decision in question has been all but unanimously approved of.

The admirable execution of the piece, so far as it goes, leaves nothing to wish for ; the only criticism has been, that the catastrophe appears unworthy of the preparation. Burns might have avoided this error—if error it be—had he followed not the Ayrshire, but the Galloway edition of the legend. According to that tradition, the *Cutty-Sark* who attracted the special notice of the bold intruder on the Satanic ceremonial, was no other than the pretty wife of a farmer residing in the same village with himself, and of whose unholy propensities no suspicion had ever been whispered. The " Galloway *Tam* " being thoroughly sobered by terror, crept to his bed the moment he reached home after his escape, and said nothing of what had happened to any of his family. He was awakened in the morning with the astounding intelligence that his horse had been found dead in the stable, and a woman's hand, clotted with blood, adhering to the tail. Presently it was reported that *Cutty-Sark* had burnt her hand grievously over-night, and was ill in bed, but obstinately refused to let her wound be examined by the village leech. Hereupon Tam, disentangling the bloody hand from the hair of his defunct favourite's tail, proceeded to the residence of the fair witch, and forcibly pulling her stump to view, showed his trophy, and narrated the whole circumstances of the adventure. The poor victim of the black art was constrained to confess her guilty practices in presence of the priest and the laird, and

---

mid confirms the statement, and adds, that the poet, having committed the verses to writing on the top of his *sod-dyke* over the water, came into the house and read them immediately in high triumph at the fireside.

was forthwith burnt alive under their joint auspices, within water mark, on the Solway Firth.[1]

Such, Mr. Cunningham informs me, is the version of this story current in Galloway and Dumfries-shire: but it may be doubted whether, even if Burns was acquainted with it, he did not choose wisely in adhering to the Ayr-shire legend, as he had heard it in his youth. It is seldom that tales of popular superstition are effective in proportion to their completeness of solution and catastrophe. On the contrary, they, like the creed to which they belong, suffer little in a picturesque point of view by exhibiting a maimed and fragmentary character, that in nowise satisfies strict taste, either critical or moral. Dreams based in darkness may fitly terminate in a blank: the cloud opens, and the cloud closes. The absence of definite scope and purpose, appears to be of the essence of the mythological grotesque.

Burns lays the scene of this remarkable performance almost on the spot where he was born; and all the terrific circumstances by which he has marked the progress of Tam's midnight journey are drawn from local tradition.

> "By this time he was cross the ford
> Where in the snaw the chapman smoor'd,
> And past the birks and meikle stane,
> Where drucken Charlie brak's neck-bane;
> And through the whins, and by the cairn,
> Where hunters fand the murdered bairn;
> And near the thorn, aboon the well,
> Where Mungo's mither hanged hersel."

None of these tragic memoranda were derived from ima-gination. Nor was "Tam o' Shanter" himself an imagi-nary character. Shanter is a farm close to Kirkoswald, that smuggling village, in which Burns, when sixteen

---

[1] [This pretended "Galloway version" of the legend is a mere inven-tion of Allan Cunningham, who tried here to impose on Mr. Lockhart, as in former years he had hoaxed Cromek.]

years old, studied mensuration, and "first became acquainted with scenes of swaggering riot." The then occupier of Shanter, by name Douglas Graham, was, by all accounts, equally what the Tam of the poet appears,—a jolly, careless rustic, who took much more interest in the contraband traffic of the coast than the rotation of crops. Burns knew the man well; and to his dying day Graham, nothing loath, passed among his rural compeers by the name of Tam o' Shanter.[1]

A few words will bring us to the close of Burns's career at Elliesland. Mr. Ramsay of Auchtertyre, happening to pass through Nithsdale, in 1790, met Burns riding rapidly near Closeburn. The poet was obliged to pursue his professional journey, but sent on Mr. Ramsay and his fellow-traveller to Elliesland, where he joined them as soon as his duty permitted him, saying, as he entered, "I come, to use the words of Shakespeare, *stewed in haste.*" Mr. Ramsay was "much pleased with his *uxor Sabina qualis*, and his modest mansion, so unlike the habitation of ' ordinary rustics." He told his guest he was preparing to write a drama, which he was to call "Rob M'Quechan's Elshin," from a popular story of King Robert the Bruce being defeated on the Carron, when the heel of his boot having loosened in the flight, he applied to one Robert M'Quechan to fix it on, who, to make sure, ran his awl nine inches up the King's heel. The evening was spent delightfully. A gentleman of dry temperament, who looked in accidentally, soon partook the contagion, and sat listening to Burns with the tears running over his cheeks. "Poor Burns!" says Mr. Ramsay, "from that time I met him no more."

The summer after, some English travellers, calling at Elliesland, were told that the poet was walking by the river. They proceeded in search of him, and presently,

---

[1] [The above information is derived from Mr. R. Chambers.]

" on a rock that projected into the stream, they saw a man employed in angling, of a singular appearance. He had a cap made of fox's skin on his head; a loose great coat, fastened round him by a belt, from which depended an enormous Highland broadsword." (Was he still dreaming of the Bruce?) "It was Burns. He received them with great cordiality, and asked them to share his humble dinner." These travellers also classed the evening they spent at Elliesland with the brightest of their lives.[1]

Whether Burns ever made any progress in the actual composition of a drama on " Rob M'Quechan's Elshin," we know not. He had certainly turned his ambition seriously to the theatre almost immediately after his first establishment in Dumfriesshire. In a letter (unpublished) to Lady H. Don, dated December 23rd, 1789, he thus expresses himself :—" No man knows what nature has fitted him for till he try; and if, after a preparatory course of some years' study of men and books, I should find myself unequal to the task, there is no great harm done. Virtue and study are their own reward. I have got Shakespeare, and begun with him; and I shall stretch a point, and make myself master of all the dramatic authors of any repute in

---

[1] [Like Thomas Carlyle, Mrs. Burns had no faith in this story. "Burns," she said, " was no fisher, and her belief was that he had never attempted to practise the art : he had a fox-skin cap, and two swords, one of these an *Andrea Ferrara;* but she never saw him so foolish as to wear them." (M'Diarmid's memoranda.) Professor Shairp, in a recent " Essay on Burns," thus snaps at Carlyle's incredulity—" Burns himself mentions the broadsword as a frequent accompaniment of his when he went out by the river." The professor ought to verify his quotations before displaying a spirit of contradiction in this form. He is thinking of our poet's " gilt-headed Wangee rod," thus referred to in a letter to Mrs. Dunlop, who had sent him some good news,—" an instrument indispensably necessary in the moment of inspiration and rapture : I seized it in my left hand, and stride—stride—quick, and quicker — out skipt I among the broomy banks of Nith."

both English and French—the only languages which I know." And in another letter to the same person, he recurs to the subject in these terms :—" Though the rough material of fine writing is undoubtedly the gift of genius, the workmanship is as certainly the united effort of labour, attention, and pains. Nature has qualified few, if any, to shine in every walk of the muses I shall put it to the test of repeated trials, whether she has formed me capable of distinguishing myself in any one." [1]

Towards the close of 1791, the poet, finally despairing of his farm, determined to give up his lease, which the kindness of his landlord rendered easy of arrangement; and procuring an appointment to the Dumfries division, which raised his salary from the revenue to £70 per annum, removed his family to the county town, in which he terminated his days. His conduct as an excise-officer had hitherto met with uniform approbation; and he nourished warm hopes of being promoted, when he had thus avowedly devoted himself altogether to the service.

He left Ellisland, however, with a heavy heart. The affection of his neighbours was rekindled in all its early fervour, by the thoughts of parting with him ; and the *roup* of his farming-stock and other effects, was, in spite of whisky, a very melancholy scene. " The competition for his chattels (says Allan Cunningham) was eager, each being anxious to secure a memorandum of Burns's residence among them."

It is pleasing to know, that among other "titles manifold " to their respect and gratitude, Burns, at the suggestion of Mr. Riddel of Friars' Carse, had superintended the

---

[1] [The words here quoted are almost identical with one sentence in a letter dated January 22, 1789 (first printed by Chambers in 1851), which that editor supposed to have been addressed to Lady Don's relative, the Hon. Harry Erskine.]

formation of a subscription-library in the parish.   His letters to the booksellers on this subject do him much honour : his choice of authors (which business was naturally left to his discretion) being in the highest degree judicious.   Such institutions are now common, almost universal, indeed, in the rural districts of southern Scotland ; but it should never be forgotten that Burns was among the first, if not the very first, to set the example.   " He was so good," says Mr. Riddel, " as to take the whole management of this concern ; he was treasurer, librarian, and censor, to our little society, who will long have a grateful sense of his public spirit and exertions for their improvement and information."[1]

Once, and only once, did Burns quit his residence at Elliesland to revisit Edinburgh.   His object was to close accounts with Creech ; that business accomplished, he returned immediately, and he never again saw the capital.[2] He thus writes to Mrs. Dunlop :—" To a man who has a home, however humble and remote, if that home is, like mine, the scene of domestic comfort, the bustle of Edinburgh will soon be a business of sickening disgust—

'Vain pomp and glory of the world, I hate you.'

" When I must skulk into a corner, lest the rattling equipage of some gaping blockhead should mangle me in the mire, I am tempted to exclaim—what merits had he had, or what demerits have I had, in some state of pre-existence, that he is ushered into this state of being with the sceptre

---

[1] Letter to Sir John Sinclair, Bart., in the Statistical Account of Scotland—Parish of Dunscore.

[2] [The " only once " here referred to was in the latter part of February, 1789, and the poet tells in a letter that he returned to Elliesland on the last day of that month.   But he did again visit Edinburgh (certainly for the last time) at the close of November, 1791, his object being to take a " last farewell " of Clarinda.]

of rule, and the key of riches in his puny fist, and I kicked into the world, the sport of folly, or the victim of pride? . . . . Often as I have glided with humble stealth through the pomp of Prince's Street, it has suggested itself to me as an improvement on the present human figure, that a man, in proportion to his own conceit of his consequence in the world, could have pushed out the longitude of his common size, as a snail pushes out his horns, or as we draw out a perspective-glass." There is bitterness in this badinage.

It may naturally excite some surprise, that of the convivial conversation of so distinguished a convivialist, so few specimens have been preserved in the Memoirs of his life. The truth seems to be, that those of his companions who chose to have the best memory for such things, happened also to have the keenest relish for his wit and his humour when exhibited in their coarser phases. Among a heap of MSS. memoranda with which I have been favoured, I find but little that one could venture to present in print : and the following specimens of that little must, for the present, suffice.

A gentleman who had recently returned from the East Indies, where he had made a large fortune, which he showed no great alacrity about spending, was of opinion, it seems, one day, that his company had had enough of wine, rather sooner than they came to that conclusion : he offered another bottle in feeble and hesitating terms, and remained dallying with the corkscrew, as if in hopes that some one would interfere and prevent further effusion of Bourdeaux. "Sir," said Burns, losing temper, and betraying in his mood something of the old rusticity—"Sir, you have been in Asia, and for aught I know, on the Mount of Moriah, and you seem to hang over your *tappit-hen* as remorsefully as Abraham did over his son Isaac—Come, Sir, to the sacrifice!"[1]

---

[1] [Robert Chambers, in 1826, had this anecdote from the lips of a then

At another party, the society had suffered considerably from the prosing of a certain well-known provincial *Bore* of the first magnitude; and Burns, as much as any of them, although overawed, as it would seem, by the rank of the nuisance, had not only submitted, but condescended to applaud. The Grandee being suddenly summoned to another company in the same tavern, Burns immediately addressed himself to the chair, and demanded a bumper. The president thought he was about to dedicate his toast to the distinguished absentee : "I give," said the Bard, "I give you the health, gentlemen all,—of the waiter that called my Lord —— out of the room."

He often made extempore rhymes the vehicle of his sarcasm : thus, for example, having heard a person, of no very elevated rank, talk loud and long of some aristocratic festivities in which he had the honour to mingle, Burns, when called upon for his song, chanted some verses, of which one has been preserved :—

> " Of lordly acquaintance you boast,
>   And the dukes that you dined wi' yestreen,
> Yet an insect's an insect at most,
>   Tho' it crawl on the curl of a queen."

I believe I have already alluded to Burns's custom of carrying a diamond pencil with him in all his wanderings, and constantly embellishing inn-windows and so forth with his epigrams. On one occasion, being storm-stayed at Lamington, in Clydesdale, he went to church ; and the indig-

---

living witness of the incident—John Syme of Ryedale. "I particularly remember (said Chambers) the old gentleman glowing over the discomfiture of a too considerate Amphitryon who, when entertaining the narrator along with Burns and some others, lingered with screw in hand over a fresh bottle, which he evidently wished to be forbidden to draw —till Burns transfixed him by a comparison of his present position with that of Abraham lingering over the filial sacrifice."—" Life and Works of Burns," 1856, vol. iv., p. 155.]

nant beadle, after the congregation dispersed, invited the attention of the clergyman to this stanza on the window by which the noticeable stranger had been sitting :

> " As cauld a wind as ever blew ;
>   A cauld kirk, and in't but few ;
>   As cauld a minister's ever spak ;
>   Ye'se a' be het or I come back."

Sir Walter Scott possesses a tumbler, on which are the following verses, written by Burns on the arrival of a friend, Mr. W. Stewart, factor to a gentleman of Nithsdale. The landlady being very wroth at what she considered the disfigurement of her glass, a gentleman present appeased her, by paying down a shilling, and carried off the relic.

> " You're welcome, Willie Stewart,
>   You're welcome, Willie Stewart ;
> There's ne'er a flower that blooms in May,
>   That's half sae welcome's thou art.
>
> Come, bumpers high, express your joy,
>   The bowl we maun renew it ;
> The tappit-hen gae bring her ben,
>   To welcome Willie Stewart.
>
> May foes be strang, and friends be slack,
>   Ilk action may he rue it ;
> May woman on him turn her back,
>   That wrangs thee, Willie Stewart ! "

[The gentleman of Nithsdale for whom " Willie Stewart " acted as factor was the Rev. James Stuart Menteith of Closeburn Hall. Willie's sister was the wife of Mr. Bacon, landlord of the Inn at Brownhill where Burns was accustomed frequently—perhaps too frequently—to bait when on his excise journeys. The factor had a pretty daughter, who often assisted her aunt in the business of the Inn, and the poet celebrated her charms in a lively song, "O lovely Polly Stewart." If proof were wanting of the intimacy that subsisted between Burns and the father of Polly, the following hitherto unpublished verses, here taken from the poet's holograph, should evince it :—

" Brownhill, Monday even.

DEAR SIR,

> In honest Bacon's ingle neuk,
> Here maun I sit and think ;
> Sick o' the warld an' warld's folk,
> And sick, d—mn'd sick—o' drink !
>
> I see, I see there is nae help,
> But still down I maun sink,
> Till some day, *laigh eneugh*, I yelp—
> ' Wae worth that cursed drink ! '
>
> Yestreen, alas ! I was sae fou,
> I could but yisk an' wink ;
> And now, this day, sair, sair I rue
> The weary, weary drink.
>
> Satan ! I fear thy sooty claws,
> I hate thy brunstane stink,
> And ay I curse the luckless cause,
> The wicked sowp o' drink !
>
> In vain I wad forget my woes
> In idle ryming clink,
> For, past redemption d—mn'd in prose,
> I can dow noucht but—drink !
>
> For you, my trusty, weel-tried friend,
> May heav'n still on you blink !
> And may your life flow to the end,
> Sweet as a dry man's drink !

ROBT. BURNS."]

Since we are among such small matters, perhaps some readers will smile to hear, that Burns very often wrote his name on his books thus—" Robert Burns, Poet ; " and that Allan Cunningham remembers a favourite *collie* at Elliesland having the same inscription on his collar.

CHAPTER VIII.

" The King's most humble servant, **I**
Can scarcely spare a minute;
But I am your's at dinner-time,
Or else the devil's in it."[1]

THE four principal biographers of our poet, Heron,
Currie, Walker, and Irving, concur in the general
statement, that his moral course, from the time when he
settled in Dumfries, was downwards. Heron knew more
of the matter personally than any of the others, and his
words are these:—" In Dumfries, his dissipation became
still more deeply habitual. He was here exposed, more
than in the country, to be solicited to share the riot of the
dissolute and the idle. Foolish young men, such as writers'
apprentices, young surgeons, merchants' clerks, and his
brother excisemen, flocked eagerly about him, and from
time to time pressed him to drink with them, that they
might enjoy his wicked wit.[2] The Caledonian Club, too,
and the Dumfries and Galloway Hunt, had occasional

---

[1] " The above answer to an invitation was written extempore on a
leaf torn from his pocket-book."—*Cromek's MSS.*

[2] [Mrs. Burns remarked on hearing this read to her:—" There is
much nonsense here. Dr. Mundel, Dr. Brown, and Dr. Copeland, occasionally looked in upon him. As to writers' apprentices, the bard never
associated with persons so juvenile ! Mr. Kerr, afterwards Clerk of the
Peace, and Provost of Dumfries, was a friend of Lewars, and with him
Burns might meet at times. But he was always respectable and careful
in his choice of company, and a fit associate for the best."

meetings at Dumfries after Burns came to reside there, and the poet was of course invited to share their hospitality, and hesitated not to accept the invitation. The morals of the town were, in consequence of its becoming so much the scene of public amusement, not a little corrupted, and, though a husband and a father, Burns did not escape suffering by the general contamination in a manner which I forbear to describe. In the intervals between his different fits of intemperance, he suffered the keenest anguish of remorse and horrible afflictive foresight. His Jean behaved with a degree of maternal and conjugal tenderness and prudence, which made him feel more bitterly the evils of his misconduct, though they could not reclaim him."

This picture, dark as it is, wants some distressing shades that mingle in the parallel one by Dr. Currie; it wants nothing, however, of which truth demands the insertion. That Burns, dissipated enough long ere he went to Dumfries, became still more dissipated in a town, than he had been in the country, is certain. It may also be true that his wife had her own particular causes, sometimes, for dissatisfaction. But that Burns ever sunk into a toper—that he ever was addicted to solitary drinking—that his bottle ever interfered with his discharge of his duties as an exciseman—or that, in spite of some transitory follies, he ever ceased to be a most affectionate husband—all these charges have been insinuated—and they are all false. His intemperance was, as Heron says, in *fits;* his aberrations of all kinds were occasional, not systematic; they were all to himself the sources of exquisite misery in the retrospect ; they were the aberrations of a man whose moral sense was never deadened, of one who encountered more temptations from without and from within, than the immense majority of mankind, far from having to contend against, are even able to imagine;—of one, finally, who prayed for

pardon, where alone effectual pardon could be found;—
and who died ere he had reached that term of life up to
which the passions of many, who, their mortal career being
regarded as a whole, are honoured as among the most
virtuous of mankind, have proved too strong for the control
of reason. We have already seen that the poet was careful
of decorum in all things during the brief space of his prosperity at Elliesland, and that he became less so on many
points, as the prospects of his farming speculation dark-
ened around him. It seems to be equally certain, that he
entertained high hopes of promotion in the Excise at the
period of his removal to Dumfries; and that the comparative recklessness of his latter conduct there, was consequent on a certain overclouding of these professional
expectations. The case is broadly stated so by Walker and
Paul; and there are hints to the same effect in the narrative of Currie.

The statement has no doubt been exaggerated, but it has
its foundation in truth; and by the kindness of Mr. Train,
supervisor at Castle Douglas, in Galloway, I shall presently
be enabled to give some details which may throw light on
this business.[1]

Burns was much patronised when in Edinburgh by the
Honourable Henry Erskine, Dean of the Faculty of Advocates, and other leading Whigs of the place—much more
so, to their honour be it said, than by any of the influential
adherents of the then administration. His landlord at

---

[1] [Mr. Joseph Train (born in 1779) became an excise-officer, at Largo,
in 1811, and was transferred to Newton Stewart in 1813; to Cupar-Fife,
as supervisor, in 1820; to Kirkintilloch, in 1821; to Queensferry, in
1822; to Falkirk, in 1823; to Wigton, in 1824; to Dumfries, in 1825;
and from thence to Castle Douglas in 1827. Mr. Train seems to have
made it the chief business of his life to hunt up " ferlies " for Sir Walter
Scott. Several of these have since been proved " ingenious fabrications
of his own." He survived till 1852.]

Elliesland (Mr. Miller of Dalswinton), his neighbour, Mr. Riddel of Friars' Carse, and most of the other gentlemen who showed him special attention, belonged to the same political party; and, on his removal to Dumfries, it so happened, that some of his immediate superiors in the revenue service of the district, and other persons of standing and authority, into whose society he was thrown, entertained sentiments of the same description.

Burns, whenever in his letters he talks seriously of political matters, uniformly describes his early Jacobitism as mere "matter of fancy." It may, however, be easily believed, that a fancy like his, long indulged in dreams of that sort, was well prepared to pass into certain other dreams, which had, as calm men now view the matter, but little in common with them, except that both alike involved some feeling of dissatisfaction with "the existing order of things." Many of the old elements of political disaffection in Scotland, put on a new shape at the outbreaking of the French Revolution; and Jacobites became half-Jacobins, ere they were at all aware in what the doctrines of Jacobinism were to end. The Whigs naturally regarded the first dawn of freedom in France with feelings of sympathy, delight, exultation; in truth, few good men of any party regarded it with more of fear than of hope. The general, the all but universal tone of feeling was favourable to the first assailants of the Bourbon despotism; and there were few who more ardently participated in the general sentiment of the day than Burns.

The revulsion of feeling that took place in this country at large, when wanton atrocities began to stain the course of the French Revolution, and Burke lifted up his powerful voice to denounce its leaders, as, under pretence of love for freedom, the enemies of all social order, morality, and religion, was violent in proportion to the strength and ardour of the hopes in which good men have been eager to indulge, and cruelly disappointed. The great body of the Whigs, however, were slow to abandon the cause which they had espoused; and although their chiefs were wise enough to draw back when they at length perceived that serious plans for overturning the political institutions of our own country had been hatched and fostered, under the pretext of admiring and comforting the destroyers of a foreign tyranny —many of their provincial retainers, having uttered their sentiments all along with provincial vehemence and openness, found it no easy matter to retreat gracefully along with them. Scenes more painful at the time, and more so even now in the retrospect, that had for generations afflicted Scotland, were the consequences of the rancour into which party feelings on both sides now rose and fermented. Old and dear ties of friendship were torn in sunder; society was for a time shaken to its centre. In the most extravagant dreams of the Jacobites there had always been much to command respect, high chivalrous devotion, reverence for old affections, ancestral loyalty, and the generosity of romance. In the new species of hostility, every thing seemed mean as well as perilous; it was scorned even more than hated. The very name stained whatever it came near; and men that had known and loved each other from boyhood, stood aloof, if this influence interfered, as if it had been some loathsome pestilence.

There was a great deal of stately Toryism at this time in the town of Dumfries, which was the favourite winter retreat of many of the best gentlemen's families of the south of Scotland. Feelings that worked more violently in Edinburgh than in London, acquired additional energy still, in this provincial capital. All men's eyes were upon Burns. He was the standing marvel of the place; his toasts, his jokes, his epigrams, his songs, were the daily food of conversation and scandal; and he, open and careless, and thinking he did no great harm in saying and singing what many of his superiors had not the least objection to hear and applaud, soon began to be considered among the local admirers and disciples of the good old King and minister, as the most dangerous of all the apostles of sedition,—and to be shunned accordingly.

A gentleman of that county, whose name I have already more than once had occasion to refer to, has told me,[1] that he was seldom more grieved, than when, riding into Dumfries one fine summer's evening to attend a country ball, he saw Burns walking alone, on the shady side of the principal street of the town, while the opposite part was gay with successive groups of gentlemen and ladies, all drawn together for the festivities of the night, not one of whom appeared willing to recognise him. The horseman dismounted and joined Burns, who, on his proposing to him to cross the street, said, "Nay, nay, my young friend, —that's all over now;" and quoted, after a pause, some verses of Lady Grizel Baillie's pathetic ballad,—

> "His bonnet stood ance fu' fair on his brow,
> His auld ane look'd better than mony ane's new;
> But now he lets't wear ony way it will hing,
> And casts himsel dowie upon the corn-bing.
>
> "O were we young, as we ance hae been,
> We suld hae been galloping doun on yon green,
> And linking it ower the lily-white lea,—
> *And werena my heart light I wad die.*"

It was little in Burns's character to let his feelings on certain subjects escape in this fashion. He immediately after citing these verses assumed the sprightliness of his most pleasing manner; and taking his young friend home with him, entertained him very agreeably until the hour of the ball arrived, with a bowl of his usual potation, and Bonie Jean's singing of some verses which he had recently

---

[1] Mr. David M'Culloch, see pp. 103 and 205 *ante.*

composed. But this incident belongs, probably, to a somewhat later period of our poet's residence in Dumfries.

The records of the Excise-Office are silent concerning the suspicions which the Commissioners of the time certainly took up in regard to Burns as a political offender—according to the phraseology of the tempestuous period, a *democrat*. In that department, as then conducted, I am assured that nothing could have been more unlike the usual course of things, than that a syllable should have been set down in writing on such a subject, unless the case had been one of extremities. That an inquiry was instituted, we know from Burns's own letters—and what the exact termination of the inquiry was, can no longer, it is probable, be ascertained.

According to the tradition of the neighbourhood, Burns, *inter alia*, gave great offence by demurring in a large mixed company to the proposed toast, " The health of William Pitt; " and left the room in indignation, because the society rejected what he wished to substitute, namely, " The health of a greater and a better man, George Washington." I suppose the warmest admirer of Mr. Pitt's talents and politics would hardly venture now-a-days to dissent substantially from Burns's estimate of the comparative merits of these two great men. The name of Washington, at all events, when contemporary passions shall have finally sunk into the peace of the grave, will unquestionably have its place in the first rank of heroic virtue,—a station which demands the exhibition of victory pure and unstained, over temptations and trials extraordinary in kind, as well as strength. But at the time when Burns, being a servant of Mr. Pitt's government, was guilty of this indiscretion, it is obvious that a great deal " more was meant than reached the ear."

In the poet's own correspondence, we have traces of another occurrence of the same sort. Burns thus writes to

a gentleman at whose table he had dined the day before:—
"I was, I know, drunk last night, but I am sober this
morning.   From the expressions Captain ——— made use
of to me, had I had nobody's welfare to care for but my
own, we should certainly have come, according to the
manner of the world, to the necessity of murdering one
another about the business.   The words were such as generally, I believe, end in a brace of pistols; but I am still
pleased to think that I did not ruin the peace and welfare
of a wife and children in a drunken squabble.   Farther,
you know that the report of certain political opinions being
mine, has already once before brought me to the brink of
destruction.   I dread lest last night's business may be interpreted in the same way.   You, I beg, will take care to
prevent it.   I tax your wish for Mrs. Burns's welfare with
the task of waiting on every gentleman who was present to
state this to him; and, as you please, show this letter.
What, after all, was the obnoxious toast?   *May our success
in the present war be equal to the justice of our cause*—a
toast that the most outrageous frenzy of loyalty cannot
object to."

Burns has been commended, sincerely by some, and ironi-
cally by others, for putting up with the treatment which he
received on this occasion, without calling Captain ———
to account the next morning; and one critic, the last, I am
sure, that would have wished to say anything unkindly
about the poet, has excited indignation in the breast of Mr.
Alexander Peterkin, by suggesting that Burns really had
not, at any period of his life, those delicate feelings on certain
matters, which it must be admitted, no person in Burns's
original rank and station is ever expected to act upon.[1]   The
question may be safely intrusted to the good sense of all who
can look to the case without passion or personal irritation.

---

[1] The critic was Sir Walter Scott.   See *infra*, page 251.

No human being will ever dream that Robert Burns was a coward; as for the poet's toast about the success of the war, there can be no doubt that only one meaning was given to it by all who heard it uttered; and as little that a gentleman bearing the King's commission in the army, if he was entitled to resent the sentiment at all, lost no part of his right to do so, because it was announced in a quibble.

Burns, no question, was guilty of unpoliteness as well as indiscretion, in offering any such toasts as these in mixed company; but that such toasts should have been considered as attaching any grave suspicion to his character as a loyal subject, is a circumstance which can only be accounted for by reference to the exaggerated state of political feelings on all matters, and among all descriptions of men, at that melancholy period of disaffection, distrust, and disunion. Who, at any other than that lamentable time, would ever have dreamed of erecting the drinking, or declining to drink, the health of a particular minister, or the approving, or disapproving, of a particular measure of government, into the test of a man's loyalty to his King? The Dumfries poet, eager of temper, loud of tone, and with declamation and sarcasm equally at command, was, we may easily believe, to the local champions of the administration of which he ventured to disapprove, the most hated, because the most dreaded, of human beings. But that he ever, in his most ardent moods, upheld the principles of the miscreants, or madmen, whose applause of the French Revolution was but the mask of revolutionary designs at home, after such principles had been really developed by those who maintained them, and understood by him, it may be safely denied. There is not assuredly in all his correspondence, (and I have seen much of it that never has been, nor ought to be, printed), one syllable to give countenance to such a charge.

His indiscretion, however, did not always confine itself

to words; and though an incident now about to be recorded, belongs to the year 1792, before the French war broke out, there is reason to believe that it formed the main subject of the inquiry which the Excise Commissioners thought themselves called upon to institute, touching the politics of our poet.

At that period a great deal of contraband traffic, chiefly from the Isle of Man, was going on along the coasts of Galloway and Ayrshire, and the whole of the revenue officers from Gretna Green to Dumfries, were placed under the orders of a superintendent, residing in Annan, who exerted himself zealously in intercepting the descent of the smuggling vessels. On the 27th February, a suspicious-looking brig was discovered in the Solway Frith, and Burns was one of the party whom the superintendent conducted to watch her motions. She got into shallow water the day afterwards, and the officers were enabled to discover that her crew were numerous, armed, and not likely to yield without a struggle. Lewars, a brother exciseman, an intimate friend of our poet, was accordingly sent to Dumfries for a guard of dragoons; the superintendent, Mr. Crawford, proceeded himself on a similar errand to Ecclefechan, and Burns was left with some men under his orders, to watch the brig, and prevent landing or escape. From the private journal of one of the excisemen (now in my hands),[1] it appears that Burns manifested considerable impatience while thus occupied, being left for many hours in a wet-salt marsh, with a force which he knew to be inadequate for the purpose it was meant to fulfil. One of his comrades hearing him abuse his friend Lewars in particular, for being slow about his journey, the man answered,

---

[1] [It is to be hoped that this "private journal" and relative productions in support of so incredible a story are still in existence at Abbotsford.]

that he also wished the devil had him for his pains, and that Burns, in the meantime, would do well to indite a song upon the sluggard: Burns said nothing; but after taking a few strides by himself among the reeds and shingle, re-joined his party, and chanted to them the well-known ditty, "The Deil's awa' wi' the Exciseman."[1] Lewars arrived shortly afterwards with his dragoons; and Burns, putting himself at their head, waded, sword in hand, to the brig, and was the first to board her. The crew lost heart, and submitted, though their numbers were greater than those of the assailing force. The vessel was condemned, and, with all her arms and stores, sold by auction next day at Dumfries: upon which occasion, Burns, whose behaviour had been highly commended, thought fit to purchase four carronades, by way of trophy. But his glee went a step further;—he sent the guns, with a letter, to the French Con-vention, requesting that body to accept of them as a mark of his admiration and respect. The present, and its accom-paniment, were intercepted at the Custom House at Dover; and here, there appears to be little room to doubt, was the principal circumstance that drew on Burns the notice of his jealous superiors.

We were not, it is true, at war with France; but every one knew and felt that we were to be so ere long; and

---

[1] The account in the "Reliques," of this song being composed for "a festive meeting of all the Excise officers in Scotland," is therefore in-correct. Mr. Train, moreover, assures me, that there never was any such meeting. [Cromek's account is here suspiciously misquoted. All that Cromek says regarding the origin of the song is, that the poet extemporarily delivered it "at a meeting of his brother Excisemen in Dumfries." The correctness of the account in the "Reliques" is now corroborated by the recent recovery of a letter of Burns addressed to an Excise official in Edinburgh, in which he tells the very same fact, thus: —"Mr. Mitchell mentioned to you a ballad which I composed and sung at one of his Excise Court dinners: here it is—'The deil's awa',' " &c.]

nobody can pretend that Burns was not guilty, on this occasion, of a most absurd and presumptuous breach of decorum.[1]

When he learned the impression that had been created by his conduct, and its probable consequences, he wrote to his patron, Mr. Graham of Fintry, the following letter :—

"*December*, 1792.

"SIR, I have been surprised, confounded, and distracted, by Mr. Mitchell, the collector, telling me, that he has received an order from your board to inquire into my political conduct, and blaming me as a person disaffected to government. Sir, you are a husband and a father. You

---

[1] [In the absence of any confirmatory documents, this queer story depends on the "*ipse dixit*" of Mr. Train. The late Dr. Carruthers, editor of the Inverness "Courier," was at some pains to inquire concerning it, but could get nothing more satisfactory than the following farther particulars, by corresponding with Train himself. John Lewars died in October, 1826, about a year after his retirement from the supervisorship in Dumfries, to which office Train succeeded. The latter, having heard a rumour that Lewars died possessed of certain documents of importance in relation to Burns that evinced his strong sympathy with the revolutionary party in France, applied to his widow concerning them, and succeeded in obtaining—(1) A memorandum by Lewars detailing the foregoing narrative. (2) A list of arms and stores that had been captured along with the smuggling craft, in the handwriting of Burns. (3) A report of the sale, also in the poet's writing, with the price obtained for the various items, in which the name of Burns is placed opposite four carronades bought by him for £3. These documents Mr. Train said he had transmitted to Sir Walter Scott, who communicated them to Lockhart. He added that Sir Walter, to test the truth of the story, had, besides searching files of the "Moniteur" for some reference to the communication from Burns, applied to the Custom House officials in London, who, after a search, reported the capture at Dover of the poet's present to the French Assembly.

The man who could, for Sir Walter's delectation, manufacture so plausible a myth about "Mollance Meg," would have no difficulty in fabricating the story of Burns's "four carronades."]

know what you would feel to see the much-loved wife of your bosom, and your helpless, prattling little ones, turned adrift into the world; degraded and disgraced from a situation in which they had been respectable and respected, and left almost without the necessary support of a miserable existence. Alas! Sir, must I think that such soon must be my lot? and from the damned dark insinuations of hellish, groundless envy, too? I believe, sir, I may aver it, and in the sight of Omniscience, that I would not tell a deliberate falsehood, no, not though even worse horrors, if worse can be, than those I have mentioned, hung over my head. And I say, that the allegation, whatever villain has made it, is a lie. To the British Constitution, on revolution principles, next, after my God, I am most devoutly attached. You, sir, have been much and generously my friend. Heaven knows how warmly I have felt the obligation, and how gratefully I have thanked you. Fortune, sir, has made you powerful, and me impotent; has given you patronage, and me dependence. I would not, for my single self, call on your humanity: were such my insular, unconnected situation, I would disperse the tear that now swells in my eye; I could brave misfortune; I could face ruin; at the worst, 'death's thousand doors stand open.' But, good God! the tender concerns that I have mentioned, the claims and ties that I see at this moment, and feel around me, how they unnerve courage, and wither resolution! To your patronage, as a man of some genius, you have allowed me a claim; and your esteem, as an honest man, I know is my due. To these, sir, permit me to appeal. By these may I adjure you to save me from that misery which threatens to overwhelm me; and which, with my latest breath, I will say I have not deserved."

On the 2nd of January, 1793 (a week or two afterwards), we find him writing to Mrs. Dunlop in these terms:—(The good lady had been offering him some interest with the Excise Board, in the view of promotion.) " Mr. Corbet can be of little service to me at present; at least, I should be shy of applying. I cannot probably be settled as a supervisor for several years. I must wait the rotation of lists, &c. Besides, some envious malicious devil has raised a little demur on my political principles, and I wish to let that matter settle before I offer myself too much in the eye of my superiors. I have set henceforth a seal on my lips, as to these unlucky politics; but to you I must breathe my sentiments. In this, as in everything else, I shall show the undisguised emotions of my soul. War I deprecate: misery and ruin to thousands are in the blast that announces the destructive demon. But ——"

" The remainder of this letter," says Cromek, "has been torn away by some barbarous hand." I can have no doubt that it was torn away by one of the kindest hands in the world—that of Mrs. Dunlop herself.[1]

---

1 [Neither Cromek nor Lockhart were right in their respective surmises regarding the motive for dissevering the two halves of this letter. Dr. Currie had published one of these in 1800, although under the erroneous date, " January 5, 1792," for " January 5, 1793," the holograph MS. of which we have inspected. A doquet on the back explains the " barbarity " that shocked the veneration of Cromek. It is in the handwriting of Gilbert Burns, and the words are these : — " The inner sheet intemperate—Politics.—G. B." Curiously enough, Dr. Currie preferred making use of the " intemperate " sheet, and the harmless one ultimately falling into the hands of Cromek, was gladly printed by him in the " Reliques." Currie's object in dealing with the dangerous portion becomes apparent on comparing his printed copy with the MS. Through his deletions and interpolations, it would be a *misnomer* to call it a letter of Burns. And that he dealt judiciously with some parts of it may be evinced by here transcribing an excised passage referring to " the inquisitorial spies and informers who have plotted my destruction." He says :—" Can such things be ? Oui! telles choses se font ! Je viens d'en faire un epreuve maudite,—By the way, I don't know whether this is French ; and much would it go against my soul to mar anything be-

The exact result of the Excise-Board's investigation is hidden, as has been said above, in obscurity; nor is it at all likely that the cloud will be withdrawn hereafter. A general impression, however, appears to have gone forth that the affair terminated in something which Burns himself considered as tantamount to the destruction of all hope of future promotion in his profession ; and it has been insinuated by almost every one of his biographers, that the crushing of these hopes operated unhappily, even fatally, on the tone of his mind, and, in consequence, on the habits of his life. In a word, the early death of Burns has been (by implication at least) ascribed mainly to the circumstances in question. Even Sir Walter Scott has distinctly intimated his acquiescence in this prevalent notion. "The political predilections," says he, "for they could hardly be termed principles, of Burns, were entirely determined by his feelings. At his first appearance he felt, or affected a propensity to Jacobitism. Indeed, a youth of his warm imagination in Scotland, thirty years ago,[1] could hardly escape this bias. The side of Charles Edward was that not surely of sound sense and sober reason, but of romantic gallantry and high achievement. The inadequacy of the means by which that prince attempted to regain the crown forfeited by his fathers—the strange and almost poetical adventures which he underwent—the Scottish martial character, honoured in his victories, and degraded and crushed in his defeat—the tales of the veterans who had followed his adventurous standard, were all calculated to impress upon the mind of a poet a warm interest in the cause of the House of Stuart. Yet the impression was not of a very serious cast; for Burns himself acknowledges in a note to one of

---

longing to that gallant people, though my real sentiments of them shall be confined alone to my correspondence with you.]

[1] " Quarterly Review " for February, 1809.

his Jacobite songs—'Strathallan's Lament,' that 'to tell the matter of fact, except when my passions were heated by some accidental cause, my Jacobitism was merely by way of *vive la bagatelle*.' The same enthusiastic ardour of disposition swayed Burns in his choice of political tenets, when the country was agitated by revolutionary principles. That the poet should have chosen the side on which high talents were most likely to procure celebrity ; that he to whom the fastidious distinctions of society were always odious, should have listened with complacence to the voice of French philosophy, which denounced them as usurpations on the rights of man, was precisely the thing to be expected. Yet we cannot but think, that if his superiors in the Excise department had tried the experiment of soothing rather than irritating his feelings, they might have spared themselves the *disgrace* of rendering desperate the possessor of such uncommon talents. For it is *but too certain*, that from the moment his hopes of promotion were utterly blasted, his tendency to dissipation hurried him precipitately into those excesses which shortened his life. We doubt not, that in that awful period of national discord, he had done and said enough to deter, in ordinary cases, the servants of government from countenancing an avowed partisan of faction. But this partisan was Burns ! Surely the experiment of lenity might have been tried, and perhaps successfully. The conduct of Mr. Graham of Fintry, our poet's only shield against actual dismission and consequent ruin, reflects the highest credit on that gentleman.''

In the general strain of sentiment in this passage, who can refuse to concur ? But I am bound to say, that after a careful examination of all the documents printed, and MSS., to which I have had access, I have great doubts as to some of the principal facts assumed in the eloquent statement. I have before me, for example, a letter of Mr.

Findlater, formerly Collector at Glasgow, who was, at the period in question, Burns's immediate superior in the Dumfries district, in which that very respectable person distinctly says:—"I may venture to assert, that when Burns was accused of a leaning to democracy, and an inquiry into his conduct took place, he was subjected, in consequence thereof, to no more than perhaps a verbal or private caution to be more circumspect in future. Neither do I believe his promotion was thereby affected, as has been stated. That, had he lived, would, I have every reason to think, have gone on in the usual routine. His good and steady friend, Mr. Graham, would have attended to this. What cause, therefore, was there for depression of spirits on this account? or how should he have been hurried thereby to a premature grave? I never saw his spirit fail till he was borne down by the pressure of disease and bodily weakness; and even then it would occasionally revive, and like an expiring lamp, emit bright flashes to the last."[1]

When the war had fairly broken out, a battalion of volunteers was formed in Dumfries, and Burns was an original member of the corps. It is very true that his accession was objected to by some of his neighbours; but these were overruled by the gentlemen who took the lead in the business, and the poet soon became, as might have been expected, the greatest possible favourite with his brothers in arms. His commanding officer, Colonel De Peyster, attests his zealous discharge of his duties as a member of the corps; and their attachment to him was on the increase to the last. He was their laureate, and in that capacity did more good service to the government of the country, at a crisis of the darkest alarm and danger, than perhaps any one person of his rank and station, with

---

[1] Letter, Alex. Findlater to Donald Horne, Esq., W.S.

the exception of Dibdin, had the power or the inclination to render. "Burns," says Allan Cunningham, "was a zealous lover of his country, and has stamped his patriotic feelings in many a lasting verse.—His 'Poor and Honest Sodger,' laid hold at once on the public feeling, and it was everywhere sung with an enthusiasm which only began to abate when Campbell's 'Exile of Erin' and 'Wounded Hussar' were published. Dumfries, which sent so many of her sons to the wars, rung with it from port to port; and the poet, wherever he went, heard it echoing from house and hall. I wish this exquisite and useful song, with 'Scots wha hae wi' Wallace bled'—the 'Song of Death,' and 'Does haughty Gaul Invasion threat,'—all lyrics which enforce a love of country, and a martial enthusiasm into men's breasts, had obtained some reward for the poet. His perishable conversation was remembered by the rich to his prejudice—his imperishable lyrics were rewarded only by the admiration and tears of his fellow-peasants."

Lastly, whatever the rebuke of the Excise Board amounted to—Mr. James Gray, at that time schoolmaster in Dumfries, and seeing much of Burns both as the teacher of his children, and as a personal friend and associate of literary taste and talent, is the only person who gives anything like an exact statement; and according to him Burns was admonished "that it was his business to act, not to think"—in whatever language the censure was clothed, the Excise Board did nothing from which Burns had any cause to suppose that his hopes of ultimate promotion were extinguished. Nay, if he had taken up such a notion, rightly or erroneously, Mr. Findlater, who had him constantly under his eye, and who enjoyed all his confidence, and who enjoyed then, as he still enjoys, the utmost confidence of the Board, must have known the fact to be so. Such, I cannot help thinking, is the fair view of the case: at all events, we know that Burns, within two years before he died, was permitted to *act* as a *Supervisor;* a thing not likely to have occurred had there been any resolution against promoting him in his proper order to a permanent situation of that superior rank.

On the whole, then, I am of opinion that the Excise Board have been dealt with harshly, when men of eminence have talked of their conduct to Burns as affixing *disgrace* to them. It appears that Burns, being guilty unquestionably of great indiscretion and indecorum both of word and deed, was admonished in a private manner, that at such a period of national distraction, it behoved a public officer, gifted with talents and necessarily with influence like his, very carefully to abstain from conduct which, now that passions have had time to cool, no sane man will say became his situation ; that Burns's subsequent conduct effaced the unfavourable impression created in the minds of his superiors ; and that he had begun to taste the fruits of their recovered approbation and confidence, ere his career was closed by illness and death. These Commissioners of Excise were themselves subordinate officers of the government, and strictly responsible for those under them. That they did try the experiment of lenity to a certain extent, appears to be made out; that *they* could have been justified in trying it to a farther extent, is at the least doubtful. But with regard to the government of the country itself, I must say, I think it is much more difficult to defend them. Mr. Pitt's ministry gave Dibdin a pension of £200 a year for writing his Sea Songs;[1] and one cannot help remembering, that when Burns did begin to excite the ardour and patriotism of his countrymen by such songs as Mr. Cunningham has been alluding to, there were persons who had

---

[1] By the way, Mr. Fox's ministry gained no credit by diminishing Dibdin's pension during their brief sway, by one-half.

every opportunity of representing to the Premier the claims of a greater than Dibdin. Lenity, indulgence, to whatever length carried in such quarters as these, would have been at once safe and graceful. What the minor politicians of the day [1] thought of Burns's poetry, I know not; but Mr. Pitt himself appreciated it as highly as any man. It could not be said of *him*,

> " Vaces oportet, Eutyche, à negotiis
> Ut liber animus sentiat vim carminis."

" I can think of no verse," said the great Minister, when Burns was no more,—" I can think of no verse since Shakspeare's, that has so much the appearance of coming sweetly from nature." [2]

Had Burns put forth some newspaper squibs upon Lepaux or Carnot, or a smart pamphlet " On the State of the Country," he might have been more attended to in his lifetime. It is common to say, " what is everybody's business is nobody's business;" but one may be pardoned for thinking that in such cases as this, that which the general voice of the country does admit to be everybody's business, comes in fact to be the business of those whom the nation intrusts with national concerns.

To return to Sir Walter Scott's reviewal—it seems that he has somewhat overstated the political indiscretions of which Burns was actually guilty. Let us hear the counter-statement of Mr. Gray, who, as has already been mentioned, enjoyed Burns's intimacy and confidence during his resi-

---

[1] Since the first edition of this Life was published, I have found, that repeated applications in Burns's behalf *were* made by Mr. Addington, now Viscount Sidmouth. I hope this fact will not be omitted in any future narrative of Burns's history.

[2] I am assured that Mr. Pitt used these words at the table of the late Lord Liverpool, soon after Burns's death. How that even might come to be a natural topic at that table, will be seen in the sequel.

dence at Dumfries. No one who knows anything of that excellent man, will for a moment suspect him of giving any other than what he believes to be true.

" Burns," says he, " was enthusiastically fond of liberty, and a lover of the popular part of our constitution ; but he saw and admired the just and delicate proportions of the political fabric, and nothing could be further from his aim than to level with the dust the venerable pile reared by the labours and the wisdom of ages. That provision of the constitution, however, by which it is made to contain a self-correcting principle, obtained no inconsiderable share of his admiration ; he was, therefore, a zealous advocate of constitutional reform. The necessity of this he often supported in conversation with all the energy of an irresistible eloquence ; but there is no evidence that he ever went farther. He was a member of no political club. At the time when, in certain societies, the mad cry of revolution, was raised from one end of the kingdom to the other, his voice was never heard in their debates, nor did he ever support their opinions in writing, or correspond with them in any form whatever. Though limited to an income which any other man would have considered poverty, he refused £50 a year offered to him for a weekly article, by the proprietors of an opposition paper ; and two reasons, equally honourable to him, induced him to reject this proposal. His independent spirit spurned the idea of becoming the hireling of party ; and whatever may have been his opinion of the men and measures that then prevailed, he did not think it right to fetter the operations of that government by which he was employed."

In strong confirmation of the first part of this statement by Mr. Gray,[1] we have the following deliberate expression

---

[1] Mr. Gray removed from the school of Dumfries to the High School of Edinburgh, in which eminent seminary he for many years laboured

of his sentiments in the famous letter to Erskine of Mar.
—" Whatever may be my sentiments of republics, ancient
or modern, I ever abjured the idea of such changes here.
A constitution which, in its original principles, experience
has proved to be every way fitted for our happiness,
it would be insanity to abandon for an untried visionary
theory." This surely is not the language of one of those
who then said and sung broadly and boldly,

> " Of old things all are over old;
>   Of good things none are good enough :
> We'll show that we can help to frame
> A world of other stuff." [1]

As to the delicate and intricate question of Parliamentary
Reform—it is to be remembered that Mr. Pitt advocated
that measure at the outset of his career, and never abandoned the principle, although the events of his time were
too well fitted to convince him of the inexpediency of
making any farther attempts at carrying it into practice;
and it is also to be considered that Burns, in his humble
and remote situation, was much more likely to seize right
principles, than to judge of the safety or expediency of
carrying them into effect.

The statement about the newspaper, refers to Mr. Perry
of the " Morning Chronicle," who, at the suggestion of
Major Miller of Dalswinton, made the proposal referred to,
and received for answer a letter which may be seen in the
General Correspondence of our poet, and the tenor of which
is in accordance with what Mr. Gray has said. Mr. Perry
afterwards pressed Burns to settle in London as a regular
writer for his paper, and the poet declined to do so, alleging

---

with distinguished success. He then became Professor of Latin in the
institution at Belfast, and is now in holy orders, and a chaplain of the
East India Company in the presidency of Bombay. [His labours in
India were very brief; he died there in 1830.]

[1] Wordsworth's " Rob Roy."

that however small, his Excise appointment was a certainty, which, in justice to his family, he could not think of abandoning.[1]

In conclusion, Burns's abstinence from the political clubs, and affiliated societies of that disastrous period, is a circumstance, the importance of which will be appreciated by all who know anything of the machinery by which the real revolutionists of the era designed, and endeavoured, to carry their purposes into execution.

Burns, after the Excise inquiry, took care, no doubt, to avoid similar scrapes; but he had no reluctance to meddle largely and zealously in the squabbles of country politics and contested elections; and thus, by merely espousing, on all occasions, the cause of the Whig candidates, kept up very effectually the spleen which the Tories had originally conceived on tolerably legitimate grounds. Of his political verses, written at Dumfries, hardly any specimens have as yet appeared in print; it would be easy to give many of them, but perhaps some of the persons lashed and ridiculed are still alive—their children certainly are so.

One of the most celebrated of such effusions, and one of the most quotable, was written while he was still at Elliesland, in December, 1789, on a desperately contested election for the Dumfries district of boroughs, between Sir James Johnstone of Westerhall, and Captain Patrick Miller, the younger, of Dalswinton; Burns, of course, maintained the cause of his patron's family. There is much humour in

THE FIVE CARLINS.

    1. There were five Carlins in the south,
        They fell upon a scheme,
    To send a lad to Lunnun town
        To bring them tidings hame.

---

[1] This is stated on the authority of Major Miller.

Nor only bring them tidings hame,
    But do their errands there ;
And aiblins gowd and honour baith
    Might be that laddie's share.

2. There was Maggy by the banks of Nith,[1]
    A dame wi' pride eneugh ;
And Margory o' the Monylochs,[2]
    A carlin auld and teugh :
And blinkin Bess o' Annandale,[3]
    That dwelt near Solway side,
An' Whisky Jean [4] that took her gill
    In Galloway so wide.
And black Joán frae Crichton Peel,[5]
    O' gipsy kith and kin,
Five wighter carlins were na found
    The south countrie within.

3. To send a lad to Lunnun town,
    They met upon a day,
And mony a knight and mony a laird
    Their errand fain wad gae,
But nae ane could their fancy please ;
    O ne'er a ane but twae.

4. The first he was a belted knight,[6]
    Bred o' a border clan,
And he wad gae to Lunnun town,
    Might nae man him withstan',
And he wad do their errands weel,
    And meikle he wad say,
And ilka ane at Lunnun court
    Wad bid to him gude day.

5. The next cam' in a sodger youth,[7]
    An' spak wi' modest grace,
And he wad gae to Lunnun town
    If sae their pleasure was ;

---

[1] Dumfries.   [2] Lochmaben.   [3] Annan.   [4] Kirkcudbright.
[5] Sanquhar.   [6] Sir J. Johnston.   [7] Capt. P. Miller.

He wadna hecht them courtly gifts,
    Nor meikle speech pretend,
But he wad hecht an honest heart,
    Wad ne'er desert a friend.

6. Now, wham to chuse, an' wham refuse,
    At strife thir carlins fell,
For some had gentle folks to please,
    And some wad please themsel'.

7. Then out spak mim-mou'd Meg o' Nith,
    An' she spak up wi' pride,
An' she wad send the sodger youth
    Whatever might betide;
For the auld Gudeman [1] o' Lunnun court
    She didna care a pin;
But she wad send the sodger youth
    To greet his eldest son. [2]

8. Then up sprang Bess o' Annandale,
    An' a deadly aith she's taen,
That she wad vote the Border Knight,
    Though she should vote her lane;
For far-aff fowls hae feathers fair,
    And fools o' change are fain;
But I hae tried the Border Knight,
    And I'll try him yet again.

9. Says Black Joan frae Crichton Peel,
    A carlin stoor and grim,
The auld Gudeman, and the young Gudeman,
    For me may sink or swim;
For fools will prate o' right or wrang,
    While knaves laugh them to scorn;
But the sodger's freends hae blawn the best,
    So he shall bear the horn.

10. Then Whisky Jean spak owre her drink,
    Ye weel ken, kimmers a',
The auld Gudeman o' Lunnun court,
    His back's been at the wa'; [3]

---

[1] The King. [2] The Prince.
[3] Referring to the King's recent illness.

And mony a freend that kiss'd his caup
    Is now a fremit wight,
But it's ne'er be said o' Whisky Jean—
    I'll send the Border Knight.

11. Then slow raise Marjory o' the Lochs,
    And wrinkled was her brow,
Her ancient weed was russet grey,
    Her auld Scots blude was true ;
There's some great folk set light by me,
    I set as light by them ;
But I will send to Lunnun toun
    Wham I like best at hame.

12. Sae how this weighty plea may end,
    Nae mortal wight can tell ;
God grant the King and ilka man
    May look weel to himsel' !

The above is far the best humoured of these productions.
The election to which it refers was carried in Mr. Miller's
favour, but after a severe contest, which lasted for nine
months, and at a very heavy expense.

These political conflicts were not to be mingled in with
impunity by the chosen laureate, wit, and orator of the
district. He himself, in an unpublished piece, speaks of
the terror excited by

   . . . . . "Burns's venom, when
He dips in gall unmix'd his eager pen,
And pours his vengeance in the burning line ;"

and represents his victims as forming "a string of cox-
combs" triumphing over the bard's temporary banishment
from the smile of Maria Riddell, and shouting that

   . . . . . "his heresies in Church and State
Might well award him Muir and Palmer's fate." [1]

---

[1] [The piece here quoted from has been long since published—
"Epistle from Esopus to Maria."]

But what rendered him more and more the object of aversion to one set of people, was sure to connect him more and more strongly with the passions,[1] and, unfortunately for himself and for us, with the pleasures of the other; and we have, among many confessions to the same purpose, the following, which I quote as the shortest, in one of the poet's letters from Dumfries to Mrs. Dunlop:—" I am better, but not quite free of my complaint, (he refers to the palpitation of heart.) You must not think, as you seem to insinuate, that in my way of life I want exercise. Of that I have enough; but occasional hard drinking is the devil to me." He knew well what he was doing whenever he mingled in such debaucheries: he had, long ere this, described himself as parting " with a slice of his constitution " every time he was guilty of such excess.

This brings us back to a subject on which it can give no one pleasure to expatiate. As has been already sufficiently intimated, the statements of Heron and Currie on this head, still more those of Mr. Walker and Dr. Irving, are not to be received without considerable deduction. No one of these biographers appears to have had any considerable intercourse with Burns during the latter years of his life, which they have represented in such dark colours every way; and the two survivors of their number are, I doubt not, among those who must have heard, with the highest satis-

---

[1]   " Lord Frederick heard of all his youthful zeal,
And felt as lords upon a canvass feel;
He read the satire, and he saw the use
That such cool insult and such keen abuse
Might on the wavering minds of voting men produce.
I much rejoice, he cried, such worth to find;
To this the world must be no longer blind.
His glory will descend from sire to son,
The Burns of English race, the happier Chatterton."
                                   CRABBE, in the " Patron."

faction, the counter-statements which their narratives were the means of calling forth from men as well qualified as themselves in point of character and attainment, and much more so in point of circumstance and opportunity, to ascertain and estimate the real facts of a case, which is, at the best, a sufficiently melancholy one.

"Dr. Currie," says Gilbert Burns,[1] "knowing the events of the latter years of my brother's life, only from the reports which had been propagated, and thinking it necessary, lest the candour of his work should be called in question, to state the substance of these reports, has given a very exaggerated view of the failings of my brother's life at that period—which is certainly to be regretted."

"I love Dr. Currie," says the Reverend James Gray, already more than once referred to, "but I love the memory of Burns more, and no consideration shall deter me from a bold declaration of the truth. The poet of 'The Cotter's Saturday Night,' who felt all the charms of the humble piety and virtue which he sung, is charged (in Dr. Currie's Narrative), with vices which would reduce him to a level with the most degraded of his species.—As I knew him during that period of his life emphatically called his evil days, *I am enabled to speak from my own observation*. It is not my intention to extenuate his errors, because they were combined with genius; on that account, they were only the more dangerous, because the more seductive, and deserve the more severe reprehension; but I shall likewise claim that nothing may be said in malice even against

---

[1] Letter to Mr. Peterkin, 1814.—Peterkin's Review, p. 82. [This attempt by Gilbert Burns to shift the obloquy from himself to the venerable shade of Dr. Currie has never been admired. Some of our notes have set evidence before the reader that Gilbert was Currie's chief adviser in preparing the Memoir of his brother, and that he selected, and had even some hand in cooking, the materials placed in that Biographer's hands for his great and, on the whole, nobly executed undertaking.]

him.[1] . . . It came under my own view professionally, that he superintended the education of his children with a degree of care that I have never seen surpassed by any parent in any rank of life whatever. In the bosom of his family, he spent many a delightful hour in directing the studies of his eldest son, a boy of uncommon talents. I have frequently found him explaining to this youth, then not more than nine years of age, the English poets, from Shakspeare to Gray, or storing his mind with examples of heroic virtue, as they live in the pages of our most celebrated English historians. I would ask any person of common candour, if employments like these are consistent with *habitual drunkenness*? It is not denied that he sometimes mingled with society unworthy of him. He was of a social and convivial nature. He was courted by all classes of men for the fascinating powers of his conversation, but over his social scene uncontrolled passion never presided. Over the social bowl, his wit flashed for hours together, penetrating whatever it struck, like the fire from heaven; but even in the hour of thoughtless gaiety and merriment, I never knew it tainted by indecency. It was playful or caustic by turns, following an allusion through all its windings; astonishing by its rapidity, or amusing by its wild originality, and grotesque, yet natural combinations, but never, within my observation, disgusting by its grossness. In his morning hours, I never saw him like one suffering from the effects of last night's intemperance. He appeared then clear and unclouded. He was the eloquent advocate of humanity, justice, and political freedom. From his paintings, virtue appeared more lovely, and piety assumed a more celestial

---

[1] [Chambers, at p. 305, vol. iv., of his "Life and Works of Burns," 1856, says :—" A friend of Mr. Gray has assured me that he used, in private, to speak of the irregularities of the poet in much the same terms as other surviving observers."]

mien. While his keen eye was pregnant with fancy and feeling, and his voice attuned to the very passion which he wished to communicate, it would hardly have been possible to conceive any being more interesting and delightful. I may likewise add, that to the very end of his life, reading was his favourite amusement. I have never known any man so intimately acquainted with the elegant English authors. He seemed to have the poets by heart. The prose authors he could quote either in their own words, or clothe their ideas in language more beautiful than their own. Nor was there ever any decay in any of the powers of his mind. To the last day of his life, his judgment, his memory, his imagination, were fresh and vigorous, as when he composed the 'Cotter's Saturday Night.' The truth is, that Burns was seldom *intoxicated*. The drunkard soon becomes besotted, and is shunned even by the convivial. Had he been so, he could not long have continued the idol of every party. It will be freely confessed, that the hour of enjoyment was often prolonged beyond the limit marked by prudence; but what man will venture to affirm, that in situations where he was conscious of giving so much pleasure, he could at all times have listened to her voice?

" The men with whom he generally associated, were not of the lowest order. He numbered among his intimate friends, many of the most respectable inhabitants of Dumfries and the vicinity. Several of those were attached to him by ties that the hand of calumny, busy as it was, could never snap asunder. They admired the poet for his genius, and loved the man for the candour, generosity and kindness of his nature. His early friends clung to him through good and bad report, with a zeal and fidelity that prove their disbelief of the malicious stories circulated to his disadvantage. Among them were some of the most distinguished characters in this country, and not a few females, eminent for delicacy, taste, and genius. They were proud of his friendship, and cherished him to the last.moment of his existence. He was endeared to them even by his misfortunes, and they still retain for his memory that affectionate veneration which virtue alone inspires." [1]

Part of Mr. Gray's letter is omitted, only because it touches on subjects, as to which Mr. Findlater's statement must be considered as of not merely sufficient, but the very highest authority.

" My connection with Robert Burns," says that most respectable man, [2] " commenced immediately after the admission into the Excise, and continued to the hour of his death. In all that time, the superintendence of his behaviour, as an officer of the revenue, was a branch of my especial province, and it may be supposed I would not be an inattentive observer of the *general* conduct of a man and a poet, so celebrated by his countrymen. In the former capacity, he was exemplary in his attention, and was even jealous of the least imputation on his vigilance : As a proof of which, it may not be foreign to the subject to quote a part of a letter from him to myself, in a case of only *seeming* inattention. ' I know, sir, and regret deeply, that this business glances with a malign aspect on my character as an officer ; but, as I am really innocent in the affair, and as the gentleman is known to be an illicit dealer, and particularly as this is the *single* instance of the least shadow of carelessness or impropriety in my conduct as an officer, I shall be peculiarly unfortunate if my character shall fall a sacrifice to the dark manœuvres of a smuggler.' [3] This of itself affords more than a presumption of his attention to business, as it cannot

---

[1] Letter from Gray to Peterkin, 1814.

[2] Letter from Findlater to Peterkin, 1814.

[3] [This letter of Burns to Findlater has since been published in full. Paterson's Library ed., 1879, vol. v., p. 377. Findlater survived till Dec., 1839, when 81 years of age.]

be supposed he would have written in such a style *to me*, but from the impulse of a conscious rectitude in this department of his duty. Indeed, it was not till near the latter end of his days that there was any falling off in this respect; and this was amply accounted for in the pressure of disease and accumulating infirmities. I will further avow, that I never saw him, which was very frequently while he lived at Elliesland, and still more so, almost every day, after he removed to Dumfries, but in hours of business he was quite himself, and capable of discharging the duties of his office: nor was he ever known to drink by himself, or seen to indulge in the use of liquor in a forenoon. . . . I have seen Burns in all his various phases, in his convivial moments, in his sober moods, and in the bosom of his family; indeed I believe I saw more of him than any other individual had occasion to see, after he became an Excise-officer, and I never beheld any thing like the gross enormities with which he is now charged. That when set down in an evening with a few friends whom he liked, he was apt to prolong the social hour beyond the bounds which prudence would dictate, is unquestionable; but in his family, I will venture to say, he was never seen otherwise than as attentive and affectionate to a high degree."

These statements are entitled to every consideration: they come from men altogether incapable, for any purpose, of wilfully stating that which they knew to be untrue. Yet we are not, on the other hand, to throw out of view altogether the feelings of partial friendship, irritated by exaggerations such as called forth these testimonies. It is scarcely to be doubted that Dr. Currie and Professor Walker took care, ere they penned their painful pages, to converse and correspond with other persons than the enemies of the deceased poet. Here, then, as in most other cases of similar controversy, the fair and equitable conclusion would seem to be, " truth lies between."

To whatever Burns's excesses amounted, they were, it is obvious, and that frequently, the subject of rebuke and remonstrance even from his own dearest friends—even from men who had no sort of objection to potations deep enough in all conscience. That such reprimands, giving shape and form to the thoughts that tortured his own bosom, should have been received at times with a strange mixture of remorse and indignation, none that have considered the nervous susceptibility and haughtiness of Burns's character, can hear with surprise. But this was only when the good advice was oral.[1] No one knew better than he how to

[1] A statement of an isolated character, in the " Quarterly Review " (No. I. penned by Sir Walter Scott), has been noticed at much length, and very intemperately, by Mr. Alex. Peterkin, in his " Review of the Life of Burns, and of the various Criticisms on his Character and Writings," 1815. I am sure that nothing could have been farther from the writer's wishes than to represent anything to Burns's disadvantage; but the reader shall judge for himself. The passage in the critique complained of is as follows :—" The dignity, the spirit, the indignation of Burns, was that of a high-souled plebeian, untinged with the slightest shade of that spirit of chivalry which, since the feudal times, has pervaded the higher ranks of European society. The lowness of his birth, and habits of society, prevented rules of punctilious delicacy from making any part of his education. . . . A very intimate friend, from whom he used occasionally to borrow a small sum for a week or two, once ventured to hint that the punctuality with which the loan was always replaced at the appointed time was unnecessary and unkind. The consequence of this hint was, the interruption of their friendship for some weeks, the bard disdaining the very thought of being indebted to a human being one farthing beyond what he could discharge with the most rigid punctuality. It was a less pleasing consequence of this high spirit, that Burns was inaccessible to all friendly advice. To lay before him his errors, or to point out their consequences, was to touch a string that jarred every feeling within him. On such occasions, his, like Churchill's, was

' The mind which starting heaves the heartfelt groan,
And hates the form she knows to be her own.'

" It is a dreadful truth, that when racked and tortured by the well-

answer the written homilies of such persons as were most likely to take the freedom of admonishing him on points of such delicacy; nor is there any thing in all his correspondence more amusing than his reply to a certain solemn

---

meant and warm expostulations of an intimate friend, he started up in a paroxysm of frenzy, and drawing a sword-cane which he usually wore made an attempt to plunge it into the body of his adviser—the next instant he was with difficulty withheld from suicide."—" Quarterly Review," Feb., 1809.

In reply to this paragraph, Mr. Peterkin says, " The friend here referred to, Mr. John Syme, in a written statement now before us, gives an account of this murderous-looking story, which we shall transcribe *verbatim*, that the nature of this *attempt* may be precisely known. ' In my parlour at Ryedale, one *afternoon*, Burns and I were very *gracious* and confidential. *I did advise him to be temperate in all things. I might have spoken daggers*, but I did not mean them. *He shook to the inmost fibre of his frame, and drew the sword-cane*, when I *exclaimed*, What ! wilt thou thus, and in my own house ? The poor fellow was so wrung with remorse, that he dashed himself down on the floor.' And this is gravely laid before the world at second-hand, as an *attempt* by Burns to murder a friend, and to commit suicide, from which he was with difficulty withheld ? So much for the manner of telling a story. The whole amount of it, by Mr. Syme's account, and none else can be correct, seems to be, that being ' gracious ' one afternoon, (perhaps a little ' glorious ' too, according to ' Tam o' Shanter '), he, in his own house, thought fit to give Burns a lecture on temperance in all things; in the course of which he acknowledges, that he ' *might have spoken daggers* ' —and that Burns, in a moment of irritation, perhaps of justly offended pride, merely *drew* the sword, (which, like every other Excise-officer, he wore *at all times* professionally in a staff,) in order—as a soldier would touch his sword—to repel indignity. But by Mr. Syme's own testimony, Burns only *drew* the sword from the cane : nothing is said of an *attempt* to stab; but on the contrary, Mr. Syme declares expressly that a mock-solemn *exclamation*, pretty characteristic we suspect of the whole affair, wound up the catastrophe of this tragical scene. Really it is a foolish piece of business to magnify such an incident into a ' dreadful truth,' illustrative of the ' untamed and plebeian ' spirit of Burns. We cannot help regretting that Mr. Syme should unguardedly have communicated such an anecdote to any of his friends, considering that this ebullition

lecture of William Nicol,[1] the same exemplary schoolmaster who " brewed the peck o' maut " which " Rob and Allan cam to pree." . . . " O thou, wisest among the wise, meridian blaze of prudence, full moon of discretion, and chief of many councillors ! how infinitely is thy puddle-

---

of momentary irritation was followed, as he himself states, by a friendship more ardent than ever betwixt him and Burns. He should have been aware, that the story, when told again and again by others, would be twisted and tortured into the scandalous form which it at last assumed in the ' Quarterly Review.' The antics of a good man in the delirium of a fever, might with equal propriety be narrated in blank verse, as a proof that he was a bad man when in perfect health. A momentary gust of passion, excited by acknowledged provocation, and followed by nothing but drawing or brandishing a weapon accidentally in his hand, and an immediate and strong conviction that even this was a great error, cannot, without the most outrageous violence of construction, be tortured into an attempt to commit murder and suicide. All the artifice of language, too, is used to give a horrible impression of Burns. The sword-cane is spoken of without explanation as a thing ' which he usually wore,'—as if he had habitually carried the concealed stiletto of an assassin : The reviewer should have been much more on his guard."

The reader may probably be of opinion, upon candidly considering and comparing the sentiments of the reviewer and the re-reviewer :— 1st, That the facts of the case are, in the two stories substantially the same ; 2nd, That when the reviewer spoke of Burns's sword-cane as a weapon which he " usually wore," he did mean " which he wore in *his capacity of Exciseman ;* " 3rd, That Mr. Syme ought never to have told the story, nor the reviewer to have published it, nor the re-reviewer to have given it additional importance by his attempt to explain into nothing what in reality amounted to little. Burns was, according to Mr. Peterkin's story, " glorious " at the time when the incident occurred ; and if there was no harm at all in what he did in that moment of unfortunate excitement and irritation, what means Mr. Syme's own language about " the poor fellow being stung with *remorse ?* " &c.

1 [The " solemn lecture " here referred to is very ironical, as the following excerpt from it will show :—" Edinburgh, 10 Feb., 1793.— Dear Christless Bobbie,—What is become of thee ? Has the devil flown off with thee, as the gled does with a bird ? If he should do so, there is little matter, if the reports concerning thy ' imprudence ' be true. What

headed, rattle-headed, wrong-headed, round-headed slave indebted to thy supereminent goodness, that from the luminous
path of thy own right-lined rectitude thou lookest benignly
down on an erring wretch, of whom the zig-zag wanderings
defy all the powers of calculation, from the simple copula-
tion of units, up to the hidden mysteries of fluxions! May
one feeble ray of that light of wisdom which darts from
thy sensorium, straight as the arrow of heaven, and bright
as the meteor of inspiration, may it be my portion, so that
I may be less unworthy of the face and favour of that
father of proverbs and masters of maxims, that antipode
of folly, and magnet among the sages, the wise and witty
Willy Nicol! Amen! amen! Yea, so be it!

"For me! I am a beast, a reptile, and know nothing!"
&c. &c. &c.

To how many that have moralized over the life and
death of Burns might not such a *Tu quoque* be addressed!

The strongest argument in favour of those who denounce
the statements of Heron, Currie, and their fellow biographers, concerning the habits of the poet, during the latter
years of his career, as culpably and egregiously exaggerated, still remains to be considered. On the whole, Burns
gave satisfaction by his manner of executing the duties of
his station in the revenue service; he, moreover, as Mr.
Gray tells us, (and upon this ground Mr. Gray could not
possibly be mistaken), took a lively interest in the education of his children, and spent more hours in their private
tuition than fathers who have more leisure than his excise-
manship left him, are often in the custom of so bestow-

---

concerns it thee whether the lousy Dumfriesian fiddlers play 'ca Ira,'
or 'God save the King'? Suppose you *had* an aversion to the King,
you could not, as a gentleman, wish God to use him worse than he has
done. The infliction of idiocy is no sign of divine friendship," &c.]

ing; [1] and, *lastly*, although he to all men's regret executed, after his removal to Dumfries-shire, no more than one poetical piece of considerable length, ("Tam o' Shanter"), his epistolary correspondence, and his songs contributed to "Johnson's Museum," and to the great collection of Mr. George Thomson, furnish undeniable proof that, in whatever fits of dissipation he unhappily indulged, he never could possibly have sunk into anything like that habitual grossness of manners and sottish degradation of mind, which the writers in question have not hesitated to hold up to the deepest commiseration, if not more than this, of mankind.

Of his letters written at Elliesland and Dumfries, nearly three octavo volumes have been already printed by Currie

---

[1] "He was a kind and attentive father, and took great delight in spending his evenings in the cultivation of the minds of his children. Their education was the grand object of his life, and he did not, like most parents, think it sufficient to send them to public schools; he was their private instructor, and even at that early age, bestowed great pains in training their minds to habits of thought and reflection, and in keeping them pure from every form of vice. This he considered as a sacred duty, and never, to the period of his last illness, relaxed in his diligence. With his eldest son, a boy of nine years of age, he had read many of the favourite poets, and some of the best historians in our language; and what is more remarkable, gave him considerable aid in the study of Latin. This boy attended the Grammar School of Dumfries, and soon attracted my notice by the strength of his talent, and the ardour of his ambition. Before he had been a year at school, I thought it right to advance him a form, and he began to read Cæsar, and gave me translations of that author of such beauty as I confess surprised me. On inquiry, I found that his father made him turn over his dictionary, till he was able to translate to him the passage in such a way that he could gather the author's meaning, and that it was to him he owed that polished and forcible English with which I was so greatly struck. I have mentioned this incident merely to show what minute attention he paid to this important branch of parental duty."—*Letter from the Rev. James Gray, to Mr. Gilbert Burns.* See his edition, 1820, vol. i., Appendix, No. v.

and Cromek; and it would be easy to swell the collection to double this extent. Enough, however, has been published to enable every reader to judge for himself of the character of Burns's style of epistolary composition. The severest criticism bestowed on it has been that it is too elaborate—that, however natural the feelings, the expression is frequently more studied and artificial than belongs to that species of composition. Be this remark altogether just in point of taste, or otherwise, the fact on which it is founded, furnishes strength to our present position. The poet produced in these years a great body of elaborate prose-writing.[1]

We have already had occasion to notice some of his contributions to "Johnson's Museum." He continued, to the last month of his life, to take a lively interest in that work; and besides writing for it some dozens of excellent original songs, his diligence in collecting ancient pieces hitherto unpublished, and his taste and skill in eking out fragments, were largely, and most happily exerted all along for his benefit. Mr. Cromek saw, among Johnson's papers, no fewer than 184 of the pieces which enter into the collection, in Burns's hand-writing.

His connexion with the more important work of Mr. Thomson, commenced in September, 1792; and Mr. Gray justly says, that whoever considers his correspondence with the editor, and the collection itself, must be satisfied,

---

[1] One of the reviewers of this memoir (John Wilson) says, "Burns never considered letter-writing as a species of composition at all," and attributes the excellence of his epistolary style to its "utter carelessness and rapidity." I am reminded by this criticism of a fact, which I should have noticed before; namely, that Burns often gave the same paragraph in different letters addressed to different persons. I have seen some MSS. letters of the poet to Lady Harriet Don, in which several of the finest and best known passages of his printed letters to Mrs. Dunlop appear *verbatim*. Such was his "utter rapidity and carelessness."

that from that time till the commencement of his last illness, not many days ever passed over his head without the production of some new stanzas for its pages. Besides old materials, for the most part embellished with lines, if not verses of his own, and a whole body of hints, suggestions, and criticisms, Burns gave Mr. Thomson about sixty original songs. It is, however, but justice to poor Heron to add, that comparatively few of this number had been made public at the time when he drew up that rash and sweeping statement, which Dr. Currie adhered to in some particulars without sufficient inquiry.

The songs in this collection are, by many eminent critics, placed decidedly at the head of all our poet's performances: It is by none disputed that very many of them are worthy of his most felicitous inspiration. He bestowed much more care on them than on his contributions to the "Museum;" and the tact and caution of the editor secured the work against any intrusions of that over-warm element which was too apt to mingle in his amatory effusions. Burns knew that he was now engaged on a book destined for the eye and ear of refinement; he laboured throughout, under the salutary feeling, "virginibus puerisque canto;" and the consequences have been happy indeed for his own fame— for the literary taste, and the national music of Scotland; and, what is of far higher importance, the moral and national feelings of his countrymen.

In almost all these productions—certainly in all that deserve to be placed in the first rank of his compositions— Burns made use of his native dialect. He did so, too, in opposition to the advice of almost all the lettered correspondents he had—more especially of Dr. Moore, who, in his own novels, never ventured on more than a few casual specimens of Scottish colloquy — following therein the examples of his illustrious predecessor Smollett; and not foreseeing that a triumph over English prejudice, which

S

Smollett might have achieved, had he pleased to make the effort, was destined to be the prize of Burns's perseverance in obeying the dictates of native taste and judgment. Our poet received such suggestions, for the most part in silence —not choosing to argue with others on a matter which concerned only his own feelings; but in writing to Mr. Thomson, he had no occasion either to conceal or disguise his sentiments. "These English songs," says he, "gravel me to death. I have not that command of the language that I have of my native tongue; in fact, I think my ideas are more barren in English than in Scottish." And again, "so much for namby-pamby. I may, after all, try my hand at it in Scots verse: There I am always most at home." He, besides, would have considered it as a sort of national crime to do anything that might tend to divorce the music of his native land from her peculiar idiom. The "genius loci" was never worshipped more fervently than by Burns. "I am such an enthusiast," says he, "that in the course of my several peregrinations through Scotland, I made a pilgrimage to the individual spot from which every song took its rise, "Lochaber" and the "Braes of Ballenden" excepted. So far as the locality, either from the title of the air or the tenor of the song, could be ascertained I have paid my devotions at the particular shrine of every Scottish muse.[1] With such feelings, he was not likely to touch with an irreverent hand the old fabric of our national song, or to meditate a lyrical revolution for the pleasure of strangers. "There is," says he, "a naiveté, a pastoral simplicity in a slight intermixture of Scots words and phraseology, which is more in unison (at least to my taste, and I will add to every genuine Caledonian taste), with the simple pathos or rustic sprightliness of our native music, than any English verses whatever.[2] One hint more let me

---

[1] To George Thomson, Jan. 26, 1793.

[2] It may amuse the reader to hear, that, in spite of all Burns's success

give you. Whatever Mr. Pleyel does, let him not alter one *iota* of the original airs; I mean in the song department, but let our Scottish national music preserve its native features. They are, I own, frequently wild and irreducible to the more modern rules; but on that very eccentricity, perhaps, depends a great part of their effect."

Of the delight with which Burns laboured for Mr. Thomson's Collection, his letters contain some lively descriptions. "You cannot imagine," says he, 7th April, 1793, "how much this business has added to my enjoyments. What with my early attachment to ballads, your book and ballad-making are now as completely my hobbyhorse as ever fortification was Uncle Toby's; so I'll e'en canter it away till I come to the limit of my race (God grant I may take the right side of the winning-post), and then cheerfully looking back on the honest folks with whom I have been happy, I shall say or sing, ' Sae merry as we a' hae been,' and raising my last looks to the whole human race, the last words of Coila shall be, ' Good night, and joy be wi' you a' ! '

"Until I am complete master of a tune in my own singing, such as it is, I can never," says Burns, " compose for it. My way is this. I consider the poetic sentiment correspondent to my idea of the musical expression,—then choose my theme,—compose one stanza. When that is composed, which is generally the most difficult part of the business, I walk out,—sit down now and then,—look out for objects in Nature round me that are in unison or harmony with the cogitations of my fancy, and workings of my bosom,—humming every now and then the air, with

---

in the use of his native dialect, even the eminently spirited bookseller to whom the manuscript of "Waverley" was submitted, hesitated for some time about publishing it, on account of the Scots dialect interwoven in the novel.

the verses I have framed. When I feel my muse beginning to jade, I retire to the solitary fireside of my study, and there commit my effusions to paper; swinging at intervals on the hind legs of my elbow-chair, by way of calling forth my own critical strictures, as my pen goes. Seriously, this at home is almost invariably my way. What cursed egotism!"[1]

In this correspondence with Mr. Thomson, and in Cromek's later publication, the reader will find a world of interesting details about the particular circumstances under which these immortal songs were severally written. They are all, or almost all, in fact, part and parcel of the poet's personal history. No man ever made his muse more completely the companion of his own individual life. A new flood of light has just been poured on the same subject in Mr. Allan Cunningham's "Collection of Scottish Songs;" unless therefore I were to transcribe volumes, and all popular volumes too, it is impossible to go into the details of this part of the poet's history. The reader must be contented with a few general *memoranda; e.g.*

"Do you think that the sober gin-horse routine of existence could inspire a man with life, and love, and joy—could fire him with enthusiasm, or melt him with pathos, equal to the genius of your book? No, no. Whenever I want to be more than ordinary *in song*—to be in some degree equal to your divine airs—do you imagine I fast and pray for the celestial emanation? *Tout au contraire.* I have a glorious recipe, the very one that for his own use was invented by the Divinity of healing and poetry, when erst he piped to the flocks of Admetus,—I put myself on a regimen of admiring a fine woman."[2]

"I can assure you I was never more in earnest. Con-

[1] To George Thomson, Sept., 1793.
[2] To George Thomson, Oct., 1794.

jugal love is a passion which I deeply feel, and highly
venerate; but somehow, it does not make such a figure in
poesy as that other species of the passion,

> ' Where love is liberty, and nature law.'

Musically speaking, the first is an instrument, of which the
gamut is scanty and confined, but the tones inexpressibly
sweet; while the last has powers equal to all the intellectual modulations of the human soul. Still I am a very
poet in my enthusiasm of the passion. The welfare and
happiness of the beloved object is the first and inviolate
sentiment that pervades my soul; and—whatever pleasures
I might wish for, or whatever raptures they might give me
—yet, if they interfere with that first principle, it is having
these pleasures at a dishonest price; and justice forbids,
and generosity disdains the purchase."——So says Burns
in introducing to Mr. Thomson's notice one of his many
songs in celebration of the "Lassie wi' the lint-white locks."[1]
"The beauty of Chloris," (nevertheless says Allan Cunningham,) "has added many charms to Scottish song; but that
which has increased the reputation of the poet, has lessened
that of the man. Chloris was one of those who believe in
the dispensing power of beauty, and thought that love
should be under no demure restraint. Burns sometimes
thought in the same way himself; and it is not wonderful,
therefore, that the poet should celebrate the charms of a
liberal beauty, who was willing to reward his strains, and
who gave him many opportunities of catching inspiration
from her presence." And in a note on the ballad which
terminates with the delicious stanza,

> " Let others love the city,
>   And gaudy show at summer noon,
> Give me the lonely valley,
>   The dewy eve and rising moon,

---

[1] Nov. 1794. " My Chloris, mark how green the groves."

> Fair-beaming and streaming
>   Her silver light the boughs amang,
> When falling—recalling,
>   The amorous thrush concludes her sang;
> There, dearest Chloris, wilt thou rove,
>   By wimpling burn and leafy shaw,
> And hear my vows of truth and love,
>   And say thou lo'es me best of a'!"

the same commentator adds—" such is the glowing picture which the poet gives of youth, and health, and voluptuous beauty.   But let no lady envy the poetic elevation of poor Chloris ; her situation in poetry is splendid—her situation in life merits our pity—perhaps our charity."

Of all Burns's love songs, the best, in his own opinion, was that which begins,

> " Yestreen I had a pint o' wine,
>   A place where body saw na'."

Allan Cunningham says, " if the poet thought so, I am sorry for it ;" while Mr. Hamilton Paul fully concurs in the author's own estimate of the performance. " I believe, however," says Cunningham, " ' Annie wi' the gowden locks ' was no imaginary person. Like the dame in the old song, she 'brew'd gude ale for gentlemen;' and while she served the bard with a pint of wine, allowed her customer leisure to admire her, ' as hostler wives should do.'"

There is in the same collection a love-song, which unites the suffrages, and ever will do so, of all men. It has furnished Byron with a motto, and Scott has said that that motto is " worth a thousand romances."[1]

---

[1] [" Worth more than that," eloquently added a more recent writer of some celebrity (Mrs. Johnstone), " these four lines are in themselves a complete romance—the alpha and omega of feeling, and contain the essence of an existence of pain and pleasure distilled into one burning drop."]

> " Had we never loved sae kindly,
> Had we never loved sae blindly,
> Never met,—or never parted,
> We had ne'er been broken-hearted."

The " Nancy " of this moving strain was the poet's " Clarinda," of a somewhat earlier date than we are now dealing with. The song was the outcome of a farewell interview betwixt the *quondam* lovers at Edinburgh, on 6th December, 1791, when she was on the eve of sailing to join her husband (Mr. McLehose) in the West Indies.

I envy no one the task of inquiring minutely in how far these traditions, for such unquestionably they are, rest on the foundation of truth. They refer at worst to occasional errors. " Many insinuations," says Mr. Gray, " have been made against the poet's character as a husband, but without the slightest proof ; and I might pass from the charge with that neglect which it merits ; but I am happy to say that I have in exculpation the direct evidence of Mrs. Burns herself, who, among many amiable and respectable qualities, ranks a veneration for the memory of her departed husband, whom she never names but in the terms of the profoundest respect and the deepest regret, to lament his misfortunes, or to extol his kindnesses to herself, not as the momentary overflowings of the heart in a season of penitence for offences generously forgiven, but an habitual tenderness, which ended only with his life. I place this evidence, which I am proud to bring forward on her own authority, against a thousand anonymous calumnies."[1]

---

[1] [This " clencher " of the reverend apologist we reckon to be equivalent to a public announcement that Mrs. Burns had condoned any of her husband's offences of the nature referred to ; and—" O thou impertinent meddler with what is no concern of thine—Is thine eye evil because I am good ? " Robert Chambers (" Life and Works of Burns," 1852) records that on March 31, 1791, the poet's " Anna wi' the gowden locks," above spoken of, was delivered of a female infant, which Burns acknowledged

Among the effusions, not amatory, which Burns contributed to Mr. Thomson's collection, the famous song of "Bannockburn" holds the first place. We have already seen in how lively a manner Burns's feelings were kindled when he visited that glorious field. According to tradition, the tune played when Bruce led his troops to the charge, was "Hey tuttie tattie;" and it has been alleged by Mr. John Syme (still alive, 1829) that it was while humming this old air, as he rode along with him through Glenkens, in Galloway, during a terrific storm of wind and rain, that the poet composed his immortal lyric in its first and noblest form.[1] This is one more instance of his delight in the sterner aspects of nature;

---

as his own offspring. But more than this, he also tells us (p. 260, vol. iii.) that Mrs. Burns, whose son, William Nicol, was born on April 9, 1791, (just nine days after the other,) magnanimously caused the bantling of the Globe inn to be brought to Elliesland, where it was nursed at the same breast with her own son!]

[1] The last line of each stanza was subsequently lengthened and weakened, in order to suit the tune of "Lewie Gordon," which Mr. Thomson preferred to "Hey tuttie tattie." However, almost immediately after having prevailed on the poet to make this alteration, Mr. Thomson saw his error, and discarded both the change and the air which it was made to suit. [Alas! not so soon as "almost immediately" was the restoration yielded to by Thomson. In July, 1799, he published his second volume of songs, in which "Scots wha hae" is found, arranged to the paltry tune of "Lewie Gordon;" and not until December, 1801, did he, in consequence of universal public protest, publish the lyric "in its first and noblest form," to its proper melody. The result of Thomson's pertinacity is the galling fact, for ever to be lamented, that while several holograph copies of "Scots wha hae" still exist in the *Thomsonian* form, not one is to be found, written "after the poet's own heart." The only exceptions are (1) a rough draft, penned on the evening of August 31, 1793 (the night before the bard communicated his finished copy to Thomson); and (2) that same "finished copy" now possessed by Lord Dalhousie. Frederick Locker, author of "London Lyrics," is the proud owner of the rough draft.]

> " Come, winter, with thine angry howl,
> And raging bend the naked tree—"

" There is hardly," says he in his earliest Journal (1784), " there is scarcely any earthly object gives me more—I do not know if I should call it pleasure—but something which exalts me, something which enraptures me—than to walk in the sheltered side of a wood in a cloudy winter day, and hear the stormy winds howling among the trees, and raving over the plain. It is my best season for devotion: my mind is wrapt up in a kind of enthusiasm to *Him*, who in the pompous language of the Hebrew bard, ' walks on the wings of the wind.'" When Burns entered a druidical circle of stones on a dreary moor, he has already told us that his first movement was " to say his prayers." His best poetry was to the last produced amid scenes of solemn desolation.

I may mention here, that during the later years of his life, his favourite book, the usual companion of his solitary rambles, was " Cowper's Task." It is pleasing to know that these illustrious contemporaries, in spite of the widely different circumstances under which their talents were developed, and the, at first sight, opposite sets of opinions which their works express, did justice to each other. No English writer of the time eulogised Burns more generously than Cowper. And in truth they had much in common,

> " The stamp and clear impression of good sense;"

the love of simplicity; the love of nature; sympathy with the poor, humour, pathos, satire, warm and manly hearts; the pride, the independence, and the melancholy of genius.

Some readers may be surprised to find two such names placed together otherwise than by way of contrast. Let it not be forgotten that Cowper had done little more than building bird-cages and rabbit-hutches at the age when the grave closed on Burns.

CHAPTER IX.

"I dread thee, Fate, relentless and severe,
With all a poet's, husband's, father's fear."

WE are drawing near the close of this great poet's
mortal career; and I would fain hope the details
of the last chapter may have prepared the humane reader
to contemplate it with sentiments of sorrow, pure comparatively, and undebased with any considerable intermixture of less genial feelings.

For some years before Burns was lost to his country, it
is sufficiently plain that he had been, on political grounds,
an object of suspicion and distrust to a large portion of
the population that had most opportunity of observing him.
The mean subalterns of party had, it is very easy to suppose, delighted in decrying him on pretexts, good, bad, and
indifferent, equally—to their superiors; and hence, who
will not willingly believe it?—the temporary and local
prevalence of those extravagantly injurious reports, the
essence of which Dr. Currie, no doubt, thought it his duty,
as a biographer, to extract and circulate.

The untimely death of one who, had he lived to anything
like the usual term of human existence, might have done
so much to increase his fame as a poet, and to purify and
dignify his character as a man, was, it is too probable, hastened by his own intemperances and imprudences; but it
seems to be extremely improbable, that even if his manhood had been a course of saintlike virtue in all respects,

the irritable and nervous bodily constitution which he inherited from his father, shaken as it was by the toils and miseries of his ill-starred youth, could have sustained to anything like the Psalmist's "allotted span," the exhausting excitements of an intensely poetical temperament. Since the first pages of this narrative were sent to the press, I have heard from an old acquaintance of the bard, who often shared his bed with him at Mossgiel, that even at that early period, when intemperance assuredly had had nothing to do with the matter, those ominous symptoms of radical disorder in the digestive system, the "palpitation and suffocation" of which Gilbert speaks, were so regularly his nocturnal visitants, that it was his custom to have a great tub of cold water by his bed-side, into which he usually plunged more than once in the course of the night, thereby procuring instant, though but shortlived relief.[1] On a frame thus originally constructed, and thus early tried with most severe afflictions, external and internal, what

---

[1] [It would have been worth the author's while to indicate who was this informant—this " old acquaintance of the bard who often shared his bed with him at Mossgiel." We do not doubt the fact stated; Chambers also records it, while he leads his reader to understand that the cold water was thus applied to restore the tone of his nervous system, weakened by over-exercise of the softer passions. That careful annotator, and latterly biographer, of Burns was long imposed upon by fictitious stories imparted to him by John Blane, who was, in 1828, driver of a stage-coach betwixt Glasgow and South Ayrshire. The old man alleged he had been a farm-servant in the Burns family both at Lochlea and Mossgiel, and for a long time slept in the same bed with Burns in the stable-loft at Mossgiel, while he was composing the poems that were published in 1786. He stated he was about 18 years old when the poet was 26, and was the identical gaudsman who chased the mouse "with murdering pettle" when Burns turned up its nest with the plough in November, 1785. When Chambers afterwards got acquainted with Mrs. Begg, the poet's sister, she cautioned him to beware of Blane's stories, for he was "a leein body."]

must not have been, under any subsequent course of circumstances, the effect of that exquisite sensibility of mind, but for which the world would never have heard anything either of the sins, or the sorrows, or the poetry of Burns !

"The fates and characters of the rhyming tribe," thus writes the poet himself to Miss Craik in 1790, "often employ my thoughts when I am disposed to be melancholy. There is not, among all the martyrologies that ever were penned, so rueful a narrative as the lives of the poets. In the comparative view of wretches, the criterion is not what they are doomed to suffer, but how they are formed to bear. Take a being of our kind, give him a stronger imagination and a more delicate sensibility, which between them will ever engender a more ungovernable set of passions than are the usual lot of man; implant in him an irresistible impulse to some idle vagary, such as arranging wild flowers in fantastic nosegays, tracing the grasshopper to his haunt by his chirping song, watching the frisks of the little minnows in the sunny pool, or hunting after the intrigues of wanton butterflies—in short, send him adrift after some pursuit which shall eternally mislead him from the paths of lucre, and yet curse him with a keener relish than any man living for the pleasures that lucre can purchase; lastly, fill up the measure of his woes by bestowing on him a spurning sense of his own dignity, and you have created a wight nearly as miserable as a poet." In these few short sentences, as it appears to me, Burns has traced his own character far better than any one else has done it since. But with this lot what pleasures were not mingled? "To you, Madam," he proceeds, "I need not recount the fairy pleasures the muse bestows to counterbalance this catalogue of evils. Bewitching poetry is like bewitching woman; she has in all ages been accused of misleading mankind from the counsels of wisdom and the paths of prudence, involving them in difficulties, baiting them with poverty, branding them with infamy, and plunging them in the whirling vortex of ruin : yet, where is the man but must own that all our happiness on earth is not worthy the name—that even the holy hermit's solitary prospect of paradisiacal bliss is but the glitter of a northern sun, rising over a frozen region, compared with the many pleasures, the nameless raptures, that we owe to the lovely Queen of the heart of man ! "

"What is a poet?" asks one well qualified to answer his own question. " He is a man endowed with more lively sensibility, more enthusiasm and tenderness, who has a greater knowledge of human nature, and a more comprehensive soul, than are supposed to be common among mankind ; a man pleased with his own passions and volitions, and who rejoices more than other men in the spirit of life that is in him; delighting to contemplate similar volitions and passions as manifested in the goings on of the universe, and habitually impelled to create them where he does not find them. To these qualities he has added a disposition to be affected, more than other men, by absent things, as if they were present : an ability of conjuring up in himself passions which are far indeed from being the same as those produced by real events, yet (especially in those parts of the general sympathy which are pleasing and delightful) do more nearly resemble the passions produced by real events than anything which, from the motions of their own minds merely, other men are accustomed to feel in themselves." [1] So says one of the rare beings who have been able to sustain and enjoy, through a long term of human years, the tear and wear of sensibilities, thus quickened and refined beyond what falls to the lot of the ordinary brothers of their race—feeling more than others can dream of feeling, the joys and the sorrows that come to them as individuals

---

[1] Preface to the second edition of Wordsworth's Poems.

—and filling up all those blanks which so largely interrupt the agitations of common bosoms, with the almost equally agitating sympathies of an imagination to which repose would be death. It is common to say of those who over-indulge themselves in material stimulants, that they *live fast;* what wonder that the career of the poet's thick-coming fancies should, in the immense majority of cases, be rapid too ?

That Burns *lived fast,* in both senses of the phrase, we have abundant evidence from himself; and that the more earthly motion was somewhat accelerated as it approached the close, we may believe, without finding it at all neces-sary to mingle anger with our sorrow. "Even in his earliest poems," as Mr. Wordsworth says, in a beautiful passage of his letter to Mr. Gray, "through the veil of assumed habits and pretended qualities, enough of the real man appears to show that he was conscious of sufficient cause to dread his own passions, and to bewail his errors ! We have rejected as false sometimes in the letter, and of necessity as false in the spirit, many of the testimonies that others have borne against him;—but, by his own hand—in words the import of which cannot be mistaken—it has been recorded that the order of his life but faintly corresponded with the clearness of his views. It is probable that he would have proved a still greater poet, if, by strength of reason, he could have controlled the propensities which his sensibility engendered; but he would have been a poet of a different class : and certain it is, had that desirable restraint been early established, many peculiar beauties which enrich his verses could never have existed, and many accessary in-fluences, which contribute greatly to their effect, would have been wanting. For instance, the momentous truth of the passage,

> ' Then gently scan your brother man,
>   Still gentlier sister woman—

> Tho' they may gang a kennin' wrang;
>   To step aside is human :
> One point must still be greatly dark
>   The moving *why* they do it:
> And just as lamely can ye mark,
>   How far perhaps they rue it,'

could not possibly have been conveyed with such pathetic force by any poet that ever lived, speaking in his own voice, unless it were felt that, like Burns, he was a man who preached from the text of his own errors; and whose wisdom, beautiful as a flower, that might have risen from seed sown from above, was, in fact, a scion from the root of personal suffering. Whom did the poet intend should be thought of as occupying that grave over which, after modestly setting forth the moral discernment and warm affections of its 'poor inhabitant,' it is supposed to be inscribed, that,

> ' ————Thoughtless follies laid him low,
>   And stain'd his name ? '

Who but himself,—himself anticipating the too probable termination of his own course? Here is a sincere and solemn avowal—a public declaration from his own will— a confession at once devout, poetical, and human—a history in the shape of a prophecy? What more was required of the biographer than to put his seal to the writing, testifying that the foreboding had been realized, and that the record was authentic ? "

In how far the "thoughtless follies" of the poet did actually hasten his end, it is needless to conjecture. They had their share, unquestionably, along with other influences which it would be inhuman to characterise as mere follies— such, for example, as that general depression of spirits, which haunted him from his youth ;—or even a casual expression of discouraging tendency from the persons on whose goodwill all hopes of substantial advancement in the scale of worldly promotion depended—which, in all likelihood, sat more heavily on such a being as Burns, than a man of plain common sense might guess—or that *partial* exclusion from the species of society our poet had been accustomed to adorn and delight, which, from however inadequate causes, certainly did occur during some of the latter years of his life. All such sorrows as these must have acted with two-fold harmfulness upon Burns ; harassing, in the first place, one of the most sensitive minds that ever filled a human bosom, and, alas ! by consequence, tempting to additional excesses ;—impelling one who, under other circumstances, might have sought and found far other consolation, to seek too often for it

> " In fleeting mirth, that o'er the bottle lives,
> In the false joy its inspiration gives,
> And in associates pleased to find a friend
> With powers to lead them, gladden, and defend,
> In all those scenes where transient ease is found,
> For minds whom sins oppress, and sorrows wound." [1]

The same philosophical poet tells us, that

> "——Wine is like anger, for it makes us strong ;
> Blind and impatient, and it leads us wrong ;
> The strength is quickly lost, we feel the error long : "

but a short period was destined for the sorrows and the errors equally of Burns.

How he struggled against the tide of his misery, let the following letter speak. It was written February 25, 1794, and addressed to Mr. Alexander Cunningham, an eccentric being, but generous and faithful in his friendship to Burns, and, when Burns was no more, to his family.

" Canst thou minister," says the poet, " to a mind dis-

---

[1] Crabbe's " Edward Shore," a tale in which that poet has obviously had Burns in his view.

eased ? Canst thou speak peace and rest to a soul tost on a sea of troubles, without one friendly star to guide her course, and dreading that the next surge may overwhelm her ? Canst thou give to a frame, tremblingly alive to the tortures of suspense, the stability and hardihood of the rock that braves the blast ? If thou canst not do the least of these, why would'st thou disturb me in my miseries with thy inquiries after me?

" For these two months I have not been able to lift a pen. My constitution and frame were, *ab origine*, blasted with a deep incurable taint of hypochondria, which poisons my existence. Of late a number of domestic vexations, and some pecuniary share in the ruin of these ***** times —losses which, though trifling, were yet what I could ill bear—have so irritated me that my feelings at times could only be envied by a reprobate spirit listening to the sentence that dooms it to perdition.

" Are you deep in the language of consolation ? I have exhausted in reflection every topic of comfort. *A heart at ease* would have been charmed with my sentiments and reasonings ; but as to myself, I was like Judas Iscariot preaching the gospel ; he might melt and mould the hearts of those around him, but his own kept its native incorrigibility. Still there are two great pillars that bear us up, amid the wreck of misfortune and misery. The ONE is composed of the different modifications of a certain noble, stubborn something in man, known by the names of courage, fortitude, magnanimity. The OTHER is made up of those feelings and sentiments, which, however the sceptic may deny, or the enthusiast disfigure them, are yet, I am convinced, original and component parts of the human soul ; those *senses of the mind*, if I may be allowed the expression, which connect us with, and link us to those awful obscure realities—an all-powerful and equally beneficent God— and a world to come, beyond death and the grave. The first

T

gives the nerve of combat, while a ray of hope beams on the field; the last pours the balm of comfort into the wounds which time can never cure.

"I do not remember, my dear Cunningham, that you and I ever talked on the subject of religion at all. I know some who laugh at it, as the trick of the crafty FEW, to lead the undiscerning MANY; or at most as an uncertain obscurity, which mankind can never know anything of, and with which they are fools if they give themselves much to do. Nor would I quarrel with a man for his irreligion, any more than I would for his want of a musical ear. I would regret that he was shut out from what, to me and to others, were such superlative sources of enjoyment. It is in this point of view, and for this reason, that I will deeply imbue the mind of every child of mine with religion. If my son should happen to be a man of feeling, sentiment, and taste, I shall thus add largely to his enjoyments. Let me flatter myself that this sweet little fellow, who is just now running about my desk, will be a man of a melting, ardent, glowing heart; and an imagination, delighted with the painter, and rapt with the poet. Let me figure him, wandering out in a sweet evening, to inhale the balmy gales, and enjoy the growing luxuriance of the spring; himself the while, in the blooming youth of life. He looks abroad on all nature and through nature, up to nature's God. His soul, by swift delighted degrees, is rapt above this sublunary sphere, until he can be silent no longer, and bursts out into the glorious enthusiasm of Thomson,—

> 'These, as they change, Almighty Father, these
> Are but the varied God,—The rolling year
> Is full of thee;'

and so on, in all the spirit and ardour of that charming hymn. These are no ideal pleasures; they are real delights; and I ask what of the delights among the sons of men are superior, not to say equal to them ? And they have this precious, vast addition, that conscious virtue stamps them for her own, and lays hold on them to bring herself into the presence of a witnessing, judging, and approving God."

They who have been told that Burns was ever a degraded being—who have permitted themselves to believe that his only consolations were those of "the opiate guilt applies to grief," will do well to pause over this noble letter and judge for themselves. The enemy under which he was destined to sink had already beaten in the outworks of his constitution when these lines were penned.

The reader has already had occasion to observe, that Burns had in those closing years of his life to struggle almost continually with pecuniary difficulties, than which nothing could have been more likely to pour bitterness intolerable into the cup of his existence. His lively imagination exaggerated to itself every real evil; and this among, and perhaps above, all the rest; at least, in many of his letters we find him alluding to the probability of his being arrested for debts, which we now know to have been of a very trivial amount at the worst, which we believe he himself lived to discharge to the utmost farthing, and in regard to which it is impossible to doubt that his personal friends in Dumfries would have at all times been ready to prevent the law taking its ultimate course. This last consideration, however, was one which would have given slender relief to Burns. How he shrunk with horror and loathing from the sense of pecuniary obligation, no matter to whom, we have had abundant indications already.[1]

---

[1] The following extract from one of his letters to Mr. Macmurdo, dated December, 1793, will speak for itself :—

"Sir, it is said, that we take the greatest liberties with our greatest friends, and I pay myself a very high compliment in the manner in which

The question naturally arises: Burns was all this while
pouring out his beautiful songs for the " Museum " of Johnson and the greater work of Thomson; how did he happen
to derive no pecuniary advantages from this continual
exertion of his genius in a form of composition so eminently
calculated for popularity ?   Nor, indeed, is it an easy matter
to answer this very obvious question.   The poet himself, in
a letter to Mr. Carfrae, dated 1789, speaks thus : " The
profits of the labours of a man of genius are, I hope, as
honourable as any profits whatever ; and Mr. Mylne's relations are most justly entitled to that honest harvest which
fate had denied himself to reap."   And yet so far from
looking to Mr. Johnson for any pecuniary remuneration for
the very laborious part he took in his work, it appears from
a passage in " Cromek's Reliques," that the poet asked a
single copy of the "Museum" to give to a fair friend, by way
of a great favour to himself—and that that copy and his
own were really all he ever received at the hands of the
publisher.   Of the secret history of Johnson and his book
I know nothing ; [1] but the Correspondence of Burns with

I am going to apply the remark.   I have owed you money longer than
ever I owed it to any man.   Here is Ker's account, and here are six guineas;
and now, I don't owe a shilling to man, or woman either.   But for these
damned dirty, dog's-eared little pages (Scotch bank-notes), I had done
myself the honour to have waited on you long ago.   Independent of the
obligations your hospitality has laid me under, the consciousness of your
superiority in the rank of man and gentleman, of itself was fully as much
as I could ever make head against, but to owe you money too, was more
than I could face."

[1] [Johnson was an honest music-engraver, in very humble circumstances, to whom Burns was introduced in Edinburgh by Wm. Dunbar, W.S., " Colonel of the Crochallan Fencibles."   The poet had a
warm appreciation of the man and his undertaking.   Of him he said,
" I have met with few people whose company and conversation gave me
so much pleasure, because I have met with few whose sentiments are so
congenial to my own."   His name appears in the subscription list for

Mr. Thomson contains curious enough details concerning his connexion with that gentleman's more important undertaking. At the outset, September, 1792, we find Mr. Thomson saying, "We will esteem your poetical assistance a particular favour, besides paying any reasonable price you shall please to demand for it. Profit is quite a secondary consideration with us, and we are resolved to save neither pains nor expense on the publication." To which Burns replies immediately, "As to any remuneration, you may think my songs either above or below price, for they shall absolutely be the one or the other. In the honest enthusiasm with which I embark in your undertaking, to talk of money, wages, fee, hire, &c., would be downright prostitution of soul. A proof of each of the songs that I compose or amend I shall receive as a favour. In the rustic phrase of the season, ' *Gude speed the wark.* ' " The next time we meet with any hint as to money matters in the Correspondence is in a letter of Mr. Thomson, 1st July, 1793, where he says,—" I cannot express how much I am obliged to you for the exquisite new songs you are sending me; but thanks, my friend, are a poor return for what you have done : as I shall be benefited by the publication, you must suffer me to enclose a small mark of my gratitude, and to repeat it afterwards when I find it convenient. Do not return it, for by Heaven, if you do, our correspondence is at an end." [1] To which letter (it enclosed £5) Burns thus replies :—" I assure you, my dear sir, that you truly hurt me with your pecuniary parcel. It degrades me in my own

---

behoof of the poet's widow for Four Pounds, while that of George Thomson is set down for Two Guineas.]

[1] [What could possibly have put the idea into Thomson's head that Burns would return the five pounds ? Did Thomson's letter really contain such an anticipation, accompanied by the thundering threat—" By Heaven ! if you do, our correspondence is at an end"? What has become of the MS. of Thomson's portion of this correspondence ?]

eyes. However, to return it would savour of affectation; but as to any more traffic of that debtor and creditor kind, I swear by that honour which crowns the upright statue of Robert Burns's integrity—on the least motion of it, I will indignantly spurn the bypast transaction, and from that moment commence to be an entire stranger to you. Burns's character for generosity of sentiment and independence of mind will, I trust, long outlive any of his wants which the cold unfeeling ore can supply; at least, I will take care that such a character he shall deserve." In November, 1794, we find Mr. Thomson writing to Burns, "Do not, I beseech you, return any books." In May, 1795, "You really make me blush when you tell me you have not merited the drawing from me" (this was a drawing of the "Cotter's Saturday Night," by Allan). "I do not think I can ever repay you or sufficiently esteem and respect you, for the liberal and kind manner in which you have entered into the spirit of my undertaking, which could not have been perfected without you. So I beg you would not make a fool of me again by speaking of obligation." On February, 1796, we have Burns acknowledging a "handsome elegant present to Mrs. B———," which was a worsted shawl. Lastly, on the 12th July of the same year (that is little more than a week before Burns died), he writes to Mr. Thomson in these terms : "After all my boasted independence, cursed necessity compels me to implore you for five pounds. A cruel . . . . of a haberdasher, to whom I owe an account, taking it into his head that I am dying, has commenced a process, and will infallibly put me into jail. Do, for God's sake, send me that sum, and that by return of post. Forgive me this earnestness ; but the horrors of a jail have put me half distracted. I do not ask this gratuitously ; for, upon returning health, I hereby promise and engage to furnish you with five pounds' worth of the neatest song genius you have seen." To which Mr.

Thomson replies—"Ever since I received your melancholy letter by Mrs. Hyslop, I have been ruminating in what manner I could endeavour to alleviate your sufferings. Again and again I thought of a pecuniary offer; but the recollection of one of your letters on this subject, and the fear of offending your independent spirit, checked my resolution. I thank you heartily, therefore, for the frankness of your letter of the 12th, and with great pleasure inclose a draft for the very sum I proposed sending. Would I were Chancellor of the Exchequer but one day for your sake!———Pray, my good sir, is it not possible for you to muster a volume of poetry? . . . Do not shun this method of obtaining the value of your labour; remember Pope published the 'Iliad' by subscription. Think of this, my dear Burns, and do not think me intrusive with my advice."

Such are the details of this matter, as recorded in the correspondence of the two individuals concerned. About thirteen years after Burns's death, Mr. Thomson was attacked on account of his behaviour to the poet, in an anonymous novel, which I have never seen, called "Nubilia." In Professor Walker's Memoirs, which appeared in 1811, Mr. Thomson took the opportunity of defending himself;[1]

---

[1] "I have been attacked with much bitterness, and accused of not endeavouring to remunerate Burns for the songs which he wrote for my Collection; although there is the clearest evidence for the contrary, both in the printed correspondence between the poet and me, and in the public testimony of Dr. Currie. My assailant, too, without knowing anything of the matter, states, that I had enriched myself by the labours of Burns, and of course, that my want of generosity was inexcusable.

"Now the fact is, that notwithstanding the united labours of all the men of genius who have enriched my collection, I am not yet even compensated for the precious time consumed by me in poring over musty volumes, and in corresponding with every amateur and poet by whose means I expected to make any valuable additions to our national music and song; for the exertion and money it cost me to obtain accompani-

and Professor Walker, who enjoyed the personal friendship
of Burns, and who also appears to have had the honour of

ments from the greatest masters of harmony in Vienna; and for the
sums paid to engravers, printers, and others. On this subject, the testimony of Mr. Preston in London, a man of unquestionable and well-known
character, who has printed the music for every copy of my work, may
be more satisfactory than anything I can say. In August, 1809, he
wrote me as follows: 'I am concerned at the very unwarrantable attack
which has been made upon you by the author of "Nubilia;" nothing could
be more unjust than to say you had enriched yourself by Burns's labours;
for the whole concern, though it includes the labours of Haydn, has
scarcely afforded a compensation for the various expenses, and for the
time employed on the work. When a work obtains any celebrity, publishers are generally supposed to derive a profit ten times beyond the
reality; the sale is greatly magnified, and the expenses are not in the
least taken into consideration. It is truly vexatious to be so grossly and
scandalously abused for conduct, the very reverse of which has been
manifest through the whole transaction.'

"Were I the sordid man that the anonymous author calls me, I had a
most inviting opportunity to profit much more than I did by the lyrics
of our great bard. He had written above fifty songs expressly for my
work; they were in my possession unpublished at his death; I had the
right and the power of retaining them till I should be ready to publish
them; but when I was informed that an edition of the poet's works was
projected for the benefit of his family, I put them in immediate possession
of the whole of his songs, as well as letters;* and thus enabled Dr. Currie

* [This allegation on Thomson's part would have been more weighty
had it been true; but facts are very stubborn things. When Thomson
became aware, immediately after the death of Burns, that he would be
required to surrender the songs and letters of Burns to be published for
behoof of the bereaved widow and family, he pushed forward his own
undertaking with remarkable vigour; and betwixt 1796 and the close of
1799, published for his own behoof the cream of the songs, numbering
thirty-nine, over and above those he had printed in the poet's lifetime.
Moreover, he demanded back all his own letters, and stipulated that the
arrangement of that correspondence for Currie's work must devolve on
himself. All which was submitted to; and, as a consequence, Thomson
had the opportunity to reconstruct his own letters to Burns.]

Mr. Thomson's intimate acquaintance, has delivered an opinion on the whole merits of the case, which must necessarily be far more satisfactory to the reader than anything which I could presume to offer in its room. "Burns," says this writer, " had all the unmanageable pride of Samuel

---

to complete the four volumes, which were sold for the family's behoof to Messrs. Cadell and Davies. And I have the satisfaction of knowing that the most zealous friends of the family, Mr. Cunningham, Mr. Syme, Dr. Currie, and the poet's own brother, considered my sacrifice of the prior rights of publishing the songs, as no ungrateful return for the disinterested and liberal conduct of the poet. Accordingly, Mr. Gilbert Burns, in a letter to me, which alone might suffice for an answer to all the novelist's abuse, thus expresses himself: ' If ever I come to Edinburgh, I will certainly call on a person whose handsome conduct to my brother's family has secured my esteem, and confirmed me in the opinion, that musical taste and talents have a close connection with the harmony of the moral feelings.' Nothing is farther from my thoughts than to claim any merit for what I did. I never would have said a word on the subject, but for the harsh and groundless accusation which has been brought forward, either by ignorance or animosity, and which I have long suffered to remain unnoticed, from my great dislike to any public appearance."

To these passages I now add part of a letter addressed to myself by Mr. Thomson, since this memoir was first published. " After the manner in which Burns received my first remittance, I dared not, in defiance of his interdict, repeat the experiment upon a man so peculiarly sensitive and sturdily independent. It would have been presumption, I thought, to make him a second pecuniary offer in the face of his declaration, that if I did, ' he would spurn the past transaction, and commence to be an entire stranger to me.'

" But, independently of those circumstances, there is an important fact of which you are probably ignorant, that I did not publish above a tenth part of my Collection till after the lamented death of our Bard ; and that while he was alive, I had not derived any benefit worth mentioning from his liberal supply of admirable songs, having only brought out half a volume of my work. It was not till some years posterior to the death, and till Dr. Currie had published all the manuscript songs which I put into his hands for the benefit of his widow and family, that I brought out the songs along with the music, harmonized by the great

Johnson; and, if the latter threw away with indignation,
the new shoes which had been placed at his chamber-door—
secretly and collectively by his companions—the former
would have been still more ready to resent any pecuniary
donation with which a single individual, after his peremptory prohibition, should avowedly have dared to insult him.
He would instantly have construed such conduct into a
virtual assertion that his prohibition was insincere, and his
independence affected; and the more artfully the transaction had been disguised, the more rage it would have
excited, as implying the same assertion, with the additional
charge, that if secretly made it would not be denied. . . .
The statement of Mr. Thomson supersedes the necessity
of any additional remarks. When the public is satisfied,
when the relations of Burns are grateful, and, above all,
when the delicate mind of Mr. Thomson is at peace with
itself in contemplating his conduct, there can be no necessity for a nameless novelist to contradict them."[1]

So far, Mr. Walker:—why Burns, who was of opinion,
when he wrote his letter to Mr. Carfrae, that "no profits

---

composers in Europe.* Those who supposed, therefore, that I had enriched myself by the publication of half a volume, were egregiously
mistaken. The fact is, that the whole five volumes have yielded me a
very scanty compensation for my various outlays upon the work, and for
the many years of labour and research which it cost me."

[1] Life prefixed to Morison's Burns, pp. cviii. cxii.

---

* [The dates of Thomson's publications contradict this assertion. The
second half-vol., embracing twenty-one songs of Burns, appeared in August, 1798; vol. ii., embracing forty songs by Burns, appeared in July,
1799. Dr. Currie's Dedication is dated 1st May, 1800. By the way,
Thomson did not, as is supposed by many, possess the exclusive copyright
of the songs written for his work by Burns. The poet dealt with him as
he did with Johnson. See letter to Thomson of April 7, 1793. "Though
I give Johnson one edition of my songs, that does not give away the
copyright."]

are more honourable than those of the labours of a man of genius," and whose own notions of independence had sustained no shock in the receipt of hundreds of pounds from Creech, should have spurned the suggestion of pecuniary recompense from Mr. Thomson, it is no easy matter to explain; nor do I profess to understand why Mr. Thomson took so little pains to argue the matter *in limine* with the poet, and convince him, that the time which he himself considered as fairly entitled to be paid for by a common bookseller, ought of right to be valued and acknowledged on similar terms by the editor and proprietor of a book containing both songs and music.

They order these things differently now; a living lyric poet, whom none will place in a higher rank than Burns, has long, it is understood, been in the habit of receiving about as much money annually for an annual handful of songs, as was ever paid to our Bard for the whole body of his writings.

Of the increasing irritability of our poet's temperament, amidst the various troubles which preceded his last illness, his letters furnish proofs, to dwell on which could only inflict unnecessary pain. Let one example suffice:—" Sunday closes a period of our curst revenue business, and may probably keep me employed with my pen until noon. Fine employment for a poet's pen! Here I sit, altogether Novemberish, a d—— melange of fretfulness and melancholy; not enough of the one to rouse me to passion, nor of the other to repose me in torpor; my soul flouncing and fluttering round her tenement, like a wild finch, caught amid the horrors of winter, and newly thrust into a cage. Well, I am persuaded that it was of me the Hebrew sage prophesied, when he foretold—' And, behold, on whatsoever this man doth set his heart, it shall not prosper!'—Pray that wisdom and bliss may be more frequent visitors of R. B."—*To Mrs. Riddell*, Nov., 1793.

[On 15th December, 1793, Burns thus addressed Mrs. Dunlop:—" I will not drawl out a heavy letter with a number of apologies for my late silence. Only one I shall mention, because I know you will sympathise in it:—these four months, a sweet little girl, my youngest child[1] has been so ill, that every day, a week or less threatened to terminate her existence.] There had much need be many pleasures annexed to the states of husband and father, for, God knows, they have many peculiar cares. I cannot describe to you the anxious, sleepless hours, these ties frequently give me. I see a train of helpless little folks, me and my exertions all their stay; and on what a brittle thread does the life of man hang! If I am nipt off at the command of fate—even in all the vigour of manhood as I am, such things happen every day—gracious God! what would become of my little flock! 'Tis here that I envy your people of fortune. A father on his deathbed, taking an everlasting leave of his children, has indeed woe enough; but the man of competent fortune leaves his sons and daughters independency and friends; while I—but I shall run distracted if I think any longer on the subject."

Towards the close of 1794 Burns was employed as an acting Supervisor of Excise. This was apparently a step to a permanent situation of that higher and more lucrative class; and from thence, there was every reason to believe the kind patronage of Mr. Graham might elevate him yet farther. [But in the same letter to Mrs. Dunlop (29th Dec.) which announces the interim appointment, and in which he says, " My political sins seem to be forgiven me," he pro-

---

[1] This letter had been mis-dated by Currie " 15th Dec., 1795;" but, *inter alia*, the expression here, " my youngest child," shows that the writer refers to transactions and feelings of 1793. His next child, James Glencairn, was born on Aug. 12, 1794. The little girl here spoken of died in Sept., 1795.]

ceeds thus gravely to moralise :—" What a transient business is life! Very lately I was a boy; but t'other day I was a young man; and I already begin to feel the rigid fibre and stiffening joints of old age coming fast o'er my frame. With all my follies of youth and, I fear, a few vices of manhood, still I congratulate myself on having had in early days religion strongly imprinted on my mind, &c." The letter from which the foregoing extract is made is one of those journal-like packets bearing a string of consecutive dates, which he was fond of addressing to that lady, especially at the Christmas season. Both in 1792, and 1793, at the same season, his correspondence exhibits very striking examples of that practice. We miss his packet to Mrs. Dunlop at Christmas, 1795, but its absence is fully accounted for in the domestic affliction and serious personal illness that overtook him during the latter months of that year. A more probable cause might be the transparent fact that this cherished correspondent of the bard had, for nearly two years, ceased to reply to his letters.]

[On 31st January, 1796, Burns resumed his correspondence with Mrs. Dunlop, in these terms :—" These many months you have been two packets in my debt (*the only published communications are those of June 25, 1794, and Christmas of same year*). What sin of ignorance I have committed against so highly valued a friend, I am utterly at a loss to guess. Alas! madam, ill can I afford, at this time, to be deprived of any of the small remnant of my pleasures.] I have lately drunk deep of the cup of affliction. The autumn robbed me of my only daughter and darling child, and that at a distance too, and so rapidly, as to put it out of my power to pay the last duties to her.[1]   I

---

[1] [The child died and was buried at Mauchline, where she had been conveyed in the hope of receiving benefit by the change, under the nursing of Mrs. Burns's mother.]

had scarcely begun to recover from that shock, when I became myself the victim of a most severe rheumatic fever, and long the die spun doubtful; until, after many weeks of a sick-bed, it seems to have turned up *life*, and I am beginning to crawl across my room, and once indeed have been before my own door in the street.

> ' When pleasure fascinates the mental sight,
>   Affliction purifies the visual ray,
>   Religion hails the drear, the untried night,
>   That shuts, for ever shuts! life's doubtful day.' "

But a few days after this, Burns was so exceedingly imprudent as to join a festive circle at a tavern dinner, where he remained till about three in the morning. The weather was severe, and he, being much intoxicated, took no precaution in thus exposing his debilitated frame to its influence. It has been said, that he fell asleep upon the snow on his way home. It is certain, that next morning he was sensible of an icy numbness through all his joints—that his rheumatism returned with tenfold force upon him—and that from that unhappy hour, his mind brooded ominously on the fatal issue. The course of medicine to which he submitted was violent; confinement—accustomed as he had been to much bodily exercise—preyed miserably on all his powers; he drooped visibly, and all the hopes of his friends that health would return with summer, were destined to disappointment.

" *4th June,* 1796 (King's Birthday.) — I am in such miserable health as to be utterly incapable of showing my loyalty in any way. Rackt as I am with rheumatisms, I meet every face with a greeting like that of Balak to Balaam—' Come, curse me Jacob: and come defy me Israel.' "

" *7th July.*—I fear the voice of the Bard will soon be heard among you no more. For these eight or ten months

I have been ailing, sometimes bedfast and sometimes not; but these last three months I have been tortured with an excruciating rheumatism, which has reduced me to nearly the last stage. You actually would not know me if you saw me—pale, emaciated, and so feeble, as occasionally to need help from my chair.—My spirit's fled! fled! But I can no more on the subject."

This last letter was addressed to Mr. Cunningham of Edinburgh, from the small village of Brow on the Solway Firth, about ten miles from Dumfries, to which the poet removed on Monday, 4th of July; "the medical folks," as he says, "having told him that his last and only chance was bathing, country quarters, and riding." In separating himself by their advice from his family for these purposes, he carried with him a heavy burden of care. "The deuce of the matter," he writes, "is this, when an exciseman is off duty, his salary is reduced. What way, in the name of thrift, shall I maintain myself and keep a horse in country quarters on £35?" He implored his friends in Edinburgh to make interest with the Board to grant him his full salary; "if they do not, I must lay my account with an exit truly *en poete*—if I die not of disease, I must perish with hunger." The application was, I believe, successful; but Burns lived not to profit by the indulgence, or the justice, of his superiors.[1]

---

[1] [In this latter particular, Mr. Lockhart has been guided by a statement to that effect in Dr. Currie's first edition of the Biography. But under better information Currie in his second edition makes the following correction:—"In the first edition it is supposed that the Board of Excise deviated from their usual rule (a shocking one it is!) in our poet's favour. It now appears that the members of the Board were not guilty of any such weakness. The bard's full emoluments were, however, continued to him by the kindness of Mr. Stobbie, a young expectant in the Excise, who performed the duties of his office without fee or reward; and Mr. Graham, of Fintry, on hearing of the poet's illness,

Mrs. Riddel of Glenriddel, a beautiful and very accomplished woman, to whom many of Burns's most interesting letters, in the latter years of his life, were addressed, happened to be in the neighbourhood of Brow when Burns reached his bathing quarters, and exerted herself to make him as comfortable as circumstances permitted. Having sent her carriage for his conveyance, the poet visited her on the 5th July ; and she has, in a letter published by Dr. Currie, thus described his appearance and conversation on that occasion :

" I was struck with his appearance on entering the room. The stamp of death was impressed on his features. He seemed already touching the brink of eternity. His first salutation was, ' Well, madam, have you any commands for the other world ? ' I replied that it seemed a doubtful case which of us should be there the soonest, and that I hoped he would yet live to write my epitaph. (I was then in a poor state of health.) He looked in my face with an air of great kindness, and expressed his concern at seeing me look so ill, with his accustomed sensibility. At table he ate little or nothing, and he complained of having entirely lost the tone of his stomach. We had a long and serious conversation about his present situation, and the approaching termination of all his earthly prospects. He spoke of his death without any of the ostentation of philosophy, but with firmness as well as feeling—as an event likely to happen very soon, and which gave him concern chiefly from leaving his four children so young and unprotected, and his wife in so interesting a situation—in hourly expecta-

---

though unacquainted with its dangerous nature, made an offer of his assistance towards procuring him the means of preserving his health. Unfortunately, that offer arrived too late—his letter is dated 13th July, and probably arrived on the 15th. Burns became delirious on the 18th, and died on the 21st."]

tion of lying-in of a fifth. He mentioned, with seeming pride and satisfaction, the promising genius of his eldest son, and the flattering marks of approbation he had received from his teachers, and dwelt particularly on his hopes of that boy's future conduct and merit. His anxiety for his family seemed to hang heavy upon him, and the more perhaps from the reflection that he had not done them all the justice he was so well qualified to do. Passing from this subject, he showed great concern about the care of his literary fame, and particularly the publication of his post-humous works. He said he was well aware that his death would occasion some noise, and that every scrap of his writing would be revived against him to the injury of his future reputation : that letters and verses written with un-guarded and improper freedom, and which he earnestly wished to have buried in oblivion, would be handed about by idle vanity or malevolence, when no dread of his resent-ment would restrain them, or prevent the censures of shrill-tongued malice, or the insidious sarcasms of envy, from pour-ing forth all their venom to blast his fame. He lamented that he had written many epigrams on persons against whom he entertained no enmity, and whose characters he should be sorry to wound ; and many indifferent poetical pieces, which he feared would now, with all their imperfections on their head, be thrust upon the world. On this account he deeply regretted having deferred to put his papers into a state of arrangement, as he was now quite incapable of that exertion. The conversation was kept up with great evenness and animation on his side. I have seldom seen his mind greater or more collected. There was frequently a considerable degree of vivacity in his sallies, and they would probably have had a greater share, had not the con-cern and dejection I could not disguise, damped the spirit of pleasantry he seemed not unwilling to indulge. We parted about sun-set on the evening of that day (the 5th

U

of July, 1799), and the next day I saw him again, and we parted to meet no more!"

I do not know the exact date of the following, but it must have been either the 7th or 14th July :—

To Mrs. Burns.—" Brow, Thursday.—My dearest Love, I delayed writing until I could tell you what effect sea-bathing was likely to produce. It would be injustice to deny that it has eased my pains, and I think has strength-ened me; but my appetite is still extremely bad. No flesh nor fish can I swallow, porridge and milk are the only things I can taste. I am very happy to hear, by Miss Jess Lewars, that you are all well. My very best and kindest compliments to her and to all the children. I will see you on Sunday. Your affectionate husband, R. B."

There is a very affecting letter to Gilbert, dated the 10th, in which the poet says,—" I am dangerously ill, and not likely to get better. God keep my wife and children." On the 12th, he wrote the letter to Mr. George Thomson, before quoted (page 278), requesting £5 ; and addressed another, still more painful, to his affectionate relative, Mr. James Burnes of Montrose, by whose favour it is now before the reader.

" My Dearest Cousin,

    " When you offered me money assistance, little did I think I should want it so soon. A rascal of a haber-dasher, to whom I owe a considerable bill, taking it into his head that I am dying, has commenced a process against me, and will infallibly put my emaciated body into jail. Will you be so good as to accommodate me, and that by return of post, with ten pounds ? O, James! did you know the pride of my heart, you would feel doubly for me! Alas! I am not used to beg! The worst of it is, my health was coming about finely. You know, and my physician assures me, that melancholy and low spirits are half my disease; guess, then, my horrors since this business began. If I had it settled, I would be, I think, quite well in a manner. How shall I use this language to you ? O, do not disappoint me! but strong necessity's curst command ——

"I have been thinking over and over my brother's affairs, and I fear I must cut him up ; but on this I will correspond another time, particularly as I shall want your advice.

"Forgive me for once more mentioning *by return of post.* Save me from the horrors of a jail !

"My compliments to my friend James, and to all the rest. I do not know what I have written. The subject is so horrible, I dare not look it over again. Farewell.

July 12*th.* "R. B."

The same date appears also on a letter to his friend Mrs. Dunlop. Of these three productions of the 12th of July, who would not willingly believe that the following was penned last ?

"Madam, I have written you so often, without receiving any answer, that I would not trouble you again, but for the circumstances in which I am. An illness which has long hung about me, in all probability will speedily send me beyond that *bourne whence no traveller returns.* Your friendship, with which for many years you honoured me, was the friendship dearest to my soul. Your conversation, and especially your correspondence, were at once highly entertaining and instructive. With what pleasure did I use to break up the seal ! The remembrance yet adds one pulse more to my poor palpitating heart.—Farewell ! "

I give the following anecdote in the words of Mr. M'Diarmid :—"Rousseau, we all know, when dying, wished to be carried into the open air that he might obtain a parting look of the glorious orb of day. A night or two before Burns left Brow, he drank tea with Mrs. Craig, widow of the minister of Ruthwell. His altered appearance excited much silent sympathy, and the evening being beautiful, and the sun shining brightly through the casement, Miss Craig (now Mrs. Henry Duncan) was afraid the light might be too much for him, and rose with the view of letting down the window blinds. Burns immediately guessed what she meant, and regarding the young lady with a look of great benignity, said, ' Thank you, my dear, for your kind attention, but oh let him shine! he will not shine long for me.'"

On the 18th, despairing of any benefit from the sea, our poet came back to Dumfries. Mr. Allan Cunningham,[1] who saw him arrive, " visibly changed in his looks, being with difficulty able to stand upright, and reach his own door," has given a striking picture, in one of his essays, of the state of popular feeling in the town during the short space which intervened between his return and his death. " Dumfries was like a besieged place. It was known he was dying, and the anxiety, not of the rich and the learned only, but of the mechanics and peasants, exceeded all belief. Wherever two or three people stood together, their talk was of Burns, and of him alone. They spoke of his history—of his person—of his works—of his family—of his fame—and of his untimely and approaching fate, with a warmth and an enthusiasm which will ever endear Dumfries to my remembrance. All that he said or was saying—the opinions of the physicians (and Maxwell was a kind and a skilful one), were eagerly caught up and reported from street to street, and from house to house."

" His good humour (Cunningham adds) was unruffled, and his wit never forsook him. He looked to one of his fellow-volunteers with a smile, as he stood by the bed-side with his eyes wet, and said, ' John, don't let the awkward

---

[1] [It has long been widely known that this finely sensational chapter on the Death-bed and Funeral of Burns is a purely " imaginary recollection" of what is described. The writer was a boy several months under twelve years old when Burns died, and it is thought Cunningham was not even in the town of Dumfries when the event occurred.]

squad fire over me.' He repressed with a smile the hopes of his friends, and told them he had lived long enough. As his life drew near a close, the eager, yet decorous solicitude of his fellow-townsmen, increased. It is the practice of the young men of Dumfries to meet in the streets during the hours of remission from labour, and by these means I had an opportunity of witnessing the general solicitude of all ranks and of all ages. His differences with them on some important points were forgotten and forgiven; they thought only of his genius—of the delight his compositions had diffused—and they talked of him with the same awe as of some departing spirit, whose voice was to gladden them no more."[1]

"A tremor now pervaded his frame," says Dr. Currie, on the authority of the physician who attended him; "his tongue was parched; and his mind sunk into delirium, when not roused by conversation. On the second and third day the fever increased, and his strength diminished." On the fourth, July 21st, 1796, Robert Burns died.

"I went to see him laid out for the grave," adds Mr. Allan Cunningham; "several elder people were with me. He lay in a plain unadorned coffin, with a linen sheet drawn over his face, and on the bed, and around the body, herbs and flowers were thickly strewn, according to the usage of the country. He was wasted somewhat by long illness; but death had not increased the swarthy hue of his face, which was uncommonly dark and deeply marked—his broad and open brow was pale and serene, and around it his sable hair lay in masses, slightly touched with grey. The room where he lay was plain and neat, and the simplicity of the poet's humble dwelling pressed the presence of death more closely on the heart than if his bier had been

---

[1] From the "London Magazine," 1824, article, "Robert Burns and Lord Byron."

embellished by vanity, and covered with the blazonry of
high ancestry and rank. We stood and gazed on him in
silence for the space of several minutes—we went, and
others succeeded us—not a whisper was heard. This was
several days after his death."

On the evening of Sunday, the 24th of July, the remains
of the poet were removed to the Trades'-Hall, where they
lay until next morning. The volunteers of Dumfries were
determined to inter their illustrious comrade (as indeed
he had anticipated) with military honours. The chief persons of the town and neighbourhood were anxious to
make part of the procession; and not a few travelled from
great distances to witness the solemnity. The streets
were lined by the fencible infantry of Angus-shire, and the
cavalry of the Cinque Ports, then quartered at Dumfries,
whose commander, Lord Hawkesbury (now Earl of Liverpool[1]), although he had always declined a personal introduction to the poet,[2] officiated as one of the chief mourners.
" The multitude who accompanied Burns to the grave,
might amount," says Cunningham, " to ten or twelve
thousand. Not a word was heard. . . . It was an impressive and mournful sight to see men of all ranks and per-
suasions and opinions mingling as brothers, and stepping
side by side down the streets of Dumfries, with the remains
of him who had sung of their loves and joys and domestic
endearments, with a truth and a tenderness which none
perhaps have since equalled. I could, indeed, have wished
the military part of the procession away. The scarlet and
gold—the banners displayed—the measured step and the
military array—with the sounds of martial instruments,
of music, had no share in increasing the solemnity of the

---

[1] The second Earl of the family, deceased since this Memoir was first
published.

[2] So Mr. Syme has informed Mr. M'Diarmid.

burial scene, and had no connection with the poet. I looked on it then, and I consider it now, as an idle ostentation, a piece of superfluous state, which might have been spared, more especially as his neglected and traduced, and insulted spirit, had experienced no kindness in the body from those lofty people who are now proud of being remembered as his coevals and countrymen. . . . I found myself at the brink of the poet's grave, into which he was about to descend for ever. There was a pause among the mourners, as if loath to part with his remains; and when he was at last lowered, and the first shovelful of earth sounded on his coffin-lid, I looked up and saw tears on many cheeks where tears were not usual. The volunteers justified the fears of their comrade, by three ragged and straggling volleys. The earth was heaped up, and the green sod laid over him, and the multitude stood gazing on the grave for some minutes, and then melted silently away. The day was a fine one, the sun was almost without a cloud, not a drop of rain fell from dawn to twilight.[1] I notice this not from any concurrence in the common superstition, that 'happy is the corpse which the rain rains on,' but to confute the pious fraud of a religious magazine, which made heaven express its wrath, at the interment of a profane poet, in thunder, in lightning, and in rain."

During the funeral solemnity, Mrs. Burns was seized with the pains of labour, and gave birth to a male infant, who quickly followed his father to the grave. Mr. Cunningham describes the appearance of the family, when they at last emerged from their house of sorrow :—" A weeping widow and four helpless sons; they came into the streets in their mournings, and public sympathy was awakened

---

[1] [Literary impudence never went beyond this ! It is a well authenticated fact that during the greater part of the day there was rainfall ; as if Nature wept for the departure of her own minstrel.]

afresh. I shall never forget the looks of his boys, and the compassion which they excited. The poet's life had not been without errors, and such errors too as a wife is slow in forgiving; but he was honoured then, and is honoured now, by the unalienable affection of his wife; and the world repays her prudence and her love by its regard and esteem."

There was much talk at the time of a subscription for a monument; but Mrs. Burns beginning, ere long, to suspect that the business was to end in talk, covered the grave at her own expense with a plain tombstone, inscribed simply with the name and age of the poet. In 1813, however, a public meeting was held at Dumfries, General Dunlop, son to Burns's friend and patroness, being in the chair; a subscription was opened, and contributions flowing in rapidly from all quarters, a costly mausoleum was at length erected on the most elevated site which the churchyard presented. Thither the remains of the poet were solemnly transferred [1] on the 19th Sept., 1815; and the spot continues to be visited every year by many hundreds of travellers. The structure, which is perhaps more gaudy than elegant, was intended to be made even more distasteful by the following inscription, which, fortunately, was never added to it.

IN AETERNUM HONOREM

ROBERTI BURNS

POETARUM CALEDONIAE SUI AEVI LONGE PRINCIPIS
CUJUS CARMINA EXIMIA PATRIO SERMONE SCRIPTA
ANIMI MAGIS ARDENTIS VIQUE INGENII
QUAM ARTE VEL CULTU CONSPICUA
FACETIIS JUCUNDITATE LEPORE AFFLUENTIA

---

[1] The original tombstone of Burns was sunk under the pavement of the mausoleum; and the grave which first received his remains is now occupied, according to her own dying request, by the eldest daughter of Mrs. Dunlop—Mrs. Perochon, who died in October, 1825.

OMNIBUS LITTERARUM CULTORIBUS SATIS NOTA
CIVES SUI NECNON PLERIQUE OMNES
MUSARUM AMANTISSIMI MEMORIAMQUE VIRI
ARTE POETICA TAM PRAECLARI FOVENTES
HOC MAUSOLEUM
SUPER RELIQUIAS POETAE MORTALES
EXTRUENDUM CURAVERE
PRIMUM HUJUS AEDIFICII LAPIDEM
GULIELMUS MILLER ARMIGER
REIPUBLICAE ARCHITECTONICAE APUD SCOTOS
IN REGIONE AUSTRALI CURIO MAXIMUS PROVINCIALIS
GEORGIO TERTIO REGNANTE
GEORGIO WALLIARUM PRINCIPE
SUMMAM IMPERII PRO PATRE TENENTE
JOSEPHO GASS ARMIGERO DUMFRISIAE PRAEFECTO
THOMA F. HUNT LONDINENSI ARCHITECTO
POSUIT
NONIS JUNII ANNO LUCIS VMDCCCXV
SALUTIS HUMANAE MDCCCXV.[1]

Immediately after the poet's death, a subscription was
opened for the benefit of his family; Mr. Miller of Dalswinton, Dr. Maxwell, Mr. Syme, Mr. Cunningham, and
Mr. M'Murdo becoming trustees for the application of the
money. Many names from other parts of Scotland appeared in the lists, and not a few from England, especially

---

[1] A far nobler statue of Burns, by Flaxman (the subscription for
which began among the Scotch gentlemen at Bombay), is now about to
be erected in Edinburgh—and, I am assured, in *the Library of the
University!* (1829.) [This statue is now in the principal exhibition
room of the Royal Scottish Academy. Its first receptacle was the Burns
Monument on the Calton Hill; but the marble was soon observed to
be suffering injury from damp, and was shifted for some years to the
College Library. It is now in its appropriate place. While the sheets
of this edition are passing through the press, Dumfries, apparently
stimulated by the example of other cities and large towns—Glasgow,
Kilmarnock, and Dundee—is placing on the pedestal in its principal
street, a magnificent statue of Burns, executed by a sister of Sir Noel
Paton, who has devoted her genius to the sculptor's art. April, 1882.]

London and Liverpool. Seven hundred pounds were in this way collected; an additional sum was forwarded from India; and the profits of Dr. Currie's Life and Edition of Burns, were also considerable. The result has been that the sons of the poet received an excellent education, and that Mrs. Burns continued to reside, enjoying a decent independence, in the house where the poet died, situated in what is now, by the authority of the Dumfries Magistracy, called Burns' Street.

"Of the (four surviving) sons of the poet," says their uncle Gilbert in 1820, "Robert, the eldest, is placed as a clerk in the Stamp-Office, London. Francis Wallace, the second, died in 1803; William Nicol, the third, went to Madras in 1806; and James Glencairn, the youngest, to Bengal, in 1812—both as cadets in the Honourable Company's service." These young gentlemen have all, it is believed, conducted themselves through life in a manner highly honourable to themselves, and to the name which they bear. One of them (James), as soon as his circumstances permitted, settled a liberal annuity on his estimable mother, which she still continues to enjoy (1829).

Gilbert, the admirable brother of the poet, survived till the 27th of April, 1827. He removed from Mossgiel, shortly after the death of Burns, to a farm in Dumfriesshire, carrying with him his aged mother. She died under his roof at a later period, when he became factor to the noble family of Blantyre, on their estates in East Lothian. The pecuniary succours which the poet afforded Gilbert Burns, and still more the interest excited in his behalf by the account of his personal character contained in Currie's Memoir, proved of high advantage to him. He trained up a large family, six sons and five daughters, and bestowed on all his boys what is called a classical education. The untimely death of one of these, a young man of very promising talents, when on the eve of being admitted to holy

orders, is supposed to have hastened the departure of the
venerable parent. It should not be omitted that, on the
publication of his edition of his brother's works, in 1820,
Gilbert repaid, with interest, the sum which the poet advanced to him in 1788. Through life, and in death, he
maintained and justified the promise of his virtuous youth,
and seems in all respects to have resembled his father, of
whom Murdoch, long after he was no more, wrote in language honourable to his own heart: " O for a world of men
of such dispositions! I have often wished, for the good of
mankind, that it were as customary to honour and per-
petuate the memory of those who excel in moral rectitude,
as it is to extol what are called heroic actions : then would
the mausoleum of the friend of my youth overtop and surpass most of those we see in Westminster Abbey!"[1]

It is pleasing to trace in all these details, the happy
influence which our poet's genius has exerted over the des-
tinies of his connections. " In the fortunes of his family,"
says Mr. M'Diarmid,[2] "there are few who do not feel the
liveliest interest; and were a register kept of the names,
and numbers, and characters, of those who from time to
time visit the humble but decent abode in which Burns
breathed his last, amid the deepest despondency for the fate
of those who were dearer to him than life, and in which his
widow is spending tranquilly the evening of her days in
the enjoyment of a competency, not derived from the public,
but from the honourable exertions of her own offspring—
the detail, though dry, would be pleasing to many, and
would weaken, though it could not altogether efface, one of
the greatest stains on the character of our country. Even
as it is, his name has proved a source of patronage to those

---

[1] These particulars are taken from an article which appeared soon
after Gilbert's death, in the " Dumfries Courier."

[2] Article in the " Dumfries Magazine," August, 1825.

he left behind him, such as the high and the noble cannot always command. Wherever his sons wander, at home or abroad, they are regarded as the scions of a noble stock, and receive the cordial greetings of hundreds who never saw their faces before, but who account it a happiness to grasp in friendly pressure the proffered hand in which circulates the blood of Burns."[1]

Sic vos non vobis. The great poet himself, whose name is enough to ennoble his children's children, was, to the eternal disgrace of his country, suffered to live and die in penury, and, as far as such a creature could be degraded by any external circumstances, in degradation. Who can open the page of Burns, and remember without a blush, that the author of such verses, the human being whose breast glowed with such feelings, was doomed to earn mere bread for his children by casting up the stock of publicans' cellars, and riding over moors and mosses in quest of smuggling stills? The subscription for his Poems was, for the time, large and liberal, and perhaps absolves a certain number of the gentry of Scotland as individuals; but that some strong movement of indignation did not spread over the whole kingdom, when it was known that Robert Burns, after being caressed and flattered by the noblest and most learned of his countrymen, was about to be established as a common gauger among

---

[1] Mr. M'Diarmid, in the article above quoted, gives a touching account of the illness and death of one of the daughters of Mr. James Glencairn Burns, on her voyage homewards from India. " At the funeral of this poor child there was witnessed," says he, "a most affecting scene. Officers, passengers, and men, were drawn up in regular order on deck; some wore crape round the right arm, others were dressed in the deepest mourning; every head was uncovered; and as the lashing of the waves on the sides of the coffin proclaimed that the melancholy ceremony had closed, every countenance seemed saddened with grief—every eye moistened with tears. Not a few of the sailors wept outright, natives of Scotland, who, even when far away, had revived their recollections of home and youth, by listening to, or repeating the poetry of Burns."

the wilds of Nithsdale—and that, after he was so established, no interference from a higher quarter arrested that unworthy career :—these are circumstances which must continue to bear heavily on the memory of that generation, and especially of those who then administered the public patronage of Scotland.

In defence, or at least in palliation, of this national crime, two false arguments, the one resting on facts grossly exaggerated, the other having no foundation whatever either on knowledge or on wisdom, have been rashly set up, and arrogantly as well as ignorantly maintained. To the one, namely, that public patronage would have been wrongfully bestowed on the Poet, because the Exciseman was a political partisan, it is hoped the details embodied in this narrative have supplied a sufficient answer : had the matter been as bad as the boldest critics have ever ventured to insinuate, Sir Walter Scott's answer would still have remained—" this partisan was BURNS." The other argument is a still more heartless, as well as absurd one ; to wit, that from the moral character and habits of the man, no patronage, however liberal, could have influenced and controlled his conduct, so as to work lasting and effective improvement, and lengthen his life by raising it more nearly to the elevation of his genius. This is indeed a candid and a generous method of judging. Are imprudence and intemperance, then, found to increase usually in proportion as the worldly circumstances of men are easy ? Is not the very opposite of this doctrine acknowledged by almost all that have ever tried the reverses of fortune's wheel themselves—by all that have contemplated from an elevation, not too high for sympathy, the usual course of manners, when their fellow-creatures either encounter or live in constant apprehension of

> " The thousand ills that rise where money fails,
> Debts, threats, and duns, bills, bailiffs, writs, and jails ?"

To such mean miseries the latter years of Burns's life were exposed, not less than his early youth, and after what natural buoyancy of animal spirits he ever possessed had sunk under the influence of time, which, surely bringing experience, fails seldom to bring care also and sorrow, to spirits more mercurial than his; and in what bitterness of spirit he submitted to his fate, let his own burning words once more tell us. "Take," says he, writing to one who never ceased to be his friend—"take these two guineas, and place them over against that . . . . account of yours, which has gagged my mouth these five or six months! I can as little write good things, as apologies, to the man I owe money to. O the supreme curse of making three guineas do the business of five! Poverty! thou half-sister of death, thou cousin-german of hell! Oppressed by thee, the man of sentiment, whose heart glows with independence, and melts with sensibility, inly pines under the neglect, or writhes, in bitterness of soul, under the contumely of arrogant, unfeeling wealth. Oppressed by thee, the son of genius, whose ill-starred ambition plants him at the tables of the fashionable and polite, must see, in suffering silence, his remark neglected, and his person despised, while shallow greatness, in his idiot attempts at wit, shall meet with countenance and applause. Nor is it only the family of worth that have reason to complain of thee; the children of folly and vice, though, in common with thee, the offspring of evil, smart equally under thy rod. The man of unfortunate disposition and neglected education is condemned as a fool for his dissipation, despised and shunned as a needy wretch, when his follies, as usual, bring him to want; and when his necessities drive him to dishonest practices, he is abhorred as a miscreant, and perishes by the justice of his country. But far otherwise is the lot of the man of family and fortune. *His* early follies and extravagance are spirit and fire; *his* consequent wants are the embarrassment of an

honest fellow ; and when to remedy the matter, he has
gained a legal commission to plunder distant provinces, or
massacre peaceful nations, he returns, perhaps, laden with
the spoils of rapine and murder ; lives wicked and respected,
and dies a . . . . and a lord. Nay, worst of all,
alas for helpless woman ! The needy prostitute, who has
shivered at the corner of the street, waiting to earn the
wages of casual prostitution, is left neglected and insulted,
ridden down by the chariot-wheels of the coroneted RIP,
hurrying on to the guilty assignation ; she, who, without the
same necessities to plead, riots nightly in the same guilty
trade. Well ! Divines may say of it what they please,
but execration is to the mind, what phlebotomy is to the
body ; the vital sluices of both are wonderfully relieved by
their respective evacuations." (To Peter Hill, 17 January,
1791.)

In such evacuations of indignant spleen the proud heart
of many an unfortunate genius, besides this, has found, or
sought relief ; and to other more dangerous indulgences,
the affliction of such sensitive spirits had often, ere this
time, condescended. The list is a long and painful one ;
and it includes some names that can claim but a scanty
share in the apology of Burns. Addison himself, the
elegant, the philosophical, the religious Addison, must be
numbered with these offenders :—Johnson, Cotton, Prior,
Parnell, Otway, Savage, all sinned in the same sort ; and
the transgressions of them all have been leniently dealt
with in comparison with those of one whose genius was
probably greater than any of theirs ; his appetites more
fervid, his temptations more abundant, his repentance
more severe. The beautiful genius of Collins sunk under
similar contaminations ; and those who have, from dulness
of head, or sourness of heart, joined in the too general
clamour against Burns, may learn a lesson of candour, of
mercy, and of justice, from the language in which one of

the best of men, and loftiest of moralists, has commented on frailties that hurried a kindred spirit to a like untimely grave.

"In a long continuance of poverty, and long habits of dissipation," says Johnson, "it cannot be expected that any character should be exactly uniform. That this man, wise and virtuous as he was, passed always unentangled through the snares of life, it would be prejudice and temerity to affirm : but it may be said that he at least preserved the source of action unpolluted, that his principles were never shaken, that his distinctions of right and wrong were never confounded, and that his faults had nothing of malignity or design, but proceeded from some unexpected pressure or casual temptation. Such was the fate of Collins, with whom I once delighted to converse, and whom I yet remember with tenderness."

Burns was an honest man: after all his struggles, his pecuniary liabilities were almost *nil* when he died. His heart was always warm and his hand open. "His charities," says Mr. Gray, "were great beyond his means;" and I have to thank Mr. Allan Cunningham for the following anecdote, for which I am sure every reader will thank him too. Mr. Maxwell of Teraughty, an old, austere, sarcastic gentleman, who cared nothing about poetry, used to say when the Excise-books of the district were produced at the meetings of the justices—"Bring me Burns's journal: it always does me good to see it, for it shows that an honest officer may carry a kind heart about with him."

Of his religious principles, we are bound to judge by what he has told us himself in his more serious moments. He sometimes doubted with the sorrow, what in the main he believed with the fervour, of a poet. "It occasionally haunts me," says he in one of his letters—"the dark suspicion, that immortality may be only too good news to be true;" and here, as on many points besides, how much did his method of thinking (I fear I must add of acting) resemble that of a noble poet more recently lost to us! " I am no bigot to infidelity," said Lord Byron, "and did not expect that because I doubted the immortality of man, I should be charged with denying the existence of a God. It was the comparative insignificance of ourselves and our world, when placed in comparison with the mighty whole, of which it is an atom, that first led me to imagine that our pretensions to immortality might be overrated." I dare not pretend to quote the sequel from memory; but the effect was, that Byron, like Burns, complained of " the early discipline of Scotch Calvinism," and the natural gloom of a melancholy heart, as having between them engendered "a hypochondriacal *disease*," which occasionally visited and depressed him through life. In the opposite scale, we are, in justice to Burns, to place many pages which breathe the ardour, nay, the exultation of faith, and the humble sincerity of Christian hope ; and as the poet himself has warned us, it well befits us " at the balance to be mute." Let us avoid, in the name of religion herself, the fatal error of those who would rashly swell the catalogue of the enemies of religion. " A sally of levity," says once more Dr. Johnson, " an indecent jest, an unreasonable objection, are sufficient, in the opinion of some men, to efface a name from the lists of Christianity, to exclude a soul from everlasting life. Such men are so watchful to censure, that they have seldom much care to look for favourable interpretations of ambiguities, or to know how soon any step of inadvertency has been expiated by sorrow and retractation, but let fly their fulminations without mercy or prudence against slight offences or casual temerities, against crimes never committed, or immediately repented. The zealot should recollect, that he is labouring, by this frequency of excommunication, against his own cause, and voluntarily adding strength to the enemies of truth. It must always be the condition of a great part of mankind, to reject and embrace tenets upon the authority of those whom they think wiser than themselves, and therefore the addition of every name to infidelity, in some degree invalidates that argument upon which the religion of multitudes is necessarily founded."[1] In conclusion, let me adopt the sentiment of that illustrious moral poet of our own time, whose generous defence of Burns will be remembered while the language lasts:—

> " Let no mean hope your souls enslave—
> Be independent, generous, brave;
> Your *Poet* such example gave,
>   And such revere;
> But be admonish'd by his grave,
>   And think and fear." [2]

It is possible, perhaps for some it may be easy, to imagine a character of a much higher cast than that of Burns, developed, too, under circumstances in many respects not unlike those of his history—the character of a man of lowly birth, and powerful genius, elevated by that philosophy which is alone pure and divine, far above all those annoyances of terrestrial spleen and passion, which mixed from the beginning with the workings of his inspiration, and in the end were able to eat deep into the great heart which they had long tormented. Such a being would have received, no question, a species of devout reverence (I mean when the grave had closed on him) to which the warmest admirers of our poet can advance no pretensions for their unfortunate favourite; but could such a being have delighted his species—could he even have instructed them like Burns ? Ought we not to be thankful for every new

---

[1] " Life of Sir Thomas Browne."
[2] Wordsworth's Address to the Sons of Burns, on visiting his grave in 1803.

variety of form and circumstance, in and under which the ennobling energies of true and lofty genius are found addressing themselves to the common brethren of the race? Would we have none but Miltons and Cowpers in poetry— but Brownes and Southeys in prose? Alas! if it were so, to how large a portion of the species would all the gifts of all the muses remain for ever a fountain shut up and a book sealed? Were the doctrine of intellectual excommunication to be thus expounded and enforced, how small the library that would remain to kindle the fancy, to draw out and refine the feelings, to enlighten the head by expanding the heart of man! From Aristophanes to Byron, how broad the sweep, how woeful the desolation!

In the absence of that vehement sympathy with humanity as it is, its sorrows and its joys as they are, we might have had a great man, perhaps a great poet; but we could have had no Burns. It is very noble to despise the accidents of fortune; but what moral homily concerning these could have equalled that which Burns's poetry, considered alongside of Burns's history, and the history of his fame, presents! It is very noble to be above the allurements of pleasure; but who preaches so effectually against them as he who sets forth, in immortal verse, his own intense sympathy with those that yield, and in verse and in prose, in action and in passion, in life and in death, the dangers and the miseries of yielding?

It requires a graver audacity of hypocrisy than falls to the share of most men, to declaim against Burns's sensibility to the tangible cares and toils of his earthly condition; there are more who venture on broad denunciations of his sympathy with the joys of sense and passion. To these, the great moral poet already quoted, speaks in the following noble passage—and must he speak in vain? "Permit me," says he, " to remind you that it is the privilege of poetic genius to catch, under certain restrictions, of

which perhaps at the time of its being exerted it is but
dimly conscious, a spirit of pleasure wherever it can be
found—in the walks of nature, and in the business of men.
The poet, trusting to primary instincts, luxuriates among
the felicities of love and wine, and is enraptured while he
describes the fairer aspects of war; nor does he shrink
from the company of the passion of love, though immo-
derate—from convivial pleasure, though intemperate—nor
from the presence of war, though savage, and recognized
as the handmaid of desolation." Frequently and admirably
has Burns given way to these impulses of nature, both
with reference to himself, and in describing the condition
of others. Who, but some impenetrable dunce or narrow-
minded puritan in works of art, ever read without delight
the picture which he has drawn of the convivial exaltation
of the rustic adventurer, "Tam o' Shanter?" The poet
fears not to tell the reader in the outset that his hero was
a desperate and sottish drunkard, whose excesses were frequent as his opportunities. This reprobate sits down to
his cups, while the storm is roaring, and heaven and earth
are in confusion—the night is driven on by song and
tumultuous noise—laughter and jest thicken as the bever-
age improves upon the palate—conjugal fidelity archly
bends to the service of general benevolence—selfishness is
not absent, but wearing the mask of social cordiality—and,
while these various elements of humanity are blended into
one proud and happy composition of elated spirits, the anger
of the tempest without doors only heightens and sets off
the enjoyment within. I pity him who cannot perceive
that, in all this, though there was no moral purpose, there
is a moral effect.

> " Kings may be blest, but Tam was glorious,
> O'er a' the *ills* of life victorious."

" What a lesson do these words convey of charitable indulgence for the vicious habits of the principal actor in this scene, and of those who resemble him! Men, who to the rigidly virtuous are objects almost of loathing, and whom therefore they cannot serve! The poet, penetrating the unsightly and disgusting surfaces of things, has unveiled, with exquisite skill, the finer ties of imagination and feeling that often bind these beings to practices productive of much unhappiness to themselves, and to those whom it is their duty to cherish—and, as far as he puts the reader into possession of this intelligent sympathy, he qualifies him for exercising a salutary influence over the minds of those who are thus deplorably deceived."[1]

That some men in every age will comfort themselves in the practice of certain vices, by reference to particular passages both in the history and in the poetry of Burns, there is all reason to fear; but surely the general influence of both is calculated, and has been found, to produce far different effects. The universal popularity which his writings have all along enjoyed among one of the most virtuous of nations, is, of itself, surely a decisive circumstance. Search Scotland over, from the Pentland to the Solway, and there is not a cottage-hut so poor and wretched as to be without its Bible; and hardly one that, on the same shelf, and next to it, does not treasure a Burns. Have the people degenerated since the adoption of this new manual? Has their attachment to the Book of Books declined? Are their hearts less firmly bound, than were the hearts of their fathers, to the old faith and the old virtues? I believe he that knows the most of the country will be the readiest to answer all these questions, as every lover of genius and virtue would desire to hear them answered.

On one point there can be no controversy; the poetry of Burns has had most powerful influence in reviving and

---

[1] Wordsworth's Letter to Gray, p. 24.

strengthening the national feelings of his countrymen. Amidst penury and labour, his youth fed on the old minstrelsy and traditional glories of his nation, and his genius divined that what he felt so deeply must belong to a spirit that might lie smothered around him, but could not be extinguished. The political circumstances of Scotland were, and had been, such as to starve the flame of patriotism; the popular literature had striven, and not in vain, to make itself English; and, above all, a new and a cold system of speculative philosophy had begun to spread widely among us. A peasant appeared, and set himself to check the creeping pestilence of this indifference. Whatever genius has since then been devoted to the illustration of the national manners, and sustaining thereby of the national feelings of the people, there can be no doubt that Burns will ever be remembered as the founder, and, alas! in his own person as the martyr, of this reformation.

That which is now-a-days called, by solitary eminence, the *wealth* of the nation, had been on the increase ever since our incorporation with a greater and wealthier state —nay, that the laws had been improving, and, above all, the administration of the laws, it would be mere bigotry to dispute. It may also be conceded easily, that the national mind had been rapidly clearing itself of many injurious prejudices—that the people, as a people, had been gradually and surely advancing in knowledge and wisdom, as well as in wealth and security. But all this good had not been accomplished without rude work. If the improvement were valuable, it had been purchased dearly. "The spring fire," Allan Cunningham says beautifully somewhere, "which destroys the furze, makes an end also of the nests of a thousand song-birds; and he who goes a trouting with lime, leaves little of life in the stream." We were getting fast ashamed of many precious and beautiful things, only for that they were old and our own.

It has already been remarked, how even Smollett, who began with a national tragedy, and one of the noblest of national lyrics, never dared to make use of the dialect of his own country; and how Moore, another enthusiastic Scotsman, followed in this respect, as in others, the example of Smollett, and over and over again counselled Burns to do the like. But a still more striking sign of the times is to be found in the style adopted by both of these novelists, especially the great master of the art, in the representations of the manners and characters of their own countrymen. In " Humphrey Clinker," the last and best of Smollett's tales, there are some traits of a better kind —but, taking his works as a whole, the impression conveyed is certainly a painful, a disgusting one. The Scotchmen of these authors are the Jockies and Archies of farce—

" Time out of·mind the Southrons' mirthmakers "—

the best of them grotesque combinations of simplicity and hypocrisy, pride and meanness. When such men, high-spirited Scottish gentlemen, possessed of learning and talents, and one of them at least, of splendid genius, felt, or fancied, the necessity of making such submissions to the prejudices of the dominant nation, and did so without exciting a murmur among their own countrymen, we may form some notion of the boldness of Burns's experiment; and on contrasting the state of things then with what is before us now, it will cost no effort to appreciate the nature and consequences of the victory in which our poet led the way, by achievements never in their kind to be surpassed.[1]

---

[1] " He was," says a writer, in whose language a brother poet will be recognized—" he was in many respects born at a happy time ; happy for a man of genius like him, but fatal and hopeless to the more common mind. A whole world of life lay before Burns, whose inmost recesses, and darkest nooks, and sunniest eminences, he had familiarly trodden from his childhood. All that world he felt could be made his own. No

"Burns," says Mr Campbell, "has given elixir vitæ to his dialect;"[1]—he gave it to more than his dialect.

The moral influence of his genius has not been confined to his own countrymen. "The range of the *pastoral*," said Johnson, "is narrow. Poetry cannot dwell upon the minuter distinctions by which one species differs from another, without departing from that simplicity of grandeur which *fills the imagination;* nor dissect the latent qualities of things, without losing its *general power of gratifying every mind by recalling its own conceptions.* Not only the images of rural life, but the occasions on which they can be properly applied, are few and general. The state of a man confined to the employments and pleasures of the country, is so little diversified, and exposed to so few of those accidents which produce perplexities, terrors, and surprises, in more complicated transactions, that he can be shown but seldom in such circumstances as attract curiosity. His ambition is without policy, and his love without intrigue. He has no complaints to make of his rival, but that he is richer than himself; nor any disasters to lament, but a cruel mistress or a bad harvest."[2] Such were the notions of the great arbiter of taste, whose dicta formed the creed of the British world, at the time when Burns made his appearance to overturn all such dogmata at a single blow; to convince the loftiest of the noble, and the daintiest of

---

conqueror had overrun its fertile provinces, and it was for him to be crowned supreme over all the

"'Lyric singers of that high-soul'd land.'

The crown that he has won can never be removed from his head. Much is yet left for other poets, even among that life where his spirit delighted to work; but he has built monuments on all the high places, and they who follow can only hope to leave behind them some far humbler memorials."—"Blackwood's Magazine," Feb., 1817.

[1] "Specimens of the British Poets," vol. vii., p. 240.

[2] "Rambler," No. 36.

the learned, that wherever human nature is at work, the eye of a poet may discover rich elements of his art—that over Christian Europe, at all events, the purity of sentiment, and the fervour of passion, may be found combined with sagacity of intellect, wit, shrewdness, humour, whatever elevates, and whatever delights the mind—not more easily amidst the most " complicated transactions " of the most polished societies, than

" In huts where poor men lie."

Burns did not place himself only within the estimation and admiration of those whom the world called his superiors—a solitary tree emerging into light and air, and leaving the parent underwood as low and as dark as before. He, as well as any man,

" Knew his own worth, and reverenced the lyre:"

but he ever announced himself as a peasant, the representative of his class, the painter of their manners, inspired by the same influences which ruled their bosoms; and whosoever sympathized with the verse of Burns, had his soul opened for the moment to the whole family of man. If, in too many instances, the matter has stopped there—the blame is not with the poet, but with the mad and unconquerable pride and coldness of the worldly heart—" man's inhumanity to man." If, in spite of Burns, and all his successors, the boundary lines of society are observed with increasing strictness among us—if the various orders of men still, day by day, feel the chord of sympathy relaxing, let us lament over symptoms of a disease in the body politic, which, if it goes on, must find sooner or later a fatal ending: but let us not undervalue the antidote which has all along been checking this strong poison. Who can doubt, that at this moment thousands of " the first-born of Egypt" look upon the smoke of a cottager's chimney with feelings which would never have been developed within their being, had there been no Burns?

Such, it can hardly be disputed, has been, and is the general influence of the poet's genius; and the effect has been accomplished, not in spite of, but by means of the most exact contradiction of, every one of the principles laid down by Dr. Johnson in a passage already cited; and, indeed, assumed throughout the whole body of that great author's critical disquisitions. Whatever Burns has done, he has done by his exquisite power of entering into the characters and feelings of individuals; as Heron has well expressed it, "by the effusion of particular, not general sentiments, and in the picturing out of particular imagery."

Currie says, that "if *fiction* be the soul of poetry, as some assert, Burns can have small pretensions to the name of poet." The success of Burns, the influence of his verse, would alone be enough to overturn all the systems of a thousand definers; but the doctor has obviously taken *fiction* in far too limited a sense. There are indeed but few of Burns's pieces in which he is found creating beings and circumstances, both alike alien from his own person and experience, and then, by the power of imagination, divining and expressing what forms life and passion would assume with, and under these—but there are some; there is quite enough to satisfy every reader of "Hallowe'en," the "Jolly Beggars," and "Tam o' Shanter" (to say nothing of various particular songs, such as "Bruce's Address," "Macpherson's Lament," &c.), that Burns, if he pleased, might have been as largely and as successfully an inventor in this way, as he is in another walk, perhaps not so inferior to this as many people may have accustomed themselves to believe; in the art, namely, of recombining and newcombining, varying, embellishing, and fixing and transmitting, the elements of a most picturesque experience, and most vivid feelings.

Lord Byron, in his letter on Pope, treats with high and just contempt the laborious trifling which has been expended on distinguishing, by air-drawn lines and technical slang-words, the elements and materials of poetical exertion; and, among other things, expresses his scorn of the attempts that have been made to class Burns among minor poets, merely because he has put forth few large pieces, and still fewer of what is called the purely imaginative character. Fight who will about words and forms, "Burns's rank," says he, "is in the first class of his art;" and, I believe, the world at large are now-a-days well prepared to prefer a line from such a pen as Byron's on any such subject as this, to the most luculent dissertation that ever perplexed the brains of writer and of reader. *Sentio, ergo sum*, says the metaphysician; the critic may safely parody the saying, and assert that that is poetry of the highest order, which exerts influence of the most powerful order on the hearts and minds of mankind."

Burns has been appreciated duly, and he has had the fortune to be praised eloquently by almost every poet who has come after him. To accumulate all that has been said of him, even by men like himself, of the first order, would fill a volume—and a noble monument, no question, that volume would be—the noblest, except what he has left us in his own immortal verses, which—were some dross removed, and the rest arranged in a chronological order—would, I believe, form, to the intelligent, a more perfect and vivid history of his life, than will ever be composed out of all the materials in the world besides.

"The impression of his genius," says Campbell, "is deep and universal; and, viewing him merely as a poet, there is scarcely another regret connected with his name, than that his productions, with all their merit, fall short of the talents which he possessed. That he never attempted any great work of fiction, may be partly traced to the cast of his genius, and partly to his circumstances, and limited education. His poetical temperament was that of fitful transports, rather than steady inspiration. Whatever he might have written, was likely to have been fraught with passion. There is always enough of *interest* in life to cherish the feelings of genius; but it requires knowledge to enlarge and enrich the imagination. Of that knowledge, which unrolls the diversities of human manners, adventures, and characters, to a poet's study, he could have no great share; although he stamped the little treasure which he possessed in the mintage of sovereign genius."[1]

"Notwithstanding," says Sir Walter Scott, "the spirit of many of his lyrics, and the exquisite sweetness and simplicity of others, we cannot but deeply regret that so much of his time and talents was frittered away in compiling and composing for musical collections. There is sufficient evidence, that even the genius of Burns could not support him in the monotonous task of writing love verses on heaving bosoms and sparkling eyes, and twisting them into such rhythmical forms as might suit the capricious evolutions of Scotch reels and strathspeys. Besides this constant waste of his power and fancy in small and insignificant compositions, must necessarily have had no little effect in deterring him from undertaking any grave or important task. Let no one suppose that we undervalue the songs of Burns. When his soul was intent on suiting a favourite air to words humorous or tender, as the subject demanded, no poet of our tongue ever displayed higher skill in marrying melody to immortal verse. But the writing of a series of songs for large musical collections, degenerated into a slavish labour which no talents could support, led to negligence, and, above all, diverted the poet from his grand plan of dramatic composition. To produce a work of this kind,

---

[1] " Specimens," vol. vii., p. 241.

neither, perhaps, a regular tragedy nor comedy, but something partaking of the nature of both, seems to have been
long the cherished wish of Burns. He had even fixed on the
subject, which was an adventure in low life, said to have
happened to Robert Bruce, while wandering in danger and
disguise, after being defeated by the English. The Scottish
dialect would have rendered such a piece totally unfit for
the stage; but those who recollect the masculine and lofty
tone of martial spirit which glows in the poem of Bannockburn, will sigh to think what the character of the gallant
Bruce might have proved under the hand of Burns. It
would undoubtedly have wanted that tinge of chivalrous
feeling which the manners of the age, no less than the disposition of the monarch, demanded; but this deficiency
would have been more than supplied by a bard who could
have drawn from his perceptions the unbending energy of
a hero sustaining the desertion of friends, the persecution
of enemies, and the utmost malice of disastrous fortune.
The scene, too, being partly laid in humble life, admitted
that display of broad humour and exquisite pathos, with
which he could, interchangeably and at pleasure, adorn his
cottage views. Nor was the assemblage of familiar sentiments incompatible in Burns, with those of the most
exalted dignity. In the inimitable tale of "Tam o' Shanter," he has left us sufficient evidence of his abilities to
combine the ludicrous with the awful, and even the horrible.
No poet, with the exception of Shakspeare, ever possessed
the power of exciting the most varied and discordant
emotions with such rapid transitions. His humorous description of death in the poem on "Dr. Hornbook," borders
on the terrific, and the witches' dance in the Kirk of Alloway, is at once ludicrous and horrible. Deeply must we
then regret those avocations which diverted a fancy so
varied and so vigorous, joined with language and expressions suited to all its changes, from leaving a more sub-

stantial monument to his own fame, and to the honour of his country."[1]

The cantata of the "Jolly Beggars," which was not printed at all until some time after the poet's death, and has not been included in the editions of his works until within these few years, cannot be considered as it deserves, with-strongly heightening our regret that Burns never lived to execute his meditated drama. That extraordinary sketch, coupled with his later lyrics in a higher vein, is enough to show that in him we had a master capable of placing the musical drama on a level with the loftiest of our classical forms. "Beggar's Bush," and "Beggar's Opera," sink into tameness in the comparison; and indeed, without pro-fanity to the name of Shakspeare, it may be said, that out of such materials, even his genius could hardly have con-structed a piece in which imagination could have more splendidly predominated over the outward shows of things —in which the sympathy-awakening power of poetry could have been displayed more triumphantly under circum-stances of the greatest difficulty. That remarkable per-formance, by the way, was an early production of the Mauchline period;[2] I know nothing but the "Tam o' Shanter" that is calculated to convey so high an impression of what Burns might have done.

As to Burns's want of education and knowledge, Mr. Campbell may not have considered, but he must admit that whatever Burns's opportunities had been at the time when he produced his first poems, such a man as he was not likely to be a hard reader (which he certainly was), and a constant observer of men and manners, in a much wider

---

[1] "Quarterly Review," No. I., p. 33.

[2] So John Richmond of Mauchline informed Chambers. See that very interesting work, the "Picture of Scotland," article "Mauchline," for some entertaining particulars of the scene that suggested the poem.

circle of society than almost any other great poet has ever moved in, from three-and-twenty to eight-and-thirty, without having thoroughly removed any pretext for auguring unfavourably on that score, of what he might have been expected to produce in the more elaborate departments of his art, had his life been spared to the usual limits of humanity. In another way, however, I cannot help suspecting that Burns's enlarged knowledge, both of men and books, produced an unfavourable effect, rather than otherwise, on the exertions, such as they were, of his later years. His generous spirit was open to the impression of every kind of excellence; his lively imagination, lending its own vigour to whatever it touched, made him admire even what other people try to read in vain; and after travelling, as he did, over the general surface of our literature, he appears to have been somewhat startled at the consideration of what he himself had, in comparative ignorance adventured, and to have been more intimidated than encouraged by the retrospect. In most of the new departments in which he made some trial of his strength (for example, his moral epistles in Pope's vein, *heroic* satires, &c.), he appears to have soon lost heart, and paused. There is indeed one magnificent exception in "Tam o' Shanter"—a piece which no one can understand without believing that had Burns pursued that walk, and poured out his stores of traditionary lore, embellished with his extraordinary powers of description of all kinds, we might have had from his hand a series of national tales, uniting the quaint simplicity, sly humour, and irresistible pathos of another Chaucer, with the strong and graceful versification, and masculine wit and sense of another Dryden.

This was a sort of feeling that must have in time subsided. But let us not waste words in regretting what might have been, where so much is. Burns, short and painful as were his years, has left behind him a volume in which there is inspiration for every fancy, and music for every mood; which lives, and will live in strength and vigour—"to soothe," as a generous lover of genius has said —"the sorrows of how many a lover, to inflame the patriotism of how many a soldier, to fan the fires of how many a genius, to disperse the gloom of solitude, appease the agonies of pain, encourage virtue, and show vice its ugliness;"[1]—a volume, in which, centuries hence, as now, wherever a Scotsman may wander, he will find the dearest consolation of his exile. Already, in the language of Childe Harold, has

> "Glory without end
> Scattered the clouds away; and on that name attend
> The tears and praises of all time."

---

[1] See the "Censura Literaria" of Sir Egerton Brydges, vol. ii., p. 55, 1796.

APPENDIX.

APPENDIX.

APPENDIX A.—Page 2.

The Paternal Ancestry of Burns.

IN 1840 Professor Wilson opened his celebrated essay on
" The Genius and Character of Burns " with the remark
that he is " by far the greatest *Poet* that ever sprung from
the bosom of the people " ; and in the same year Carlyle
wrote thus on the same theme :—" Wheresoever a Saxon
dialect is spoken, it begins to be understood that one of the
most considerable Saxon *men* of the eighteenth century was
an Ayrshire peasant, named Robert Burns." In recent
years, however, books of imposing appearance have been
produced, under the authority of big names, with the object
of showing that Burns and his ancestors were not *peasants*
—that his forefathers were farmers, entitled to rank with
" yeomen " of England, possessing cherished family traditions reaching back into the dim past of centuries ago. Be
this as it may, it must be confessed, after careful perusal of
" Notes on his Name and Family," by Sir James Burnes
(1851), and " Genealogical Memoirs of the Scottish House
of Burnes," by the " Historiographer to the Grampian
Club " (1877), that we find the result of their learned
labours in that direction to be very unsatisfactory. They
have demonstrated that persons bearing the surname
Burnes, did reside and rent small farms in Kincardineshire
upwards of two centuries ago ; but they produce no reliable
documentary links connecting any of these with Robert

Burnes, the humble tenant of a small farm called " Clochnahill," in Dunnottar parish, the known parent of William
Burnes who migrated to Ayrshire and became the father of
Burns the poet.   The genealogists have failed to show *when*
that grandfather of the poet was born, or who was *his* father;
and they do not attempt to indicate where or when he died.
The same lack of information attaches to Isabella Keith,
his wife—the paternal grandmother of our poet ; it is not
even known if she was alive at the time William Burnes and
his elder brother abandoned their native home together, and
went southward in search of employment and bread. The following table, therefore, contains all that is positively known
concerning the poet's paternal ancestry and their immediate
descendants.   The date of marriage of the grand-parents
is unknown, but the birth-date of the eldest child being
ascertained, we may assume 1715, or thereabout, to have
been the year of the marriage.

ROBERT BURNES in CLOCHNAHILL, and ISABELLA KEITH,
HIS SPOUSE, HAD ISSUE AS FOLLOWS :

1. JAMES,   born 1717, became a Burgess of Montrose, died in 1761.
2. ROBERT,   „   1719, a Gardener by trade, " poor uncle Robert,"
                               died in 1789, at Stewarton, Ayrshire.
3. WILLIAM „   1721, a Gardener, FATHER OF THE POET, died
                               in 1784, at Lochlea, in Ayrshire.
4. MARGARET, „   1723, married Andrew Walker, in Crawton.
5. ELSPET,   „   1725, married John Caird, in Denside, Dunnottar.[1]
6. JEAN,   „   1727, married a cousin, John Burnes, no issue.[2]
7. GEORGE,   „   1729, died in early life.
8. ISABEL,   „   1730, married William Brand, a dyer in Auchenblae.[3]
9. MARY,   „   1732, died unmarried.

[1] The poet refers to John Caird in his letters to James Burness of
Montrose, June 21, 1783, and Aug. 3, 1784 ; also in his letter to Gilbert
Burns, Sep. 17, 1787.

[2] The poet refers to Jean in his letter to Gilbert Burns, Sep. 17,
1787.

[3] The poet refers to Isabel and to William Brand in same letter, Sep.
17, 1787.

In the poet's autobiography, the brief reference to his paternal ancestry makes no pretence to carry the reader farther back than the time of the first Jacobite insurrection, 1715; yet he implies that his forefathers had, for an indefinite series of years, rented land in the Mearns, " under the noble Keiths of Marischal," and adds that on the suppression of that rebellion, as a consequence of their loyal adhe· sion to the cause adopted by their Chief, they " had the honour to share his fate." And afterwards, in a letter addressed by him to a Jacobite lady, he thus adverts to that circumstance:—"Although my forefathers had no illustrious honours and vast properties to hazard in the contest, they left their humble homes to follow their leaders,—what they could they did, and what they had they lost." Whatever substance the tenant of Clochnahill was possessed of prior to the date of his marriage, he certainly figures as a very poor man thereafter; yet he may have been " once better off," for the family misfortunes are clearly attributed by the grandson to the circumstance narrated. " I mention it," says he, " because it threw my father on the world at large." Sir James Burnes, in preparing his " family notes," had recourse to conjecture when his researches proved abortive. Finding little blossom to deck his " family tree " in the parish from which the poet's father and his own great-grandfather emanated, he betook himself to the parish of Glenbervie, where he found plenty footprints of former indwellers of the name he was in search of. Under many a mossy heap, the remains of these lie in the picturesque churchyard; where several headstones bear inscriptions recording the interment of many a Robert, William, James, and John of that surname, who had been tenants either of " Bogjorgan," or of " Brawlinmuir," farms that belong to the adjoining estate of Inchbreck. The oldest legible date of demise recorded of these is 1715, and there is one rather handsome and perfectly inscribed stone which Sir James set

his heart on as very likely to be that of the father and
mother of his acknowledged ancestor, Robert of Clochnahill.
It bears the following inscription :—

"Here under lyes the body of James Burnes, who was tenant of
Brawlinmuir, who died the 23 of January, 1743, aged 87 years. Also the
body of Margaret Falconer, his spouse, who departed this life the 28 of
December, 1749, aged 90 years."

Robert of Clochnahill must, of course, have had a father
either living or dead at the time his misfortunes overtook
him ; and if this James of Brawlinmuir and his spouse were
his parents, the extreme destitution of the Clochnahill family
seems inconsistent with the costly headstone here set up for
their nearest kindred, at a date when matters were at their
very worst.   Something more than alleged " local tradition"
is wanting here to supply the missing link which alone can
prove the conjecture of Sir James to be correct.   Production
of a record of the birth, or even of the marriage, of Robert
of Clochnahill might put an end to all doubt on the subject,
and until either of these be produced, the Glenbervie head-
stone does not speak to the point.

With a view, no doubt, to give a fair-spreading top to his
family-tree, the Guelphic Knight says in reference to his
great-great-grandfather of Clochnahill, "This Robert Burnes
was, about A.D. 1700, one of five brothers of substantial position in the Mearns, who could show silver utensils at their
tables, with other indications of wealth unusual in that
county."   We have no objection to this, if the statement
rests on a good foundation ; he gives no authority however,
and assumes that these five brethren were the sons of James
of Brawlinmuir, whose names and birth-dates he does not
pretend to know.   He also records an interesting circumstance regarding the common ancestor of himself and the
poet, which may be safely accepted as true, namely, that
the humble farmer of Clochnahill, with a liberal sense of the
value of education for his children, erected a school-house

on his farm, and in conjunction with some of his neighbours engaged a teacher. This was precisely the course afterwards pursued by the poet's father at Alloway in Ayrshire. At the same time the extreme poverty of the grandfather is more than implied in Gilbert's narrative of the early hardships of his own father. "Compelled along with an elder brother, Robert, to leave home and turn their steps towards the south in quest of a livelihood, I have often heard my father describe his anguish of mind when they parted on the top of a hill on the confines of their native place, each going off his several way, and scarcely knowing whither he went." Garvock hill is supposed to be the one on whose summit this affecting farewell was taken, the incident in some respects reminding one of the parting betwixt the patriarchs Abraham and Lot—"Is not the whole land before us? if thou wilt take the left hand, I will take the right; or if thou depart to the right hand, then I will go to the left." Robert took the right hand, and William the left, but here the parallel stops. In the case of the two patriarchs, "the land was not able to bear them, for their substance was so great;" in the other instance, the land was not able to bear them because of its own utter barrenness. From that hill top neither the plains of Mamre on the one side, nor the well-watered plain of Jordan on the other, could be discerned by the forlorn brothers. The elder one took the road, by way of Perth and Stirling, into England; while the poet's father took his way by Dundee and Kinghorn into Edinburgh. William obtained a job there in the only line of handicraft he had been taught; the famous Meadow-walks were then in process of formation, and he was employed on these for some time. "Still, however," adds Gilbert, "he endeavoured to spare something for the support of his aged parent; and I recollect hearing him mention his having sent a bank-note for this purpose, when money of that

kind was so scarce in Kincardineshire, that they scarcely
knew how to employ it when it arrived."

All this reads very awkwardly along with the counter
statements of the much more fortunate descendant of that
same "aged parent," which are above quoted—"silver utensils and other indications of wealth !" "Sweet are the uses
of adversity," however, if we have any faith in Shakespeare
and in Him who delivered the "sermon from the mount."
Like two mountain rills pursuing different directions from
one source, and meeting again just before reaching the
ocean, the two Kincardine brothers met again when their
locks were thinned and grey with age. At Lochlea, in
1781, the younger of them thus wrote to his north-country
relatives concerning the elder:—" My brother Robert lives
at Stewarton, by Kilmarnock; he hath two sons, named
John and William, and one douther, named Fanny. Their
circumstances are very indifferent."

APPENDIX B.—Page 30.

THE TARBOLTON LOVES OF BURNS.

IN Gilbert's narrative of his brother's early life, written
at the request of Mrs. Dunlop and published by Currie,
he says, "these connexions were numerous, and as they
were governed by the strictest rules of virtue and modesty
—from which he never deviated till he reached his twenty-
third year—he became anxious to be in a situation to
marry." The growing bard commenced his twenty-third
year on 25th January, 1781, three and a half of the
seven years comprising the Tarbolton period of his life
having then elapsed. On 4th July of that year he was
admitted an apprentice mason of St. David's Tarbolton

Lodge, and removed immediatly thereafter to Irvine, where he resided till the end of February in the following year. The Lodge-books record that he was "passed and raised" on 1st October, 1781, so that, unless such a step of promotion could have been awarded during his absence, he must have made a journey from Irvine for the occasion. After his final return from that sea-port town, all thoughts of marriage as a cure for love-sickness seem to have been banished from his mind.

The author, speaking in 1787 of his earlier productions, of a period which might embrace a year or so after his return from Irvine, thus observed :—"None of the rhymes of those days are in print, except 'Winter, a dirge' (the eldest of my printed pieces), and Songs, first, second, and third." These are (1) "The Rigs o' Barley," (2) "Now Westlin Winds," (3) "My Nannie, O." The first of these songs is not likely to have been composed prior to the Irvine days, for few modest girls would care to confess being the subject of it. Song second, the poet says, was "the ebullition of that passion" for Peggy Thomson which put a stop to his studies at Kirkoswald school, in his seventeenth year. In deciding the question of the heroineship of "My Nannie, O," we must not be guided by the natural assumption that "Nannie," or "Agnes," was her Christian name. Its matchless melody is so identified with the oft-recurring "My Nannie, O," as the refrain of each stanza, that any words—even from the pen of Burns—if not constructed so as thus to introduce the expected syllables, would be declared unsuitable for the charming undulations of that old Scotch tune. Gilbert Burns was applied to by George Thomson in 1819 for information on this subject, and he replied that on casting his memory over the list of Tarbolton young women of that Christian appellative, he could only venture to name "Agnes Fleming, a farmer's daughter, to whom Robert paid a little of that roving attention which he was constantly devoting to some one." "Her charms," he added, "were indeed mediocre, but what she had were sexual, which was the characteristic of the greater part of the poet's mistresses; for he was no Platonic lover, however he might otherwise pretend, or suppose of himself."

Lockhart has praised "The Rigs o' Barley" as the best of our poet's songs written at that time; but surely he did not mean to prefer it to such a pearl of nature as "My Nannie, O." Somehow he had formed the impression that the latter, along with "Mary Morison," and "The Lass of Cessnock Banks," were productions of the Mossgiel period (page 78 *supra*); but these all belong to a time considerably earlier, and in every probability were inspired by the fascinations of one and the same charmer. Gilbert had been also requested to inform Thomson of what he knew concerning "Mary Morison," and replied that if his brother had any particular person in his eye, certainly this was not the young woman's real name. He believed she must have been the same individual who also formed the subject of some light verses beginning,

"And I'll kiss thee yet, yet, my bonie Peggy Alison."

but who "Peggy Alison" was, Gilbert did not explain.

Some further light was thrown upon these early love-songs of our poet, about twenty years after Gilbert's death, by his then only surviving sister, Mrs. Begg. In reference to four love-letters that were addressed by the poet, in 1780 or 1781, to "My dear E.," and printed in Currie's first edition, but withdrawn from the second and all subsequent issues of that work, she communicated the following particulars. About two miles eastward from Lochlea, a shining stream, called Cessnock Water, flows past in a northerly course through Galston parish into the River Irvine. A young woman, named Ellison Begbie, the daughter of a small farmer near Galston, was then in ser-

vice with a family whose house was on Cessnock bank at
the distance mentioned from the farm of William Burnes.
The youthful poet had got acquainted with Ellison, and
was so much charmed with her superior manners and
agreeable person, that he courted her with all his ardour
during several months, with a serious view to future
marriage. It was on her he composed the very poetic
"song of similes," called "The Lass of Cessnock Banks,"
concluding a gorgeous description of her person with this
peroration—

> " But it's not her air, her form, her face,
>   Though matching beauty's fabled Queen,
> But the mind that shines in every grace,
>   And chiefly in her sparkling een."

This revelation from Mrs. Begg, taken in connection with
Gilbert's hint regarding "Peggy Alison," very naturally
suggested the inference that the latter pretty enough name
being altogether unknown in Tarbolton, it must have been
merely a euphonistic synonym invented by the poet for
"Alison Begbie," the latter name being too prosaic to be
woven into verse. The poetic warmth of the following
stanza may be thought fervid enough, but the lyric flow of
the lines is very masterly.

> " When in my arms, wi' a' thy charms,
>   I clasp my countless treasure,
> I seek nae mair o' heaven to share
>   Than sic a moment's pleasure :
> And by thy een sae bonie blue,
>   I swear I'm thine for ever,
> And on thy lips I seal my vow,
>   And break it shall I never !
> And I'll kiss thee yet, yet, &c."

The fine song addressed to "Mary Morison," which
Gilbert says his brother composed on the same fair one who
inspired the above lines, fits exactly in sentiment with the

known history of his passion for Ellison Begbie, and its disappointing issue :—

> " Yestreen when, to the trembling string,
>   The dance gaed thro' the lighted ha',
>   To thee my fancy took its wing—
>   I sat, but neither heard nor saw," &c.

The " lighted ha' " here, of course, means the country dancing school with its sanded floor, and a strolling fiddler inspiring the rustics with the magic of his " trembling string." The issue of his love-suit is painfully pictured in the closing verse :—

> " O canst thou really wreck his peace
>   Wha for thy sake wad gladly dee ?
>   Or canst thou break that heart o' his
>   Whase only faut is loving thee ?
>   If love for love thou wiltna gie,
>   At least be *pity* to me shown—
>   A thocht ungentle canna be
>   The thocht o' ' Peggy Ellison.' "

The last of the prose letters addressed to " My dear E.," concludes with the intimation that he is about to remove to some distance; and his after narrative of the distress he had to encounter in the town of Irvine is summed up thus :— " To crown all, a *belle fille* whom I adored, and who had pledged her soul to meet me in the fields of matrimony, jilted me with peculiar circumstances of mortification." It would appear that the prudent *Ellison* " had two strings to her bow," or, in plain words, had two beaux after her hand at the same time, and she chose the one that best accorded with her notions of future comfort. In 1806, Cromek traced her out, then a married woman resident in Glasgow, and took down from her recitation the words of " The lass of Cessnock Banks."

We cannot part with this subject without adding the following bit of pleasantry in connection with it. In one of our earliest rambles in the Ayrshire localities rendered

classic by the poet's former residence among them, and by
his allusions thereto in his writings, we made a close inspection of the grave-stones in Mauchline Churchyard, the
sceue of "The Holy Fair."   There, amongst others of real
interest, we were confronted with a fresh-looking head-
stone near the Church, that staggered us not a little, owing
to the strange information conveyed by its inscription,
thus :—

> "In memory of Adj. John Morrison, of the 104th
> Regiment, who died at Mauchline, 16th April, 1804,
> in the 80th year of his age :   Also his daughter,
> Mary Morrison—the poet's 'Bonnie Mary Morrison'—
> who died 29th June, 1791, aged 20."
>   Erected in 1825, by his grandson, A. N. Carmichael,
> of Edinburgh.

Here is a claim set up in behalf of an Adjutant's young
daughter, named Mary Morrison, alleging her to have been
once so beloved by Burns as to be the subject of one of the
choicest and tenderest of his early songs.   If she were but
twenty years old in 1791, when Burns was preparing to
leave Ellisland for the town of Dumfries, what would be
her age at the time the song is understood to have been
composed ?   We have the author's own express statement
that the song was " a juvenile performance ; " but he never
hinted that its inspirer was a little girl in short frocks !
This child of the retired soldier would be thirteen years
old when the poet, at the age of twenty-six, removed from
the parish of Tarbolton to that of Mauchline, in 1784.

If this " pious fraud "—the offspring of a deplorable
kind of ambition in its fabricator—were allowed to pass
unexposed, it might soon be seized on as the subject of a
pretty romance, " The Adjutant's Daughter," for instance,
in which sad liberties would be taken with the biography
of Burns.   But who is " A. N. Carmichael ? "   We lost no
time in learning all about him.   Archibald Nisbet Car-

michael, born at Muirkirk in 1794, was the eldest child of John Carmichael, schoolmaster there, and his wife Elizabeth Morrison, a surviving sister of "Mary" of the foregoing inscription. A. N. Carmichael became a famous classical scholar—was the dux-medallist of Edinburgh High School, in 1811—parish teacher of Crieff, in 1817—master of the Royal Academy, Inverness, in 1819; and finally a classical master of the New Academy of Edinburgh, which situation he held when he died, 8th January, 1847.

He was a learned and a good man; but *humanum est errare.*

While so fine a lyric as Burns's "Mary Morison" remained unfitted with a heroine, and seemed wandering through space, like a lost *Pleiad*, seeking its proper kindred connection, the temptation was irresistibly strong in a man of A. N. Carmichael's temperament, whose mother once had a little sister of the name in question resident in the poet's locality, to set up his claim in the shape above explained. His son, John Carmichael, inherited his father's talents, and was appointed a classical master of the Edinburgh High School in 1848, where his services were much appreciated, till his death in 1871.

APPENDIX C.—Page 80.

THE HIGHLAND MARY EPISODE.

IN 1842, an elegant monument was erected over the spot in the West Churchyard of Greenock, where the remains of the poet's departed Mary had been laid by her relatives fifty-six years previously. What led to the erection of that memorial was the circumstance of the then recent recovery, and final safe bestowal, of the precious volumes inscribed and delivered to her by Burns at their memorable parting in May, 1786. Campbelton, in the West Highlands, was then the domicile of Mary's parents, but in Greenock resided a cousin of Mary's mother, married to a ship-carpenter named Macpherson, whose house became to Mary a second home when requisite. One of the poet's letters to a correspondent in July, 1786, has this intimation—"I am now fixed to go to the West Indies in October;" and it seems the betrothed lovers had arranged to meet at Greenock on the occasion proposed. "She had scarce landed," says the poet in a note to one of his songs regarding her, "when she was seized with a malignant fever, which hurried my dear girl to the grave before I could even hear of her illness." The piece of ground in which she was interred had then, as now appears, been recently purchased by Macpherson from a brother carpenter, its original owner, who desired to part with it, because he was about to emigrate.

The monument committee of 1842 were doubtless careful to see that the erection was put in the rightful place, and to examine the titles to the ground before purchasing the extra adjoining space required for the pretty wide base of the structure. A register of "Lairs" kept by the superintendent, in relation to a ground plan of the churchyard, shows the following satisfactory entry, and proves to demonstration that poor Mary's remains could not have been deposited there prior to 12th October, 1786. The following is a copy of that entry, noted by Chambers in 1851, from the official record:—

"Jan . 14 . 1760 . Duncan Robertson, carpenter . . . . 6 feet . 0 . 9 . 0
Oct . 12 . 1786 . This lair is this day transferred to
Peter Macpherson, ship-carpenter, Greenock."

That portion of the register of *burials* applicable to the year 1786, in that parish, having been destroyed or lost, no venture was made to inscribe on the monument any supposed date of Mary's death. Indeed, that important item in the chronology of facts in the poet's life did not become a question with anybody till some years later, when it was started, and hunted to its conclusion, by the writer of the present article.

There can be little doubt that Burns himself had, from the beginning, resolved to keep the story of his intercourse with Mary an entire secret; and the world might never have heard her name, but for the circumstance of the production of his verses "To Mary in Heaven," composed three years after her death. He could not resist the impulse to publish them, and their surpassing beauty and pathos had the effect of rousing the curiosity of his personal friends and the public generally, to learn some particulars of that part of his history to which the verses refer. He could not avoid giving some sort of answer to the enquiries made to him on the subject, and his notes to Riddell and to George Thomson on the subject, give the substance of what these replies must have been. The Glenriddell notes were not given to the public till the appearance of Cromek's "Reliques," in 1808; and the cautious Dr. Currie, who must have received from Gilbert some hint to speak indefinitely in regard to the *date* of the Highland Mary episode, contents himself with simply quoting Burns's own words to Thomson :—" I took the following *farewell* of a dear girl, *in my very early years*, when I was thinking of going to the West Indies." The parallel passage in the Glenriddell notes is even more misleading as regards the date of the poet's intercourse with Mary ·—" This was a composition of mine *in my very early life, before I was known at all in the world*," &c. Cromek, of whose interference in the publication of the poet's writings Gilbert was extremely jealous, became perhaps the unconscious means of rivetting the impression on the public mind, that Burns's intercourse with the living Mary was a very juvenile affair. At the same time, some very interesting details of the memorable " day of parting love " betwixt the lovers, near the junction of the Fail Water with the River Ayr, which Cromek was the first to publish, must have been imparted to him by some person who knew the secret history of the transaction. That informant could not have been the poet's widow, who was the least likely person in the world to know anything whatever about it. She, it will be remembered, was not resident in Mauchline during the time of the poet's secret interviews and parting with Mary Campbell. It is known that Mary, for six months, if not a year, prior to that parting had served as a nursery-maid in the house of Gavin Hamilton, who enjoyed more of the bard's confidence at that period than perhaps any other individual in Mauchline. From that source, therefore, it is probable Cromek obtained his information, along with an express injunction to preserve the mystery regarding its date, conform to the poet's own wishes, evinced in the notes he had left behind him. In a footnote at page 35 of the " Reliques," Cromek particularly speaks of " the valuable information and kindness he received from Mr. Gavin Hamilton of Mauchline, and every branch of his family." Cromek was just the man to obey such injunctions : it is known that he refused to print an anecdote imparted to him in confidence by Creech,—his reply (now in the hands of the editor) is in these terms—" I cannot have it ; it tells against Burns, whose character must be kept sacred and dignified. Poor, dear man ! with all his faults I love him entirely ! "

If delicacy for the feelings of Mrs. Burns influenced the poet's earlier biographers and annotators, preventing them from plain speaking on the question of the date of the poet's song—" Will ye go to Indies, my Mary ? " surely, from 1834 downwards, their successors were relieved from any such trammels to free discussion. But the death of

Mrs. Burns introduced no change in that respect, and neither did the speaking inscription on the recovered bible of Mary succeed in removing their deeply sunk prejudices from the old socket of belief in which they had been embedded. Allan Cunningham, Hogg, and Motherwell, Professor Wilson, and Robert Chambers, all harped on the same string, and not a single new thought on this point could be elicited from any likely quarter. The present writer—a mere amateur in Burns-literature—had constructed, for his own use, a chronological table of the earlier compositions of Burns, and the corresponding incidents of his life, but could find no room anywhere for the Highland Mary transactions ; and at length he felt inclined to regard her as a pure myth ! Yet although he was then unaware of the entry above quoted from the Greenock "register of lairs," he arrived at the firm assurance in the end, that the year 1786 was the only year in the calendar into which the Highland Mary episode could be fitted. Wrapped up in his own solitary theories on this subject, he watched every public vehicle of intelligence for some streak of daybreak ; but the shadows would not flee away ! At length an hour arrived when he was enabled to rub his hands with the delight of cheering anticipation. At page 181 of the third volume of "Wood's Songs of Scotland," then just published (1849), he observed a note, as follows :—

"Thomas Thorburn, Esq., of Ryedale, in a letter of 9th February, 1849, to the editor, writes as follows regarding Highland Mary :—
"I lately received some particulars regarding Highland Mary which are interesting. She was born in the parish of Dunoon in 1761 or 1762, and died of an epidemic at Greenock on or about 17th September, 1784.'

The writer at once put himself in communication with Mr. Thorburn, who, after some fencing, vouchsafed at length to give his authority for the statements thus made public. That authority was old John Munro, Session Clerk at

Greenock, and he, on being plied with an argumentative protest, soon was forced to admit his mistakes, and at our request expressed his recantation to Mr. Thorburn in the completest manner.

The new, and now universally accepted theory, which fixes the exact time of this remarkable incident in the life of Burns, while showing its harmonious relation to the peculiar circumstances of the bard at that period, dates from 16th January, 1850. An exhaustive essay on the subject, by the present writer, was then read within the hall of the Scottish Antiquaries in Edinburgh, to a large assemblage of literary and scientific notables convened for the occasion. It is needless now to dilate further concerning what has become an accomplished fact, nevertheless it may be right to state, as an early practical result of the fresh light then shed on the poet's biography, that it formed the main inducement for Robert Chambers to construct and publish his valuable chronological edition of the " Life and Works of Burns," which appeared in the following year.

APPENDIX D.—Page 202.

" THE MERRY MUSES OF CALEDONIA."

THE first—indeed the only—reference found in the poet's published correspondence, to the fact that he was forming a collection of curious unpublishable songs, is in a letter of December, 1793, addressed to the Duke of Queensberry's chamberlain, Mr. John M'Murdo. The words are these—" I think I once mentioned something of a collection of Scotch songs I have for years been making : I send you a perusal of what I have got together ; I could not conveniently spare them above five or six days, and five

or six glances of them will probably more than suffice you.
A very few of them are my own. There is not another
copy of the collection in the world, and I should be sorry
if any unfortunate negligence were to deprive me of what
has cost me a good deal of pains."

Burns did not survive the date of that letter so long as
three years. Into whose hands the collection fell after his
death has never been explained : the probability is that it
would go along with the rest of his papers and MS. books,
including "even the sweepings of his study," into Dr.
Currie's hands at Liverpool. If it had been there and then
destroyed after " five or six glances " of pure inspection, so
much the better for the scapegraces of succeeding generations who might otherwise be fated to gloat over its pages !
But then, the good George Gilfillan of Dundee would have
been *minus* of his divining-rod, "to point the moral and adorn
the tale," in his last Memoir of the bard. Let us hear what
the spirit of that defunct rhetorician is now saying to the
churches :—" We own to having read those unworthy productions—the biggest literary blot on the memory of Burns
—and while we admit the plea set up in their behalf, that
many of them are not from the pen of the collector, and
those that are manifestly his are the purest, and that to his
hand we trace all those strokes of quirky humour and
naïveté which are found in the most and worst of them—
we freely grant that ' The Merry Muses ' may be called ' a
beastly book,' and is rank throughout with the very miasme
of uncleanness. A purer, sincerer, simpler being, or one
who more admired Burns, never existed, than the gentleman who showed us the copy—the late Robert White of
Newcastle. Deep sorrow, rather than anger, was in both
our hearts as we went over it together. He mentioned on
that occasion that he knew an innkeeper, whose house the
bard had frequented, who said that up to a certain point
he was most delightful society ; but beyond that, he would

otten spend the rest of the evening in singing obscene
songs. Alas! at a certain stage the poet and the man
were spirited away—the *Burns* evaporated—the *Brute* only
remained. White mentioned this to us repeatedly, and it
was undoubtedly true. . . . We gathered from the late
amiable and child-like Dr. Wightman of Kirkmahoe that
a certain degree of degradation came across the great spirit
of Burns in his latter years. He knew the poet at that
time, and judged he had become desperate, and at bay, and
it was a great affliction to be in his company. His talk
was fierce, lurid, too often loose, profane, and unhappy.
The noble ship—as we would put it—had got on fire, its
guns were going off, and it became positively dangerous to
approach it." Alas! alas! who could exist within range
of such a Dumfries desperado as that?

But, "who fired that gun? Not I, indeed. You lie! I
believe. I am not accustomed to lie, honest man." We
are entirely without information regarding the fate of the
MS. collection spoken of by Burns to M'Murdo in 1793; and
if it be in existence now, its dismembered leaves, at all
events, must have been floating in the manuscript-market
ere this—but they have never been seen. Who then was
the printer of the "mean-looking volume" that has thus
been hawked furtively about, and sold by pedlers, as
"Burns's Merry Muses"? *When* and *where* was it printed,
and from what "copy" was it set up? These are questions
which no one has attempted to answer, and which we
believe to be unanswerable. The poet Wordsworth, in
1816, thus referred to that "foundling waif":—"He must
be a miserable judge of poetical composition who can for a
moment fancy that such low, tame, and loathsome ribaldry
can possibly be the production of Burns. With the utmost
difficulty we procured a slight perusal of the abominable
pamphlet alluded to. The truth is (and we speak on the
best authority this country can produce) there is not one

verse in that miscellany that ever was publicly acknowledged by Burns, nor is there above a single page that can
be traced to his manuscript."

The late Robert Chambers, nevertheless, felt constrained,
when giving to the world, in 1851-52, his well-known " Life
and Works of Burns," in four volumes, to speak somewhat
definitely on this subject; and yet neither does he settle
the question, Who printed the "Merry Muses"? or *when*,
where, and from *what* manuscript was it taken? His words
are these—"Unluckily Burns's collection of these facetiæ,
including some of his own essays in the same walk, fell,
after his death, into the hands of one of those publishers
who would sacrifice the highest interests of humanity to
turn a penny additional into their own purses; and, to the
lasting grief of all the friends of our poet, they were
allowed the honours of the press. The mean-looking
volume which resulted, should be a warning to all honourable men of letters against the slightest connection with
clandestine literature, much more, the degradation of con-
tributing to it."

We believe that the "flying stationers" who deal in
literature of the class in question have produced several
collections professing to be the genuine "Merry Muses"
of our poet, and that no two of these are alike in the quantity and quality of their respective contents. The most
genuine-looking of these (judging from the apparent age of
the paper and printing), that has come to our hands, is a
12mo. volume of 127 pages, in pretty large type of obsolete
fount, containing about ninety songs, among which are at
least half-a-dozen that are found in every ordinary edition
of Burns's poems. There is no imprint nor compiler's
name on the title-page, of which the following is a tran-
script :—" The Merry Muses of Caledonia ; a Collection of
favourite Scotch Songs, ancient and modern ; selected for
the use of the Crochallan Fencibles.

> Say, Puritan, can it be wrong
> To dress plain truth in witty song ?
> What honest Nature says we should do ;
> What every lady does—or would do."

The language of several of the pieces is even grosser than
the ideas and sentiments they are meant to express; yet
the coarsest phrase in the collection may be found in
Bailey's Dictionary, which was the standard one prior to
the appearance of Johnson's. Besides the decent enough
productions of the bard above referred to, there are at least
a dozen of wildly witty productions that would certainly
have betrayed their own parentage, even if copies of them
did not exist, as they certainly do, in Burns's handwriting.
The douce Robert Chambers, with a charity and candour
that does him infinite credit, thus apologizes for our poet :
" He was led into this by his enthusiastic love of all the
forms of his country's elder Muse ; for, with a strange contradiction to the grave and religious character of the Scottish people, they do possess a wonderful quantity of inde-
corous traditionary verse—not of an inflammatory character, but simply expressive of a profound sense of the
ludicrous, in connection with the sexual affections." And
in palliation of the poet's aptness to indulge in levity respecting Scripture characters and incidents, he reminds us
that " the piety of old Scotch people did not exclude a very
considerable share of what may be called ' unconscious
profanity.' "

But, who were the " Crochallan Fencibles " ? many
readers may be inclined to ask. A social club so-called had
existed in Edinburgh for some years prior to our bard's
arrival in that city, composed of well-to-do gentlemen, accustomed to free-living and free-speaking. Its members
must also have had a taste for vocal music, if we judge not
only from what is known of them, but from the fact that
the club derived its name from the refrain of a Gaelic

song, which used to be sung by the Celtic landlord of the tavern in which its meetings were held. The military term "Fencibles" was adopted by way of burlesque, and the principal members were addressed by mock-official names to correspond; but the sharp practice implied in the title consisted chiefly of pot-house raillery and smart rejoinder. Burns was soon introduced, and became an important accession to the corps. William Smellie, the printer, William Dunbar, W. S., Alexander Cunningham, writer (afterwards jeweller), Robert Cleghorn, farmer, Saughton Mills, and Peter Hill, bookseller, were the members to whom the poet became most attached, and who continued his cherished correspondents through life thereafter. Of these jolly fellows, the only one particularly requiring notice in the present connection is Mr. Robert Cleghorn, who survived Burns only a very few years. To him our poet sent early copies of any fine song or poem which he considered more than usually happy in conception and execution; and to him also, it must be confessed, he communicated several of the very wildest productions of that stamp we are now commenting on. His wife was the amiable widow of a writer in his neighbourhood, named Allen, who had been early cut off, leaving behind him an only son, who was reared as one of Cleghorn's household, and who became a man of some note in London, from 1803 till his death in 1843. This was John Allen, an early associate of Lord Byron, who frequently refers to him in his letters as "Holland House Allen." There can now be little doubt that Cleghorn's papers fell into Allen's hands, and amongst these, a large bundle of Burns's letters addressed to his stepfather, which are thus noticed in Byron's Journal, 1813 :—"Allen has lent me a quantity of Burns's unpublished and never-to-be published letters. They are full of oaths and obscene songs. What an antithetical mind ! tenderness, roughness, delicacy, coarseness, sentiment, sensuality, soaring and grovelling, dirt and Deity, all mixed up in one compound of poor clay."

The letters and songs thus referred to by Byron, instead of being now quietly shelved in some public library— would the reader believe ?—are still circulating in the London manuscript market ! In one of these the hapless poet thus writes :—" There is, and *must be* some truth in ' original sin.' My violent propensity to bawdry convinces me of it. Lack a day ! if that species of composition be the sin against the ' haly ghaist,' I am the most offending soul alive." The letter from which this quotation is made is thus specially noticed by Byron in a communication to Bowles :—" Several of these are so elaborately coarse, that I do not believe they could be paralleled in our language ; and what is more strange is, that some of the grossest passages are couched as postscripts to his serious and sentimental letters. To these are often tacked either a piece of prose or some verses of the most hyperbolical obscenity. In one he says that if obscenity (he uses a much coarser word) be the sin against the Holy Ghost, he certainly cannot be saved ! "

Even while writing to his frigid correspondent, George Thomson, he could not restrain his pen from dashing into strains of the same character that must have made the cautious fiddler's hair stand on end ! But let us console ourselves with the assurance that " our poet's delight in such effusions bore no great proportion to the mere métier of the *artist* aiming at a certain literary effect."

APPENDIX E.

APPENDIX E.

BIBLIOGRAPHY OF LOCKHART'S "LIFE OF BURNS."

ANY desire to arrive at a clear knowledge of the number and respective dates of the author's editions of this work has hitherto been discouraged by confusion and mystification. The catalogues of Lowndes, Allibone, and other bibliographists refer to "third," "fourth," and "fifth" editions; but, after a painstaking search, we arrive at the conclusion that no more than *two* editions passed through the author's hands. The first of these, produced in May, 1828, for "Constable's Miscellany," was simultaneously published in *two* forms—the one, in "16mo." (as vol. xxiii. of the "Miscellany"), and the other, in "demy 8vo.," to match externally with the volumes of Currie and Cromek. The *second* edition ("revised and enlarged") is dated 1830, and appeared only as "vol. xxiii. of 'Constable's Miscellany,'" to supply the demand caused by the rapid sale and complete exhaustion of the previous issue. There was no octavo duplicate printed of that *second* edition. Unfortunately, through some misjudgment, this second issue of vol. xxiii. of "Constable's Miscellany" was termed the "third," instead of *second edition;* and much of the confusion complained of is to be attributed to that mistake. By no amount of industry can ever be found a copy of "Lockhart's Life of Burns," with "second edition" printed on its title-page. As a matter of course, any publisher having right to issue a reprint of that enlarged edition, and exercising it, would naturally inscribe "fourth edition" upon the fresh publication, and so onwards; but the true fact remains, notwithstanding, that in the absence of renewed editorial revisals, these were only *reprints of the second edition.* The last unpirated edition that we know to have been published in the author's lifetime is that of John Murray, London, 1847 (fcap. 8vo.), and it is inscribed "fifth edition." The body of the work is found to be merely a verbal reprint of the author's revised edition, 1830.

The date of the following letter, addressed by Lockhart to Mr. Archibald Constable, shows that he must have been applied to by that publisher at a very early stage of the " great project " (which the " Miscellany " was then deemed to be), to contribute to its successful starting :—

"London, *January* 29*th*, 1827.

" I trust nothing is to prevent my spending the chief part of next summer in Scotland, and shall look forward to the BURNS as my work during that time. As to *two* volumes, I doubt whether that would not be too much for a *Life* of Burns. If a selection from his poetry is to be included, the case is altered, and indeed I think it would be doing a service to his fame to place before the public those pieces by which alone he merits his place, apart altogether from his mawkish attempts in the English dialect, and also those Scotch performances, the coarseness of which overbalance their wit ; and which, at any rate, should never be included in such a work as your Miscellany."

The one volume above referred to was published, as the reader is aware, in summer of the following year, the preface being dated " April, 1828," and the whole impression (over and above a considerable issue in octavo size, for library shelves), was exhausted in six weeks. Before the year closed, Carlyle's magnificent review of Lockhart's volume was published, and raised the enthusiasm of the world on the subject. So early as 14th July, 1828, we find Sir Walter Scott thus writing to his son-in-law :—" I see, by the bye, that your ' Life of Burns ' is going to press again, and therefore send you a few letters which may be of use to you."

These manuscripts of Burns, along with a further supply he received from a son of the poet's correspondent, James Burnes of Montrose, are specially noticed in a short prefatory addendum, dated "October, 1829," which marks the time when the press-work of his second edition was ready for throwing off. In January, 1830, the new edition was in circulation. The additional matter introduced is considerable in quantity ; but as the author was restricted to a certain average thickness of the volume, he had been under the necessity of throwing the greater portion of the addenda into small-type footnotes, some of these very lengthy. The *first* edition occupies 310 pages, while the *second* is comprised in 328 pages. Each of them is embellished with an engraved title-page, having a pretty vignette showing the figure of Burns at full-length, with folded arms, walking in a musing manner by the river Doon, near the "Auld Brig," and "Alloway's auld haunted kirk."

The only poetical piece, till that time unpublished, which the first edition quotes in full, is the *Election ballad*, entitled "The Five Carlins ; " and the only fresh letter there introduced (but in part only) is a brief note addressed by the poet, early in spring, 1786, to James Smith of Mauchline. In the second edition the fresh letters introduced are these— (1) to James Burness, 3rd August, 1784; (2) to the Earl of Glencairn, 4th May, 1787; (3) portion of Tour along with Nicol, August, 1787; (4) letter to Lady W. Maxwell Constable (in part only), 16th December, 1789 ; and (5) to James Burness, 12th July, 1796. The following pieces in verse are there introduced for the first time—(1) Song— "Willie Chalmers ; " (2) Song—"You're welcome, Willie Stewart ; " (3) Epigram—"Of lordly acquaintance," &c.; and (4) Epigram—"As cauld a wind as ever blew."

The dedication "to James Hogg and Allan Cunningham " is in each of the editions, including the octavo issue of the earlier one. Hogg, by the way, seems to have regarded that compliment as equivalent to a gift made to him of the copyright of the work, for he filched chapter after chapter from it in 1834, when employed to produce a Memoir of Burns for what is termed "Hogg and Motherwell's edition." Not content with that, he imported into his motley performance nearly the whole of Carlyle's famous " Review " already referred to.

THE END.

CHISWICK PRESS :—C. WHITTINGHAM AND CO., TOOKS COURT, CHANCERY LANE.